M
KID *is*
DRIVING
ME
CRAZY

A Mom's Survival Guide for Living with a Child with Mental Illness

TAMARA ARNOLD

NEW YORK

LONDON • NASHVILLE • MELBOURNE • VANCOUVER

My Kid is Driving Me Crazy

A Mom's Survival Guide for Living with a Child with Mental Illness

© 2018 Tamara Arnold

Published in New York, New York, by Morgan James Publishing in partnership with Difference Press. Morgan James is a trademark of Morgan James, LLC. www.MorganJamesPublishing.com

The Morgan James Speakers Group can bring authors to your live event. For more information or to book an event visit The Morgan James Speakers Group at www.TheMorganJamesSpeakersGroup.com.

ISBN 9781683506911 paperback
ISBN 9781683506928 eBook
Library of Congress Control Number: 2017911968

Cover Design by:
Rachel Lopez
www.r2cdesign.com

Interior Design by:
Chris Treccani
www.3dogcreative.net

In an effort to support local communities, raise awareness and funds, Morgan James Publishing donates a percentage of all book sales for the life of each book to Habitat for Humanity Peninsula and Greater Williamsburg.

Get involved today! Visit
www.MorganJamesBuilds.com

Advance Praise

"Finally, someone has opened the windows and let the light and fresh air in! This is such a beautifully raw and honest view of living with and raising a child with mental illness. This book has given me hope for a more peaceful and happy tomorrow. I have already started implementing some of the steps suggested. My child's mental illness may have had me in the pits of despair, but Tamara has thrown down a rope to help guide me out. I am no longer alone! I now can see that the light at the end of the tunnel is not an oncoming train, but the glow of a beautiful dawn. Hope is no longer a nasty four-letter word."

–Theresa Priest-Whitehouse

My Kid is Driving Me Crazy

Dedication

This book is for my son Ethan, who has given me love, hope, and the desire to be the best mom I can be. Thank you for giving me permission to write this book.

Table of Contents

Introduction

"We live in prisons with the doors wide open."
–Rumi

There came a day when I walked into my laundry room and found my sixteen-year-old son standing there, chair in front of him, cord in his hands. Panic, fear, adrenaline, and terror shot through my body. The visual imprinted in my mind, burning into my memory. I can still see it when I close my eyes – every possible outcome playing out in one moment. As selfish as it sounds, the main thought I had was, "Oh God, no, please not in my house."

I don't think you can prepare yourself for it. I mean, I knew there was potential, but the reality was so different.

Ever since Ethan was a baby, he was different than other kids. He didn't make friends easily, exhibited strange behaviors, and drew pictures of knives and death. Seeing him in the laundry room that day, *ready to do it*, broke me.

The previous ten years of our lives had been a battle to get the right systems in place, work through different medications, find the right people to talk to – and we were losing the fight. I was losing the fight.

When your child wants to die, or at least talks about wanting to die, who can you trust to help you? Where do you go to get answers? I looked, but there were no books, people, or programs out there. Everything I found was so sterile and cold regarding mental health.

I don't know about you, but for me having a child that suffers from mental illness can feel like the loneliest island in the world. No one understands. They smile, and tell you how strong you are. If you're lucky, they ask if there's something they can do to help. You know they mean well, but when things are falling part around you, you don't want help. You want to hide.

Have you ever woken up and wondered what happened to your life? Where did it go? Who are you? After ten years of fighting with Ethan and for Ethan, I didn't even recognize myself anymore. I was a shadow fighting to stay above water, to keep the one I loved from losing himself, but in the process, I was losing myself.

Mental illness in a loved one sucks! I mean it full out blows chunks. Every thought you feel, day you wake up to, second that passes, is consumed with wondering how they are doing and how you are going to help them.

For a decade, I spent my life only being *Ethan's mom*. Appointments, putting out fires, trying to keep him safe, worrying. I lost myself in that role. I forgot all about the *me* who wanted my own things in life, who had dreams. I'm a huge ham, and I believed I was going to be an actress, in theater or on television – I wasn't picky.

When, eventually, Ethan and I "broke up" – stopped talking and parted ways, which had to happen – the real journey of my life began, the part where I rediscovered who I was without him. It was super freaking scary.

I learned how to nap through meditations, make friends with a weirdo named "the Universe," dance in the kitchen, let go of the crap that kept me paralyzed, and step into my days with excitement. My mornings shifted from lying in bed, pondering if it was worth getting up to face the day, to waking up with a smile on my face.

When I committed to understanding that my relationship with my son wasn't healthy and I had to fix it, things took on a whole new shape. I can honestly say it was the toughest journey of my life, but one that saved my life, and my son's. It is the very reason I became an intuitive life coach – to help other moms who are going through what I went through, to help them step into their power and see an incredible future ahead of them.

Let's call it an adventure. An adventure isn't always easy; you must fight the bad guys and do things that make you uncomfortable. Look at Frodo in *The Lord of the Rings*. He stepped out on his adventure and then came back completely different.

That's what this book is about – it's about courageously stepping out of your comfort zone to see if there are other possibilities, and opening yourself up to the idea that every day doesn't have to be a struggle, but can be filled with ease and joy. Three years ago, I was barely getting out of bed, and today I am writing a book. This works.

You may want to grab a journal to write your feelings as we go. If you are an anti-feeling-writing kind of person, you don't have to write your feelings down. If you do write your feelings, you might want to read the book once, and then go back through it again and write your thoughts. Do what works for you. This book is about you.

If you are writing, which will enhance your journey, name your journal something special. *The Me Book*, *I'm Badass*, *The Super Spectacular Writings of...* – there is no right or wrong. Close your eyes, take a deep breath, and ask for your journal's name for this adventure. Whatever you hear is perfect. Don't second-guess it.

Allow yourself to believe and trust what I have written here. Doing so can't be worse than losing yourself or your child.

Chapter One

How Bad Can It Get?

"The wound is the place where the light enters you."
–Rumi

I wish I could tell you things were wonderful as a new mom, and I had a rocking relationship with my first born, but I can't. For over a decade, my life was miserable. I didn't like my kid.

Ethan and I had some good moments, but most of our lives we were fighting. Fighting against each other, fighting against the school system, fighting our inner demons, which was the hardest battle of all.

Ethan's biological father walked out of his life when he was three, which I am sure ignited abandonment issues. Then "the ex," who is my daughter's father, making him write lines and blaming him for everything, definitely didn't help. By the time I met Jeff, my husband now, Ethan was fourteen, and was in no mood to listen to anything Jeff had to say. Ethan had been shunned by the men in his life who were supposed to love him. This would cause a hurt boy to lash out.

The chaos began when he was five and he stole a bouncy ball from the Butterfly Conservatory. He pulled it out over lunch, and when I asked him where he got it from, he told me he had found it at Nanny's house. Really? The bouncy ball with a butterfly in it came from a place you hadn't visited today?

When Ethan was eight, death was a regular topic of conversation. Ethan threatened to kill himself, drew extremely graphic pictures of death, and started to isolate himself from other kids. That freaked me right out! My mom doesn't exactly love life, so I was a little more sensitive to this than most people. I used to get mad at Ethan. How could he want to die? Did he even know what it would do to his family, to those who loved him? Looking back, I think I was a little intense, and probably scared him. I taught him that the more he talked like that, the more I would pour attention on him.

The first psychiatrist we ever saw took a total of twenty minutes to figure out there was something wrong with Ethan. Ethan went in and I barely had time to read a chapter of my book before "the ex" and I were called in to talk about what the problem was. The psychiatrist told me Ethan had ADHD, and that he'd require medication. What? How could someone diagnose him in only twenty minutes? Where was the proof? I was pissed off.

I was in denial, so I chose not to medicate Ethan and to smother him in love instead. This backfired and he continued to feel angrier and angrier. The next psychologist we saw told me Ethan was just a normal boy who had anger issues and that things would work themselves out. That was great news! I felt relieved that I didn't have to worry about all the behaviors Ethan was exhibiting. Life was about to get easier.

This psychologist retired shortly after seeing Ethan, which makes me believe she didn't want any more clients. I didn't care, really. I just wanted to pretend that there was nothing wrong, and we were going to live happily ever after from that point on. That was not the case. That was the moment in a sports game where everything changes (in our house we call it the TSN turning point – Canadians will know what that means). Over the next seven years, I'd stop being me and become only Ethan's mom.

Have you tried to find books to help you understand what raising a child with a mental illness feels like? I searched high and low, but everything I found read like a research paper.

Everything was a review of this, a review of that. There was nothing that said, "For years of your life, the mere thought of your kid could cause a panic attack" or "No matter how much you love your child, there will be days you don't like your child at all."

By the time Ethan was in grade six, he had been hospitalized for cutting himself, and we were told he suffered from depression and anxiety. Are you freaking kidding me? I moved out at seventeen to run away from mental health issues in my family, and now it had followed me in the worst way possible. I couldn't run away anymore. Why would the Universe do this to me?

Just when things were really going badly, I realized my relationship with the man I was with clearly needed to end. We didn't really like each other anymore and fought all the time. Ethan was eleven and his sister was three. I didn't want my kids to grow up thinking that was what love was, so I added dealing with leaving my ex to my already growing stress pile.

But the real kicker, the one that was like the awesome sauce on the homemade burger, was when Ethan's school told me that they didn't have the support systems in place to let a child who cuts himself come back to school. Pardon me! Because my son suffered from depression, they wouldn't let him sit in the class with other kids. Mama bear was pissed off. Let the games begin.

In the end, Ethan was only allowed back to school in small increments, and he wasn't allowed to sit with the other kids in his class. He got to sit in an oversized closet with a "worker" and create a popsicle stick rendition of the school. Awesome! I am sure that made him feel good about himself.

"How could things get worse from there?" you ask. I had to quit my job. There was no one in my life who had the freedom in their day to take Ethan to school and pick him up as many times as I did. He wasn't allowed to play with the other kids at recess, so that meant I had to get him every time there was lunch break. Yep, they wouldn't let him hang out with the other kids, all because he had been told by a little girl to "Go become emo and die in a hole," so he'd cut himself. (P.S., "emo" means "emotional." Don't feel bad, I didn't know either!).

I remember the day the school called to set up a meeting. I walked in to find seven faces staring at me. It was like a firing squad, not a meeting. No one had anything good to say, so like any good parent, I got majorly defensive. I didn't understand why it took so many people to have a conversation about what was best for my child. Why did every meeting feel like an attack instead of help?

There are no words for me to explain what I was going through. The worst of it all was when I tried to look at the situation through my son's eyes. All he wanted was to fit in, and instead he was being pushed further and further away from having any sense of normal in his life. We started therapy with the local mental illness association, but with their huge turnover rate, we had to tell our story over and over again. Ethan gave up. He stopped talking all together.

Because Ethan missed so much of grade six, it was decided he would start a program for his grade seven year that would help him readjust to school. Before grade seven ended, things got even worse in our house. I was a single mom with a child who hated himself, the world, and me. He wouldn't listen, was angry, had innumerable difficult behaviors, and was toxic. The summer before grade eight, I broke. I asked Ethan to leave, to live in a mental health residence. I tapped out of being a mother.

I needed a break, time to breathe. I wanted just one day where I didn't have to worry about what he was doing and how I was going to clean it up. I wanted to feel free of stress and worry. No one understood why I would do such a thing to my own child. Countless conversations occurred, with my family talking in circles. "How could I, how could I, how could I?" they would ask. How could I not! At that point, I was failing as a parent, everyone thought I was an jerk, and my kid hated me. Awesome job! Mother of the year goes to me!

My life spun out of control. I cancelled appointments with my own clients in order to take Ethan to therapy appointments. I drove back and forth to the mental health residence. I drank to forget how bad my life was. It was great fun. Highly recommend. The worst part was, that wasn't even the worst part.

There was a brief upswing in the story then, when Ethan got out of residence and joined a rowing team in grade nine, we worked out, talked about health, and didn't fight. It was a little slice of heaven amongst the entire disaster pie. I pretended that everything was going to be okay. I lived in the sparkles, not knowing that, behind the glitter, Ethan was having a terrible time. I chose to believe the façade because it was easier than looking at what was going on behind the scenes.

Then we moved into the house I currently live in – with Jeff and his two young kids. That was when the real storm began. Ethan and I had done a pretty good job of pretending things were okay, when really they weren't. When I rocked the boat and changed Ethan's routine, all the bad things I had been ignoring surfaced with a vengeance.

Mental illness is funny. It doesn't like change, and it doesn't like being told what to do. Throw in a new father figure and a couple of new siblings, and that's how you really make things fun. Luckily, the younger three kids didn't fully understand what was going on. We tried to keep that all hidden, but the emotional vibration of the house was noticeable.

Ethan spun out of control. Every morning I fought to get Ethan out of bed, he snuck out at night, suicide was constantly a topic – I honestly didn't know what to do. I was barely sleeping and barely functioning. I threw myself into work, but at the end of the day I still had to come home and face the disaster. Who knew your own home could feel like a prison? I didn't want to be there, so I drank. What's a bottle of wine a night? "It helps me sleep," I said. It mellowed me, it made me like my kid a little.

I will never forget walking in to the laundry room and finding Ethan with the chair and cord. Something in me snapped. I was falling apart, slowly losing each piece of myself. I drove Ethan to the hospital and prayed they could help. *Please take him away and fix him*. I couldn't try anymore. I was failing miserably.

Ethan was sent to the best hospital that specialized in mental illness. I was saved! Or so I thought. After three days they wanted to send him home. How could he come home? He wasn't any better. They actually diagnosed him with more while he was there. Now he was carrying ADHD, depression, *and* ODD (oppositional defiance disorder) in his back pocket. If you don't know what ODD is, it's as awesome as it sounds

– a whole lot of anger, sometimes violence (which Ethan didn't have), and a backpack full of *not going to listen*. I have never cried so hard in my life. He couldn't come home. I didn't know what to do.

I can still remember the day I drove to the town of Hamilton to give my son the ultimatum to get help or leave. He was sixteen. I was a shell. The drive up to the hospital felt like hours, though it was only a little over half an hour. The sound of the tires on the road, steady and consistent, *thump, thump, thump*, matched the beat of my broken heart and the tears that wouldn't stop. I wanted to make him better, to rub his hair, give him a big hug, and tell him everything was going to be okay, but it wasn't. I can still see the room we were placed in when I close my eyes. I can see the couch where he sat. I can see the look in his eyes when I told him he needed to get help or he couldn't come home. His eyes showed rage, disbelief, and hurt. I'd thought I was broken before, but nothing breaks a mother's heart more than hearing their child choose living in a shelter, over doing the work to come home.

For two years after that, things got *really* bad. Like, worse than you are probably thinking. This part of the story belongs to him, but in the end, we had to break up. I looked my son in the eyes and told him I didn't want to see him again. We were done. Our relationship was over. That was the hardest thing I've ever done in my life, but doing it would end up being both our savior and our grace.

Chapter Two

Codependency and My Child

"The surest way to make ourselves crazy is to get involved in other people's business, and the quickest way to become sane and happy is to tend to our own affairs."
–Melodie Beattie, Codependent No More

Having a child with high needs is all-consuming. There were times when I could barely function for fear of what my son was doing. It plagued my thoughts at work and at home while I tried to sleep. Where was he? Was he making good decisions? Who was he with? What was he doing? I made his life my responsibility. I would fix him.

When we have a child with mental health or behavioral issues, it's as though we feel extra responsible for parenting them. Smothering them will obviously fix everything. And then there is the over-worrying, blaming ourselves, guilt we made them this way, and shame we can't fix it.

Maybe it's just me, but I felt like I had to be some super parent – the caped mother teaching her child that what he was doing wasn't correct or safe, saving Ethan from endless years of harm and failure.

I don't know how many times I tried to explain the same things over and over to Ethan. Clearly, repetition would work. If at first they don't succeed, repeat the same thing again, and again, and again, and again. Any child, even the ones without mental health issues, would clearly love that.

Then there is the wonderful joy of worrying about what others parents are thinking. 'Cause when you are yelling at them on the school grounds, or talking between closed teeth, someone is going to notice.

And let's be honest here. It wasn't only at school. Chances are, you stopped going to restaurants, busy malls, parties, or other social gatherings with your kid – just in case there was a meltdown or you'd be seen getting pissed (with and without alcohol).

Life can get real poopy. It's our job to give up everything to be there for our kids. Right? We are clearly responsible for their every waking hour. If we could follow them with a broom and dust pan to pick up their messes, that would work, right?

Have you thought about what the other parents are saying? I did. These are the things I told myself they were saying about me:

"She clearly doesn't punish that child. He is out of control. She should watch Dr. Phil and teach that boy a lesson."

"What a meany. Ethan is so hard done-by at home. His mother is such a loser."

"It's not Ethan's fault. He's left to his own devices because his mother works too much. She doesn't love him enough to be home for him."

"She's crazy. There's nothing wrong with that child. Why does she put those things in his head?"

"Wow, does that woman ever exaggerate. There's no way things can be that bad."

And my favorite: "Boys will be boys. Lighten up!" (That one was actually said to my face).

I truly believed that was what people were saying. I didn't really enjoy making friends with the other parents. I became the parent that slipped in and slipped out of recitals and concerts. Who needs small talk.

All of those avoidances and pretend outcomes caused me to shut up about what was going on in my life to most people. I kept a very select group of friends to drink my cares away with and vent to, but I didn't go out of my way to do much else.

At that point in my life, I'm pretty sure if you had looked up *codependent* in the dictionary, my image would be there.

I'm not sure if you have heard of the word *codependent* before, so let me give you my take on what it is. If you in any way, shape, or form change your life, thoughts, or plans for the sole purpose of providing help for someone who has not asked for it, you are codependent. At least, this is my description.

In her book, *Codependent No More*, Melodie Beattie writes, "A codependent person is one who has let another person's behavior affect him or her, and who is obsessed with controlling that person's behavior."

To break it down even further, I recently told my son on the phone that he needed to stop worrying about everyone else's problems. It was theirs and not his. He needed to worry about his own problems. I can't blame him for his codependent behavior though. He did learn it from a master on the subject – me.

Think about all the times you've stopped what you were doing because you were worried about your child. If you went to the store, would he be okay? If you stepped out for a yoga class, would you feel too guilty to enjoy it? Every time we let what "could" happen affect our decisions, we're exhibiting codependency.

It's hard when every day is a new struggle to detach. I understand. I rebelled against that idea myself, so when my therapist suggested I read *Codependent No More*, ten years ago, I refused.

What was she talking about! I wasn't codependent. I was a good mom who understood that her role was to give up everything she had ever wanted to do in her life to stay home and fix her child, who didn't want fixing, then blame her life, her child, and everyone who didn't help for being the reason she had not become an actress.

Then I decided to write a book.

Maybe reading *Codependent No More* would help me as I started working with other moms who wore the cape of responsibility. It was a freaking gift! As soon as I started reading,

I wished I had listened to my therapist and read it when she told me to read it. It would have made a huge difference. She was so totally right. I hereby declare my position of thinking I knew everything in my twenties as being silly and unnecessary, including thinking that not listening to a professional was the right thing to do.

So how does codependency work in your life? This little demon manifests itself in many sneaky ways. What I thought was good parenting was really obsession. To give you a more detailed list of ways we adopt codependency, let me list a few of my favorites:

Changing plans to accommodate their wants. "Yes, we can stay home so you can play video games. This way we don't have to go out in public, and you will play quietly in your room while I enjoy this wine."

Giving in to their bullying about new toys/electronics/ sleeping in your bed because it is easier. "Yes, I will buy you the new version of Call of Duty every November so you stop following me around the house asking for it over and over again."

Worrying about their behaviors while you are at work. "I'm sorry. Can you repeat what you just said to me again, because my mind has wandered to what experiments my child is doing in my kitchen after school today."

Leaving an event or work to check up on them. "I'll be right back. If I get home at just the right time, I can catch him in the act."

Not sleeping at night due to worrying. "Did I hear the door? Is he sneaking out? Maybe if I sleep with one eye open, I'll be able to respond fast enough."

Blaming them for things going wrong in your life. "It's clearly your fault I don't have a boyfriend or a job."

Getting angry over what they are doing. "Stop going out and having fun. If I don't get to, neither should you."

Not forgiving them and carrying over what they have done into later arguments. "Remember when you were five and you did that thing I'm still talking about now, ten years later?"

It can be an endless cycle. When things get bad, everything goes down the toilet.

How does codependency affect your relationship with your kids? How does it not? Once they know we are willing to give up anything and everything to be there for them, codependency becomes a game.

When Ethan was in grade six, I was called to the school because he had cut his wrist with a key and was hiding under a desk. The school wanted to call an ambulance because they didn't know what else to do. I had a therapy appointment booked for him that night, so I suggested I come get him, and that I would deal with it.

"My Ex" and I took the next day off work to be with Ethan. It was a Friday, so we spent three days loving up on him, giving him what we felt he needed – movies, snuggles, candy, you name it. When Monday came, he promised he was okay and would never cut himself again. Off to school he went.

Guess what happened at school on Monday? He absolutely cut again. Why wouldn't he? We had just taught him that we would give up everything to be with him when he did.

That time, he ended up in the hospital for a week, with unlimited movies and my attention. It stopped my life. I didn't go to work, was barely home with my husband and daughter, and cancelled all the plans I had.

Luckily there were some amazing psychologists at the hospital. They saw what had happened and got through to Ethan, and he didn't cut again. They saw how codependent we were with each other, but I was still defending my stance of good parenting at that time.

I'm not alone here, people. I have heard so many stories that are like this one. Just recently, one of my coaching clients almost didn't come to her session because her son with ADHD was acting up over the Christmas holiday. She felt that she needed to be there to make sure he didn't do anything unsafe while she was out, or hurt his brother. When she showed up to see me, she was frazzled and beaten. It's so hard not to get swept up in making sure we are there all the time so that nothing goes wrong.

Another example is my good friend who kept letting her son sleep with her. Things weren't good between her and her ex. Her son was angry all the time and breaking out in a rash. She and her son fought all the time, yet, when he wanted to sleep with her, she let him. She told me she didn't want him sleeping with her, but she just didn't know how to stop it. Clearly, everything that was going on was her fault, and she didn't want to take that away from him, too. He needed her.

Fast forward to two years ago, when my therapist (the same one) finally got through to me. I want to share with you what she said. It changed my life with my son, and although things got worse for a while, they eventually got better.

My therapist said, "If anyone else treated you the way your son is treating you, would you respond the same way?"

Mic drop.

If Ethan wasn't my son but was some random person, would I look at how I responded differently? Hearing what my therapist told me that day was one of those big defining moments in my life. I look at that day as the day I took my life back, and the day Ethan and I began a real parent-child relationship.

Chapter Three

It's Not About Your Child

"We are not held back by the love we didn't receive in the past, but by the love we're not extending in the present."
–Marianne Williamson

I contracted codependency at an early age. I picked it up at the age of ten. Unfortunately, it is not a virus, like the measles or a bad cold. It takes more than antibiotics or a quick run to the local health store to fix it. I believe I will always suffer. I will always have it. Once you know the signs and symptoms though, you can catch it before it spreads through your life again.

My mom suffers from depression and anxiety, and back in the day, while she still had her uterus, severe PMS. Guys, if you are reading this, don't say a word when your wife gets her period. No one can complain about PMS unless they are in the five percent of women who have actually been diagnosed with having PMS as a hormonal imbalance. My poor mom was, and it was a real humdinger.

In a meditation one day, I asked myself how old I was when I stopped being a child. The answer was ten. Looking back, I know exactly when that was and what was happening. My sister was having problems and my mom kicked her out. She moved in with my dad. My mom started crying then. Almost every day. I wanted nothing more than to help her feel better. I would do all sorts of things – try to make her laugh, put on recitals at bedtime, whatever it took. She needed me, or that's what I told myself. I would make dinners, stay home instead of going out, and I would curl up in her chair at night to watch TV. I did that for years, even when I was in high school. At sixteen I applied to go on a Rotary Exchange through my school, and they told me I was too close to my mom to be accepted. Houston, we have a problem here. So, I moved out, mostly because I couldn't do it anymore. I wanted to be a child, not a parent. I reapplied to the Rotary program the next year, and even though I was living with my sister, I was accepted! Ten months of beautiful Brazil awaited.

That was probably the best thing that could have happened. It allowed me to find my independence and gain perspective on who I was. For the first time, I could step away from the codependency, and truly hear my own thoughts. Thanks, Dad, for funding this. I'm not sure I'd be the same if I hadn't gone. The funny part was that everyone openly bet on how long I could handle staying there. It hurt to think that my family and friends thought I was so weak.

Coming home was worse, because I walked into a codependency party. My mom, sister, my future brother in law, and my sister's best friend had all moved into a town house together. There is a lot of talk when you go on an exchange about how hard it is to leave your life. I found it so much harder to come home, to walk off the plane into a new life, one where all the characters had changed, but they looked the same. It was very *Twilight Zone*.

When the first man who seemed even somewhat cool walked in to my life, I was all in. Calgon, take me away! I quickly moved in with him, and shortly after that, had Ethan growing in my belly. Having a baby filled me with excitement. I could have *love* with me forever. It would be mine to snuggle and kiss and hold whenever I wanted. I don't think that, at nineteen, I had really thought through the other parts that went into the equation. I just knew I wanted to be needed.

If you don't have any kids, it doesn't mean you don't feel codependent with someone in your life. It could be your partner. Do they have alcoholism or any other addiction? Would you do anything to help them, make excuses for them, change your life to be there for them? What about a parent? Maybe they needed you so much that they created a victimized way of keeping you close to them, saying things like, "You are the strong one, you keep the family together" or "I couldn't do this without you." Man, it sucks to be needed so much that you feel obligated to be there. That kind of pressure can down the best of us.

Even if you had the best childhood imaginable, the minute you heft an eight-pound baby out of your vagina you feel the innate urge to protect it. Like the mother bear protecting the cub, nothing in life is going to hurt this being you created. Then the cub becomes a little terror, but you've already signed up for the best mom club, so you do whatever it takes to make things right. It's hard to find the line that separates good parenting from "Oh my God, I just gave up everything for a child that doesn't like me."

I grew up being told that family was everything. You never gave up a family gathering to be with your friends. That was a non-option. Friends would come and go, but family – family was the real deal. We weren't even Italian and I felt like I owed my family my children and my life.

The problem was that my family was broken. I mean this in the most loving way, but they didn't know how to take care of themselves, let alone take care of me. I was told I was the strong one who kept the family together, and that without me things would fall apart – and I believed them! I wanted to be that strong and important, the one who hosted all the Christmas dinners and made sure we all stayed connected.

When I didn't do what my family wanted me to, the real fun began. It's amazing how people use guilt as a form of communication, as though it's its own language – like English or German. "Good morning. Are you speaking guilt today?" Some of my favorite gems in the language of guilt were:

"If you loved me, you wouldn't go out."

"Are you my daughter? I wouldn't know because I don't hear from you."

"You have time for your friends and work, but you don't have time for me."

"You are the only one I can go out with."

"You don't love me."

"You always buy things for yourself, but never for me."

"You are ashamed of us as a family."

"Everyone is more important than me."

"If it weren't for you, I don't think I could do this."

"Why don't you love me?"

"Just forget about me over here. I'll be fine without you."

The list goes on and on. That endless string of words and sentences sucked the life out of my body. I believed I was a terrible mother, daughter, sister, and partner. Nothing I did was good enough.

How do you handle this when it hits you right in the heart? You detach yourself emotionally. I don't mean that you stop loving your child. I mean that you don't let it get to you. When they are speaking that way, they know they are going to get a desired response from you. If it doesn't work, they might even yell that they hate you, or swear. That is not how they truly feel. It is the way they get what they want from us. We get tired, beaten down, exhausted, and give up. Give in. It's easier.

I remember when I met my husband, when Ethan was fourteen. I actually said to him, "I don't discipline Ethan like other kids. I let him get away with everything. It's easier." I'd been a single mom for three years by then, and I was exhausted from the fight, and didn't want to do the work anymore. I had given up.

Having someone in my life who stood with me, and having my therapist telling me to detach myself emotionally, gave me the strength to stand firm in my decisions and, in turn, take back a huge part of myself.

At times, it's like you are living in two worlds. The imagined one is nice and normal. You see yourself fitting in at pool parties, the kids playfully splashing in the pool and the adults barbequing and sharing stories. Everything remains calm, and everyone gets along.

Then there is the other life. The one where you question if you can bring your child out today or will there be a scene. You worry they will not listen, will do something unsafe, and you won't be able to relax. You feel judged by everyone who is around you.

One of my clients described it perfectly yesterday. She said her shoulders get tense the minute her son with ADHD comes home from school, and until he falls asleep she feels she needs to be "on" to make sure nothing bad happens. But when he is at school, everything is calm and nice. There is peace, and she can relax. Nothing bad can happen.

Another client has a nephew with behavioral problems who lives with her. He is eighteen and hardly home anymore because he goes to his girlfriend's house. My client feels that the house is lighter and easier when he isn't home. There is less conflict and there are fewer arguments.

What both of those women have in common, besides children with mental illness, is that neither one of them knows who they are or what they want with their lives. They have been the mom and aunt who gave up everything to care for their child or nephew. When I asked, "What do you want to be when you grow up?" neither of them could answer that question.

Somewhere along the way, without even noticing it, they had lost the light that made them who they were. It got lost in the chaos of being the best parent or caregiver, doing what was expected, giving up more time, more energy, everything they had.

Chapter Four

I Didn't Want My Kid

"All great things are preceded by chaos."
–Deepak Chopra

There were days when I didn't want to be a parent. For real. I didn't understand why it had to be so hard. It was not what I signed up for. The weird thing was that having Ethan was like having two kids. One was Ethan the sweetheart, all snuggles. The other Ethan I could look in his eye and see that there was going to be trouble. That was not my favorite Ethan.

The worst time for us was at night. In the midnight hours, when the rest of the house was asleep, his mind couldn't settle. That meant he would find alternate ways to amuse himself.

Before bed, his pupils would tell me the story of whether it was going to be a good night or a bad night. If his pupils were dilated, this momma didn't sleep well. And a sleep-deprived parent is so much more effective.

When I peeled my eyes open the next morning, I felt that it wasn't worth it to get out of bed to deal with the realities of life and work. What was the point when something new was going to happen? Why even bother?

To be completely honest, I sometimes cringed when Ethan came home from school. It was so quiet and calm when he wasn't there. When he got home I would have to be on duty, and I wouldn't be able to relax. If I was lucky, he would go to his room and play video games. If I wasn't, he would do something else in his room, or follow me around. Quietness when Ethan was around usually meant something was happening that I would not like, but I didn't think about that. I was just happy for the moment that it was quiet.

Things got so out of hand in my house that I suggested Ethan move to a mental health residence. I was tired. I didn't want to feel that way anymore. I didn't want to dislike my own child. I needed help.

The facility required him to go in on his own. Meaning he had to make the decision to go there on his own. I couldn't admit him. Do you know how hard it is to have a conversation with your child and ask him to move away from home, into a place filled with "crazy" kids? There are no words.

But I couldn't bear our situation another day. I was so completely overwhelmed. Why did it have to be so hard? Why couldn't even one day feel easy? At that point, I didn't know that my daughter, Siena, who was only in kindergarten at the time, was affected as much as she was by the situation with Ethan. She has told me since then that she could hear us fighting after I tucked her in. It made her cry. But, when Ethan had been gone for months, she missed him. I tried so hard to keep what was going on from affecting her, but somehow she knew. Kids are funny like that. They can feel what's going on, even when we try to protect them. Siena says she always knew there was something going on, and she hated not feeling a part of it. Add that to the parental fail list!

My children are eight years apart in age. All of that happened the summer leading into grade eight for Ethan. That is one of the most influential times in a child's life.

When he started grade eight, the residence Ethan went to would drive all the kids to school. They were from several different cities. That meant the kids were up early, ready and on the road before most adults got up. He started one of the most influential years of school, but he didn't live at home. I drove Ethan to school for the first day, but after that he was on his own.

The residence was designed to help Ethan learn coping strategies, gain life skills, and help us work on our relationship. He would come home on weekends and special holidays, but for the first few months, he spent the entire week there. In the beginning, I didn't even want to see him on weekends. I wanted to be free. Driving to pick him up was hard.

We had appointments with counselors, therapists, and other workers. It was an endless cycle of driving all over, and of changing my schedule. That frustrated the snot out of me. All I wanted by the time he was home from the residence was to stay home. Maybe that's their secret plan. They make you so tired of running around, you get excited to have your child home. After nine months, we were both ready to settle back into a routine at home.

Things were so good when Ethan came home. It felt different. He was happy. And, for the first time in his life, he was medicated.

Later, I found out he was on his best behavior then because he was afraid I would send him back to the residence. It wasn't long before he stopped taking his medication and resorted back to old patterns. Eventually, we were back in the same place we'd started. What a piss-off that was! Part of the fallout was there was no support once we got him back home. There was no one to keep working with us, to help us move forward. That just ended, which brought everything back up.

Things got worse before they got better again. I mean, a lot worse. Like, throwing-in-the towel worse. There comes a point when you can look back at everything you have gone through, and know you put all the effort you could into working things out. There was no stone left unturned in helping my child.

This is funny, because I love therapy. I could sit with a therapist all day. Getting an unbiased, helpful overview of what was going on in my life was a game-changer for me. Ethan, on the other hand, hated therapy. I remember one day when Ethan told me that he would never like therapy or receiving any kind of help, because of me and my therapy-loving nature. I had overdone it, and he would never get over it. I had ruined therapy for him. How does that happen?

There have been countless words, phrases, and analogies from all kinds of therapists and counselors, that carried me through the "I'm going to kill my kid," "Why is this happening?" and "There is no hope" moments.

The first real gem that I latched on to was this: "Fresh start. Forgive." Holding on to grudges was not going to help Ethan and me build a relationship that was worthwhile. If, every day, we were tossing past hurts into our conversations, there was no way we would be able to move forward. Both of us felt completely burned by the other. I committed, each day, to waking up with a clear heart, letting go of everything that had been done, and allowing myself to start over.

It didn't stop there, either. I also had to go in and realize there was stuff that I was carrying from my own childhood which had crossed over into my parenting. That was terrible and awesome at the same time. Dealing with the past is not usually on our daily to-do lists. But doing so makes a major difference in what today looks like. Plus, when you do the work, it gets rid of crap from both the past and the present in one fell swoop. Best thing ever!

Letting go of blame, shame, guilt, and toxic bull snot is freeing, and I highly recommend it to every living person on the planet. You feel light, like a giant weight has been lifted off your shoulders.

Another philosophy I adopted from my therapist was knowing that I had done everything I could possibly have done to teach Ethan life skills. If he wasn't in a place to use them, that was not a direct reflection on me. It did not make me a bad parent. Far from it. My therapist let me know that each person begins their journey at a different age. Some kids stay home until they are in their thirties, others leave home in their teenage years. I flew the coop at seventeen, so that idea made sense to me.

Detaching myself emotionally was a big idea – being able to step out of the situation and ask myself, "If this wasn't my child, would I allow this to happen?" If he was speaking to me, or if his behaviors fell into the "no way in hell" category, it was okay for me to not tolerate it.

When Ethan and I broke up, because things did get to that point of "no way in hell," I was a lost soul. Who was I without my child? I had spent most of my adult years taking care of him. Without him, I felt lost.

That was when I had to take a look at who I was and what I wanted out of life. For years, I had told myself my life was on hold while I was parenting my child with mental health. I had put myself on autopilot and cruised through a decade of my life.

But I didn't want to do that anymore, so I had to figure out who I was and what I wanted. The one thing I had done right was ensure that my body and mind were strong. Strong enough to withstand stress, trauma, sleepless nights, and so much more. Exercise was my sanity. When things were tough, I turned to sweat to make me feel better. I was a fitness instructor, and my classes saved me. If I hadn't been paid for exercising, I may have given up on it. Another thing I had always done was take nutritional supplements. With all my systems being barraged by cortisol and other unfriendly hormones, I wanted to make sure there was a fair fight waged inside me.

Next, I needed to figure out what I loved, what fired me up inside. What could I see myself doing, day in and day out. That thought scared me. The open road was an endless highway of unknowns. If you are anything like I was, the thought of change gave me a panic attack. I'm not kidding. Full on anxiety! I had allowed myself to be comfortable in the knowledge that parenting Ethan was going to be my life forever. So imagine how my body responded when I told it otherwise. It was a good thing I was on supplements when the fight or flight response kicked into overdrive.

Stepping onto that open road led me to writing this book and to becoming an intuitive life coach. (The next six chapters include stories from beautiful people who I have been blessed to work with.)

Giving myself permission to love myself, to do self-care was terrifying. Oh, the guilt! How could I spend time on things for me while my child was in pain? What would the other parents think and say when they found out? I lived in fear that someone would call the authorities on me. "That mom is loving herself more than her child. That can't be right."

What kept me from giving up and falling back into the same codependent cycle I had been living for years was meditation? When I first started, I practically laughed at myself. I was a pathetic meditator, sleeping through every instructional video I found and tried on YouTube. I used to call it medi-napping. The minute the music began, my body shut down. I got so much good sleep in. I figured it was helping, because eventually I stayed awake during the meditations.

After all the years of being strong, holding it together, and relying on only myself, the hardest thing I faced was reconnecting to fun and play. I had become quite dour. The only fun I had was with other adults, drinking copious amounts of wine and trying to forget my life. That was not the fun I wanted anymore. I wanted to laugh sober, because life was silly and games were fun. That meant I had to have a serious conversation with my inner child, and she was pissed with me. I had shut her out of my life for quite some time, so she didn't want to play at first. It took a good many play dates before she believed I truly meant that I wanted to include fun back in my life. Sometimes she still gets mad at me. Sometimes I "adult" too hard and don't listen to her.

Through all of that, what I began to realize was the more I stopped focusing on Ethan, the better his and my relationship became. I no longer compulsively worried about him. Instead, all that energy went into me.

Codependency is like an illness. It can be the unseen demon that breaks everything apart. To break free completely of it, you need to be willing to stand on your own, because you like yourself and know you are worth fighting for.

* * *

The next six chapters are going to go into more detail about how to be more than your child's mom. They will give you a detailed plan for finding your own heartbeat. Trust me when I say it will make a huge difference in your relationship with your child. Even if you are having a hard time believing this will work, go through the chapters and do the work anyway. What's the worst thing that can happen?

Chances are, you bought this book because life sucks right now. What if taking a chance and experimenting with what I'm offering here helps, or works, or creates space for you and your child to be filled with so much love you both explode? It could be fun.

Chapter Five

It's All My Kid's Fault

"I'm working on my happiness like a full time job"
–Gabrielle Bernstein

Everything was Ethan's fault. I allowed myself to believe that. I blamed Ethan for why my life wasn't moving forward. Have you ever blamed your child for the breakdown of your relationship? Have you held your kid accountable for your stalled career? I did.

Imagine my surprise when Ethan moved out and I had no one to blame anymore. There was only me. Owning your story is hard. It was so much easier to give Ethan all the credit for ruining my life. If he still lived with me today, and I'd never experienced my own life without him around, I'd probably be exactly where I was before he left – giving him all the awards for making my life miserable.

This is the part of the book where you will either be on board, or you will find me to be a stark raving lunatic. The things that have happened since Ethan and I broke up have surprised the hell out of me, yet when I look back I see that I always knew who I was. Do you get that feeling sometimes? You find something out about yourself that throws you off guard, but when you look back, you can see it was always part of you, but you weren't listening.

That is how this chapter starts – with a little magic and intuition. However, I believe you also have intuition. I would even suggest it is how we found each other. Have you ever known something was going happen to your child before it does? Do you sense their moods, just by looking at them? Then I call you out and say you are already using intuition. You're locked and loaded, with intuition to spare.

There came a point in Ethan's and my life when I had to let him go. In a fury of anger, I told him I didn't want him in my life anymore. I said he was completely disowned, and I never wanted to hear from him again. I even kicked him off Facebook. Even writing that brings up guilt. I can't tell you exactly what happened to make me come to that decision, because I promised Ethan I wouldn't, but I can tell you it sucked big time.

For days after he was gone, I was in the fetal position. What kind of mother does this? What were people saying? Why did no one understand? Why did everyone think I was doing okay? Explaining over and over again why Ethan and I broke up was exhausting. I shut down, shut up, and hibernated. I didn't want to see anyone or talk about it.

I took to meditating. There had to be something that could pull me out of the sadness I felt. Pretending to be happy for everyone else was wearing me down to the bone. Have you felt that way – plastered smile on your face, going through the motions? I don't remember where I had read meditation helped with healing, I just really wanted to feel better. Thank God for YouTube!

Doing online searches with words like "healing meditation," "meditation for letting go," and "motivation meditation" became my drug. I would put the headphones on, start a meditation video, the music would start, and I would be out like a light, coming back to reality only when the voice told me the meditation was over. It became my thing – medi-napping. I figure it was because I wasn't ready to hear the teachings, but my subconscious was. I kept going back for more, because somehow I started to feel a little bit better.

Eventually, I started staying awake, which was even weirder, because I felt like I was doing it all wrong. Everything I had told myself about meditation seemed to involve having major out-of-body experiences, but I never went anywhere. I just sat there, listening, thinking about my grocery list. Distraction was my forte! I got mad at myself for doing meditation badly, but for some reason I kept going.

Then it happened. I was tired, emotional, raw, and I didn't feel like meditating, but someone had posted a Martha Beck meditation in Facebook and I hit play. That was the first time I cried in meditation, and the first time I got something from it.

I have always felt abandoned by men in my life. At least, that was what I found out during that meditation, which included a guided visualization. I'd end up in a castle. In that meditation, we had gone on a long walk, and the castle rose out of the depths of my mind. We were instructed to go up the stairs and into a big beautiful room with a roaring fire. There were two cozy chairs nestled close to fire – the perfect place to enjoy the heat and the surroundings. While standing in the room, we were directed to go look out the window. Being so high up afforded me with an incredible view of the forest surrounding the castle. When it was time to turn around, we were told there would be someone sitting in front of the fire who wanted to speak with us.

It was my Poppy, my grandpa who died when I was in grade three. He was so strong in my memory, always there for me, even though he worked on the ships at sea. His forearm anchor tattoo was my favorite memory of him when I was little and sitting on his lap. I can remember looking at it, running my little hands over the ink. When I sat down, he looked at me and did his Poppy smile. Man, I missed him. He told me during that meditation that he knew how sad I was, how lonely I was. The next thing he said cracked me open like an egg, and I started to cry a deeper cry then I could remember ever having cried. He told me that he had been with me all the time, that I had never been alone.

When we were done talking, he lifted me up and carried me back down the castle stairs. He placed me gently on the ground outside the big wooden door of the castle. When I was about to turn to leave, he told me he had been carrying me through all the hard times, and that he would continue to carry me for as long as I needed him. I felt safe for the first time in so long.

When I came out of that meditation, I released my body weight in tears. I cried and cried until I was empty. Then I felt lighter, like the weight of the world wasn't on my shoulders, because Poppy was there to help me.

I can't remember the name of that meditation, or where to find it, but I would love to create a space for you to have that kind of experience, too. We carry so much responsibility on ourselves. We think that everything that happens to our kids is somehow either our fault or due to something we did.

It doesn't even have to be about your kids. Have you felt responsible for your past relationships ending or for your parents, your husband, your animals, your plants? Killing a plant sucks! All you had to do was water it and you couldn't even do that! How many times have you blamed, shamed, or guilted yourself?

I say you end being responsible for all of that right now. It's time to free your body, mind, and spirit from carrying all the crap that isn't yours to carry. Dump it. Let it go. Flush it down the Universal toilet, and wipe yourself clean from it.

I have uploaded a cutting cords meditation on my website (www.theenchantedfairy.ca) that will help you let go of all the crap you are toting around like luxury luggage. Trust me, you probably don't know you are carrying so much, until you let it go and feel the difference. This is a way to let go of junk in your memory trunk that will make the rest of this process way easier.

When I did my first cord-cutting meditation I was in a room full of strangers. There is a group of women where I live named the Gifted Goddesses, who offer themselves in the service of God and Goddess to help people. I was scrolling through Facebook one day (yes, I spend a lot of time on there), and I saw a post about a free service to help people heal. I would have screamed "pick me" at the computer if I thought it would get me into that program.

When it was time to go and do that healing, I freaked out. What had I signed up for? Who goes to a complete stranger's house, where there will also be other people they've never met, because they don't know how to make themselves better. Me, that's who. I would have done anything to get out of my slump. I was desperate.

In that house, I sat in a chair facing away from the group of six women. Just being around them made me cry. They assured me I wasn't the only one who felt that way and put a box of Kleenex on my lap. For the next 45 minutes, there were a series of guided meditations they played off a boom box on the table. The cord-cutting meditation was the second one.

I bawled like a baby. I mean, racking, sobbing, ugly crying. You know the type, where you turn purple and your face expands to twice its normal size. The box of Kleenex they gave me was my savior. I could have filled a pitcher with my nose drippings. That's probably too much information, but I want you to know how much that cord-cutting meditation affected me.

When it was over and my face went sort of back to normal, I was exhausted. I could have slept for a hundred years. I didn't know if I had done it right or not, since all I wanted to do was go to bed. I later found out that feeling tired is normal and likely when you let go of stuff. Who knew? I must have let a ton go then, because I couldn't keep my eyes open.

For me, cutting the cords between Ethan and me was the hardest. I had been trying to stay ahead of the guilt and shame for so long that freeing myself of all the self-hatred and anger left me raw.

Why do we make ourselves responsible for everyone else? I've realized recently that our human bodies can't handle all that pressure. It's too much to hold. It's like a helium balloon filled with negative emotions that carries us higher into a place we can't come down from. When it gets too full, we pop and come crashing down, losing pieces of ourselves as we fall.

Chapter Six

It's Everyone Else's Fault

"Happiness is not something ready made. It comes from your own actions."
–Dalai Lama

I blamed my mom, my dad, my sister, the neighbors, the mailman, and everyone else with a pulse who wouldn't help me. I blamed them for my past, for my present, and for the future I was not living.

My mom got the most blame, because that was easiest. She was surely the reason I sucked at being a mother. She had tried to leave us kids twice, by her own hand. Who did I have as a mentor to show me the way now that I was a mother? Clearly, if she had been more motherly, none of this would have happened.

Then there was my dad. He never believed I would amount to anything because I didn't finish high school. It had to be his fault all of this with Ethan was happening. If he had accepted who I was, I would have had the approval I needed, and Ethan would never have gotten sick. Yep, Dad is definitely to blame, too.

In my mind, parents are supposed to be the ones who are there in your times of need, who save you from all the hard stuff, who protect you from the monsters and pick you up when you skin your knee. But as my life was falling apart around me, I couldn't ask them for help.

I blamed my grandmother for harsh words spoken, my sister for being older, all the men I dated for sucking my spirit from me. I could say I hadn't wanted to get pregnant, but deep within my soul, I wanted a baby. I wanted him to fill the void I felt in my heart and in my life. I wanted to feel loved.

I was a selfish mom in the beginning, choosing partying in my early twenties over being there for Ethan. I left him in the care of people who could barely take care of themselves. I often look back and wonder if that is where Ethan's illness began.

I flung myself into loveless relationship after loveless relationship, seeking the approval from men that I hadn't receive from my family. That caused me to stay in a relationship with a man I met who would end up being the downfall of my son's mental health. That man is my daughter's father, and for that I am extremely grateful. My son, however, blames him for everything. The time when we all lived together was a long eight years.

I blamed everyone in my family, every man who hurt me, and anyone who didn't fit the mold of what I needed for why my life was falling apart around me. It was their fault I was doing all that work with Ethan on my own. No one came riding in on a white horse. No one gave me the support I needed. I was so very angry.

I spent years in that cycle. Maybe you have, too. It is so much easier to give away our power than to do the work to take it back. We can stay hidden, stay small, have excuses for why life is so terrible. I lived off those excuses, ate them for breakfast, lunch, and dinner.

I built my life on a fear that all of my demons would surface. Each one carried the ability to break my façade down, to bare my dishonesty to the world. I lived in fear that truths like these would surface:

I stopped school at eighteen, and because of my dad, I was never going to be successful.

I left home at seventeen because I didn't want to deal with my mom, and that caused me to do drugs.

Being abandoned by men in my life made me promiscuous.

Because I lacked a strong relationship with anyone in my family when I was growing up, I became pregnant as a teen.

The only way my family knew how to help was with alcohol, so I drank.

Since no one was there for me, it was okay for me to run away.

I lived in the eye of a hurricane. At any minute everything could be ripped out from underneath me, and I couldn't stop it from happening. It was like being on the world's worst rollercoaster ride without being clipped in.

Cue the tiny violin. I was giving everyone else my power. How could I cry about everything going wrong in my life, when I wasn't doing anything to make it right?

Finally, after Ethan and I broke up, it was time to start digging, time to excavate why blaming everyone was easier than showing up each day, and time to learn how to stand in my power and teach my kids how to stand in theirs. Imagine what I could be teaching Ethan if, instead of wallowing in how my life was not one I wanted, I actively began to create a life I did want.

Plus, I really liked myself as a person. I love everyone. Well, mostly everyone. You, for sure. I am sensitive, empathetic, open-minded, an awesome cook, and loyal to a fault. I had to have gotten all those shining attributes from somewhere other than my ego.

Here's the truth. When you take your power back and reunite all the pieces of yourself, you can see how the puzzle of yourself fits together. Each experience, person, hiccup, bad decision, good lay, bad lay, argument, disaster, failure – all come together to make a beautiful person. The very you are reading this book right now. That's beautiful. You're beautiful. If it weren't for the events of your life unfolding exactly how they have, you may have missed that very quality that makes you so unique and special now.

You can be quite a force when you stand in your own strength.

Reuniting myself was the first time I could see that giving in to Ethan, and giving up, wasn't helping him. It allowed me to push through my weariness and say "no" to him and mean it. To be fair, I also started dating an incredible man who supported me while I was becoming my powerful self. That helped me stay firm. But I think it was me in my power that he found sexy in the first place. Poor chap. He didn't know what he was getting in to at the time.

Releasing and letting go of the thoughts, feelings, and emotions of others in your life is like taking a huge, heavy backpack off and then going for a run. It feels like you can fly. Why carry that heaviness if you don't have to? Who told you to take it and place it on your back in the first place?

Blame was my big release. There are so many emotions we hold. You may recognize yourself in several or all included in this list:

Blame
Defensiveness
Shame
Anger
Resentment
Bitterness
Hate
Guilt
Loneliness
Grief

A truly magical experience of finding one's own strength came from a client. I'll refer to her as Nadia. When we started working together, she felt a lot of sadness. Her heart was aching from being married to an alcoholic husband for eight years. Even though he had been sober for a year, there were many emotions bottled up inside her, unresolved, making it hard to breathe.

Living with an alcoholic is very similar to living with a child with mental illness. You want to help the one you love with every ounce of your being, but don't know how. Years are lost to rehab, appointments, and therapy. You feel hurt, blame, and detachment from the person you love the most.

On our first call, Nadia and I went to work sifting through her emotions and how we were going to get in and clear all the difficult things she was feeling. While we were talking, she told stories going back to being five years old, and how her grandmother, even with love in her heart, had made Nadia feel insecure and dirty about sex.

Almost forty years later, Nadia was still carrying the weight of feeling that way. She felt flawed and had been told by her mother that her alcoholic husband would be the best she could do, considering the flaws she had. With no other hope in her heart, she had married a man she knew would hurt her.

Nadia was carrying hurt from her husband, anger from her mom, guilt from her grandmother, and other emotions that had built up over the years. We needed to get in there and cut her free of feeling that way. We got to work, Jackie Chan style. Together, we sliced through layer after layer of emotion, heartache, and self-worth struggles.

Nadia went from crying to laughing, and when she told me she felt free for the first times in years, I wept with her. Nadia's cry was not the cry of holding things in and them leaking out of your eyes anyway, but the good kind of cry, the kind that gives you permission to let go, to free your body and mind from feeling that way again.

At the end of our call, Nadia told me she had been writing the word "free" on sticky notes and posting them everywhere. She felt like hugging her husband for the first time in years, and she felt hope again, hope that they could heal. Words are powerful and the word "free" mattered. Nadia had taken back her power.

Chapter Seven

Who Am I
Without My Child?

"The creative adult is the child who survives."
–Unknown

When I was at the peak of my adulting attempts, worried all the time, barely making ends meet, I became a shell of my former, younger self. I thought only about what I needed to do to pay the bills, get dinner on the table, make the appointments for the day. I lost myself to my duties, to what was expected of me. I no longer heard the calling of my heart or my purpose.

When it came to doing things with my kids, I had a hard time finding things to do that I enjoyed. My favorite pastime was calling a friend who had a kid and getting together so the kids could play and we could drink wine. I had lost my fun mojo. I even told my kids, "Mommy isn't fun." What in the world was that all about? How can one "lose" their fun?!

I had no childlike wonder, carefree play, or connection to my inner child at all. My inner child and I had had a fight, split our best friend necklace, and gone in separate directions. When I thought about doing anything with her, I saw a closed door with a "No Trespassing" sign on it.

I needed to find a way to connect to my younger self, to bring her out to play without scaring her. Frankly, I just needed to see her to believe she still existed. I think I convinced myself she had never been there in the first place, and so I was all alone.

I grew up in a house full of women – me, my mom, and my sister. Every weekend, Nanny would come over, we would all clean house, have dinner, then watch a movie. Conversations at the dinner table were filled with girl nonsense. For instance, there was the time my sister declared that "vagina" was a terrible name for the female private parts. Why couldn't it be named something pretty, like flower, or butterfly? I grew up in an openly estrogen-filled, girly world.

When I gave birth to a boy, I cried. I cried because I had no idea what I was going to do with a kid who had a penis. I only knew how to play Barbies, dolls, and dress-up. What was that thing called Lego? How do I play cars? It was like I was living in a foreign world of blue. I started to lose a part of my fun self then, mostly because I didn't try to learn his world. I kinda wanted Ethan to enter mine. When I met my daughter's father, he told me I was close to making Ethan into a girl.

Having a child with mental illness grows you up a lot. I started to believe I had to keep the world from falling apart – at home, and in the eyes of those looking in. I built up walls to protect myself from all the good stuff – happiness, fun, play, and joy. I think I didn't allow them in because it would feel too good, because when everything crashed down, which I knew it would, that would mean an even farther drop onto the ground. What if I shattered?

I wasn't a completely terrible mom. We watched movies, played countless games of Wii bowling. Ethan learned how to play games – just not board games, like Monopoly or Life (why do those games have to last for hours?). We went to water parks (where I avoided the slides), and there is probably a jar somewhere with all of those lost YouTube hours in it.

Somewhere along the way, I realized that I didn't want to have fun with Ethan anymore. I wanted my fun to happen when he wasn't around, because when he was there, I was stressed and on edge.

Ethan also had a different idea of how he wanted to play, like video games. I hated video games. Usually I hurt myself trying, and got blisters on my thumbs from rubbing the buttons so hard. I'd sweat from the pressure and get a huge case of Tourette's.

Ethan and I didn't like the same things. We still don't. I might have taught him to like shopping along the way, but that is an expensive way to spend quality time.

During the dark days of guilt after I kicked Ethan out of my life, I found a tribe of women who helped me feel comfortable being lost. It was a group of women who all seemed to be struggling to figure it out, just like me. I joined Leonie Dawson's Biz/Life Academy for a year. It was a bunch of spiritual women, basking in their feminine beauty, looking for answers to who they were and what they wanted.

While in the program for that year, I got access to loads of courses and meditations. It was in one of those courses that a simple question rocked my world for days. It wasn't crazy, nor did it require tons of work. It simply left me stumped. Absolutely lost. I was asked to write a list of 100 things I enjoyed doing.

What the world did I like doing? Seriously, I couldn't answer that question for days. I realized then that I had closed down business, shuttered the windows, and cut myself off from having any fun at all.

It was time to send in the rescue crew, and for some reason, that involved Dora the Explorer. She and Backpack had to go through Memory Forest, around Scared of Myself Lake, over Hiding from Life Mountain, to reach Free My Inner Child.

Even when I think about talking to my inner child right now, it's hard. I feel like she is scared of me writing this book. It took me so long to coax her out to play that writing about all the years I ignored her is making her want to hide again.

Something happened when I started writing out what I loved to do. It sent me back in time to my favorite townhouse where I lived with my mom. Every day, after dinner, I would sit on the couch and my mom would sit in her big oversized chair with her feet on an ottoman. I remembered so vividly that I would have a pile of stationary beside me.

Every night, while my mom watched her recorded episode of *The Young and the Restless*, I would write poetry, draw, create stories, or read. I found solace in paper. Writing words and drawing pictures became my favorite part of my day. I needed to do more of those things. I was already a stationary junkie, and after remembering that time, I knew why.

I started to craft, making fairy houses and doors out of polymer clay, and making fairy wands and houses. Magic was part of me. Reading fantasy stories, which I had done when I was younger, opened me up to a world I had forgotten. I found pictures in my basement that my aunt had given me of a fairy and a wizard. They hang in my daughter's room now. I was a princess. How could I have forgotten?

My creative cave had been reopened, and all I wanted to do was make things. I used to believe I didn't finish anything I started, but after getting back in touch with what I enjoyed, I completed a coloring agenda and an Intention Card deck. I was on fire!

The inner child work was hard. I could remember what I loved doing, and I began to bring some of that back into my life, but other kinds of play and fun still eluded me. I didn't have the same childhood as everyone else – that's what I believed. With my mom having severe depression, we didn't go anywhere there was a crowd, so no going out to movies or taking field trips to fun places. My dad would take us to the cottage every year, but that was as far as I went.

My first inner child meditation felt icky. Like I didn't want to remember what it felt like to play. My adult self had been in the driver's seat for such a long time, not allowing any detours down Have a Good Time Lane. The more intense life became, the more serious I had become.

My client Theresa couldn't get past sitting in a dark room holding on to inner child, at first. She had grown up around a lot of sadness, and all her inner child wanted to do was be held and cry. She sat and rocked her inner child and made a promise to come back to her. The more she went to sit with herself, the more her inner child trusted her to share the memories she had been holding onto so tightly. Theresa went from having no happy memories of being a kid, to remembering playing.

When I asked her what playing meant to her, she cried. She has a daughter now and she realized how serious a mom she was. Because she hadn't remembered how to play, she felt she had stolen her daughter's childhood. As we worked together, young Theresa came out to play and spent more time with her daughter, just letting loose. Her daughter, Keira, noticed.

When they were sitting together one day, Keira, who was twelve, told her mother she seemed like she was having more fun lately. She felt that her mom had taught her how to be a really great adult, but that she didn't feel she taught her how to play. Theresa felt she had stolen not only her own happiness, but her daughter's. As they talked, that wound began to heal.

For another client, Michelle, her happiest times came after work during her high school years. During our work together, she remembered how much fun she used to have. She'd lost touch with that during the eighteen years she spent raising her nephew, who had behavioral problems, and shutting down from life.

When I asked Michelle if she could take herself on a date, she decided to try it, and found herself out by Niagara Falls, drinking a coffee, walking the same path she used to walk after work, long ago. It flooded her with memories of being free, and she found herself laughing uncontrollably. Even though she felt crazy, she let go and laughed, which freed her inner child.

Thank freaking goodness we aren't stuck in our lives and can reach out to our inner child with an invitation to play whenever we want.

I can't believe how serious I became as a parent. I know I can't go back and change the fun factor in my house back then, or even how I didn't nurture my soul, but I could sure as heck make living a happy life more of a priority in the present.

Here are some of the ways we create fun in my house now:

Having games night once a week

Doing a March movie madness during the March school break (each night someone picks a movie and a snack – six people, six nights)

Taking trips to the water park (I now think waterslides are worth going down)

Ice skating (even though I suck at it)

Laughing with the kids – they are funny!

Doing what the kids ask, which means sometimes putting down my work for a few minutes; practicing somersaults is fun!

Letting the kids make a mess in the kitchen to cook

Having random dance parties

Singing loudly in the car

The list could go on and on. It's like once the tap is turned on, you can't stop the fun from flowing. It's like riding a bike – you forget how much you enjoy doing it until you are racing down the street, the wind in your hair, feeling the rush of freedom.

Chapter Eight

How Can My Child and I Get Along Better?

"When you want something, all the Universe conspires in helping you achieve it."
–Paulo Coelho

The craziest thing happened. I know it may sound completely unfamiliar and foreign, but the less I focused on Ethan, the better our lives became. Even when he lived at home, the more energy I put into things that lit me up inside, the more we seemed to revolve around each other differently. Two planets orbiting around each other in a peaceful solar system, instead of the firing meteor showers we normally were.

When I was overbearing, trying to fix him, hyper-focused on where he was and what he was doing, our lives spiraled out of control. It was as though the more I tried to control the situation, the more out of control it became.

The last two years have been about learning how to step away from being in control of Ethan, and stepping into who I wanted to be and what I wanted out of life. I took the time to work on myself, on my own mind, body, and spirit.

So many concepts are out there that allow us to see the world through different lenses. I fell in love with the idea that we can order up what we want from the Universe, like at a fast food drive-through. "Hi, I'd like to place an order please. Can I have a million-dollar sandwich, with a side of energy, an order of vacations, and a large cup of happiness? Thanks!"

What if the truth is that simple? What if our parents told us life was hard because that's what their parents told them, and their parents before them, and for hundreds of years those words defined who our ancestors were and what decisions they made? Why wouldn't we believe our parents? We looked up to them when we were little, and we looked up to our grandparents. I had taken all of my parents' belief systems and made them my own.

I heard the statements below and made them part of my DNA, creating truths that reached right into my cellular structure:

"I'll believe it when I see it." My dad told me that when I told him I was going to create online courses.

"Good luck making a living doing that." I heard that when I chose a career as a personal trainer

"Grow up." My family told me that a lot when I was a young mother.

"You're crazy." What my dad said when I told him about selling fairy houses and doors.

"You are throwing your life away." Said when I decided to stay pregnant at the age of nineteen.

"We don't have money to do things." Said by my mom, because I grew up in subsidized housing with a single mom.

"Money doesn't grow on trees." That was a Dad special.

Those are just a few. I'm sure my family meant well, but come on. Talk about stopping me from succeeding before I could even get started. Whether we mean to or not, listening to those we respect as we grow up defines how we see ourselves in life.

No way was I going to think along those lines forever. I also didn't want to find myself stuck in the parent cycle of telling my kids that their lives were going to be hard, too. I am not saying you have to spend every penny on your children's every whim, but imagine what could happen if they grew up thinking life was easy, that they could make money freely, and that anything was possible. I'm 39 and I'm just now starting to believe it.

The first creative way I tested the Universe on this theory was with a vision board. To make a vision board, cut or print out some pictures of things that you find attractive or that you want, stick them onto some Bristol board, and *boom*, your Universal menu order is complete.

My first vision board had a couch, the words "write a book," Birkenstock sandals, a stack of money, a car, a trip to Atlantis, and a puppy on it. It was a tall order! Here's the crazy part: things happened. I didn't write a book like this one, but I self-published a 52-week coloring agenda. We didn't go to Atlantis, but I went to Florida and Vegas. And we got a car. Shut the back door!

I couldn't get over how amazing it was. I did another vision board a year later, and even my husband got on board. How could he not, because my results seemed like witchy magic gone wild. We didn't do our vision boards at the same time, and his was pretty simple. But, I was ecstatic he was making one. I'm not making this up. Almost everything we put on the boards came true. Some came with life lessons, like when we paid down all our debt, then got scammed on our roof. I know some of that needed that to happen in order for me learn how I felt about money.

There are no right or wrong ways to make a vision board, as long as you have your wishes and dreams there. One of my clients hand-drew her vision board, and it was pure magic. There are so many variations and ways you can make it perfectly you. I love looking at them so much I started a gallery on my website, www.theenchantedfairy.ca. If you feel inspired, go check them out.

It's possible to go deeper still, to imagine the exact day-to-day life you desire. When my life was falling apart around me – a failing relationship, losing my job and feeling like I was losing my sanity – I would fantasize about what a normal life would look like. Me and the Beavers, waving at each other as we stepped outside in the morning to get our papers, then sipping coffee in our robes. Inside, everyone was laughing and smiling. Every day was happy.

I started to write down what my perfect day would look like, what I would be doing, how it would unfold. The simplicity of it surprised me. When I ask my clients to do that, they often told me the same thing – that their ideal life was simple. They were doing things they loved, feeling connected, walking, reading, journaling. It was far less about hustling, fighting, and forcing themselves to do things they thought they "should" do.

It might be hard to imagine that this can work. I hear you, loud and clear. When life is falling apart around you and no one is throwing you a life jacket, how can you put any stock in believing you can change it all with pictures, or with words written over and over? Whenever I ask a client to describe and write their perfect day, and then to write it again, they are confused at first.

They say they can't trust the Universe, that it can't be that easy. How strange it feels to them to have the freedom to create the life they want, different from what society told them. Almost every one of them has told me it feels forced at first, unreal and fake. Sitting there pretending to have an easy life when it's not *is* hard work. It *does* feel forced. But it gets easier.

At this point, if you are still following me and don't think I'm completely full of poop, I'm going to give you the big idea, the one that will rock your socks and blow your mind all at the same time.

You can actually place the order into the Universal drive-thru of life and *expect* it to happen. Yep, I want the million-dollar burger and that cup of happiness. Let that thought soak in. Feel your shoulders relax at the idea of having ease and flow. If you write out in detail what you want your next year to look like, you can make it happen – as long as your subconscious believes it.

Let me give you an example of why details are so important. Let's say you decide you are going to renovate your kitchen. You look through magazines, pick your countertop, backsplash, floors, and cupboards. You go shopping at different stores (in person or online), seeing and even feeling each texture. Weekends are spent on choosing the furniture and lighting fixtures you'd want. You contact a couple of contractors and designers who you feel match your style. You have a perfect vision of what your kitchen will look like when it's finished and complete.

What would happen if, instead, you hired someone to come in but gave them no clue as to what you wanted? You leave the contractor to build your kitchen, but give them no color schemes, pictures, or ideas. Do you think they would design your kitchen the way you liked it? Or would they design it how *they* thought it should look?

Your life is no different. Without knowing what you want, how can the Universe, God, Source energy, or whomever you pray to, bring you the life you desire or want? Do you feel selfish for asking for that, or guilty for wanting things a certain way?

It has taken me three years (each year including writing a book of some kind) for my dream of writing a book like this to come true. Somehow, after Ethan and I had stopped talking I went back to wanting to be a kid again. That translated into wanting to draw and color, which magically became me creating a 52-week coloring agenda. Writing goals for me needed to be soft and creative, and it felt good to see a project visually come to life. Shortly after creating the coloring agenda, I was guided to create an Intention Card deck. Words have power, and giving an intention to the day helped me set a tone that I could step into. Those were incredible feats of awesome, but I still wanted to make a different kind of book.

Knowing that you can design your life as you would design a kitchen, what would you want to create? Grab a piece of paper or your favorite journal, pull up to the Universal ordering station, and order your year.

Write out what your life will look like exactly one year from today. The more detail you provide, the more it's likely to happen. It's like telling the contractor you want white cupboards, or telling them you want Shaker-style cabinets in matte white on the top and soft grey on the bottom, with quartz counters, and designer handles. You will absolutely get the detail you put into this.

Going from feeling like your life is out of control to imagining it in fine detail can feel like a complete fairy tale, silly and not worth the time. I get that. But... what if you try it and something does change because you wrote it out? What if you write your life as it looks one year from now, detailed down to how many days you take off to play, and life starts to change to mirror it?

One of my clients wrote out their perfect day and it included quitting his job and working from home. Within weeks of putting that desire on paper, the world aligned to his wishes, and he was able to quit his job and work at home.

Chapter Nine

How to Have a Healthy Relationship with Your Child

"I believe that every single event in life happens in an opportunity to choose love over fear."
–Oprah

Stress has such a terrible effect on the body. It's such an poo head for doing that. It comes to you in the morning, can sneak up on you in the afternoon, and wants to snuggle at night when you're trying to unwind. It makes itself known in every moment of the day. Stupid stress.

I used to let stress take over my life. There were a few times when I gave up the fight. It was hard enough to get through the day, let alone take care of myself in the process. No way. Too hard. It was easier to open a bottle of wine than it was to make dinner. Feed the kids what they wanted; feed the mommy what she wanted.

To paint that picture, think of me like Superman, but in an unhealthy way. Personal Trainer by day – chip-eating, wine-guzzling maniac by night. For a while, I was drinking away my cares more frequently than I'd like to admit. It helped for a while, until it didn't. When none of my clothes fit, and I felt guilty when I was helping my clients figure out their fitness goals, I knew I needed a shift.

Self-care was a strange word that I didn't understand. How could I spend time on myself when my son was in so much pain? I don't know if it was a martyr thing, a society thing, or just my own warped way of thinking, but I felt guilty if I spent money or time on myself.

My personal saving grace was that I taught fitness classes. If I wasn't getting paid to get up on stage and work people out, I probably wouldn't have gotten any exercise. I have to be honest –during a few of those classes, I was super hungover. Have you ever tried teaching a nine a.m. step class while still kind of drunk and hungover at the same time? I don't recommend it.

When I finally made the decision to get my act together and listen to my body, I noticed the biggest shifts in my life and in all of my relationships.

I am about to unlock the secret treasures of your body and mind. Just kidding. I'm about to share how I helped Ethan and me get to a great place for a while, and how I kept myself from losing my mind.

I'm going to bring up the word *self-care* again, because it matters for what I am about to tell you. Society can often tell us that, as parents, our sole purpose is to give ourselves over to the needs of our children, to bow to them or be considered selfish. A cell has a nucleus that runs the whole thing. If the nucleus shuts down, so does that cell. You are the nucleus of your life. When you are overtired, pissed off, defeated, and done with life, everything around you will be affected by that.

Think back to a time in your life when you felt vibrant and happy. What were the people around you doing? How were they responding to you? Now think about a time when you felt like giving up and throwing in the towel. See in your mind how people in your life responded to that emotion. I nearly fell off my chair when I realized that my energy affected my whole household. It felt like a power trip. Who was I to have so much control?

So how do we go from living below zero to flying high, especially when we don't feel like it? We fake it! I'm totally not kidding. One of my favorite sayings ever is that everything is difficult before it becomes easy. Getting into a healthy, vibrant vibe is going to feel like trudging through mud. Then, all of a sudden, it will feel like the wind is at your back and you could run a marathon.

What's important is that you stay true to yourself and do things that actually make you feel good, not what everyone else says you should do to feel good. I hate running, therefore I walk, even though everyone tries to tell me that running is better for me. But running hurts my hips and makes me feel like my face is going to pop off. No thank you!

The best time in my house for me and Ethan was when he joined the rowing crew in high school and I swore off alcohol. For a brief while, we would get up early together, make his protein shake and his lunch, and I would drop him off at school. It was so cool to talk about health and fitness together. We didn't fight, I wasn't worried about what he was doing, and the whole house felt lighter. I can still remember how it felt when we got along that well. It was awesome.

It's a cliché, but true, that when you love yourself, the world loves along with you. The more you focus on getting your health and happiness in order, the more your happy vibes will bring up the energy in your space.

How do you break free from the chaos and start creating a life that makes you feel good? First, you decide what makes you feel good. What were you doing before the world told you to grow up, get a real job, and let go of your fantasies? What lit you up like a Christmas tree? Were you into sports or the arts? Did you spend all your time outside. Did you lose hours playing video games? Chances are, if you gave yourself permission to do these things now, they would still make you feel good.

A remarkable thing happens in your body when you do something you love. It floods with all sorts of happy hormones. These hormones wash you in a glow of joy that makes everything else in the world more manageable, even your kids. Think about your post-sex glow, how good you feel after, how many people notice the silly smile on your face.

Speaking of sex, it can count as an activity you love. Being intimate is like riding a bike. You may have given up on it because you became too responsible and got distracted, but once you start having fun again, you may realize how much you love it. Even if you aren't with anyone right now, a good orgasm never hurt anyone. Just saying.

Write a list of all the things you love to do. Hold nothing back. Allow your mind to remember grade school, high school, university, and what you loved to do. What were you doing when you laughed the hardest, smiled the biggest, felt the most free? Take yourself back to those moments?

When I was talking to a client the other day, she told me she used to love dancing when she was a kid. She excelled at it, and she got into doing choreography. She was involved in dance all through high school, and she even got to choreograph the major performance at the end of the year. After high school, she wanted to continue, but her parents didn't think that was acceptable. They told her she should go to school and get a job that paid well.

The next few years passed in school with increased anxiety and hating what she was learning. She admitted to me that she couldn't even remember anything she learned while getting her MBA. She knows she passed and graduated, but it was like living in a fog. She felt numb.

Within a week of us starting to work together, she had signed up for a dance class and had been asked to perform in a community fundraiser. She felt alive again.

When things were at their worst, I sometimes needed to top up the happy. I'm not afraid to admit I use nutritional supplements. If I know my vitamin and mineral levels are depleted because I am not sleeping, functioning, or feeding myself properly, I ante up. What's the point of suffering through when there are options to prevent a complete meltdown? Cortisol can be a real jerk, and it will take you down. It doesn't fight fair, so why should I? Fortifying the body's defenses for the fight makes sense to me. I want to give my body every opportunity to kick stress's ass. Vitamins, probiotics, and digestive enzymes are captains in my army of the body. They go in and fight the war in my digestive system, adrenals, and energy system so I can love my life and kids.

There are so many ways to light yourself up and get your energy flowing. Here are some ideas:

Walking
Hiking
Dancing
Recreational sports – like ultimate Frisbee and dodge ball
Going to the gym
Swimming
Singing
Art classes
Running

Do them by yourself, or invite your kids along. If you need a break from them, because they sometimes suck, then go alone. If you want to share the journey, take them with you. Don't feel bad if you need some space from them. If you come back happy, they will be happier. Even if they get pissed in the beginning, they will soon realize happy Mom is better than smothering Mom.

Theresa was defined by her daughter as being "a helicopter mom," always hovering, not allowing her to breathe. Things started to improve between them when Theresa focused on getting her life and her happiness in order. Here's the thing, though – when you get into a good head space and focus on yourself, there is going to be resistance. There came a day when her daughter, Keira, wanted to get her mom's attention, so the school called and informed Theresa that her daughter had cut herself.

Instead of running out and going to pick her up, Theresa allowed Keira to complete her day and then walk home. A couple of hours after Keira had gotten home, Theresa brought up the cutting. She asked Keira why she had felt the need to cut, and Keira said it was because she wanted to talk to her mom. After being smothered for so long, she didn't know how to get Theresa's attention without resorting to old habits.

They had an honest conversation, and when Keira was given the choice between a helicopter mom and the mom who was happy and working on herself, Keira chose the happy Mom. What changed was the fact that Theresa didn't react from a place of fear. They agreed that Keira would ask her mom for her time instead of cutting herself to get attention.

Trusting that you aren't failing as a parent when you make time for yourself is a strange feeling. Giving up guilt over this is even harder. But once you get in the flow of doing what feels good for yourself and get through the resistance about it, life takes on a soft glow of awesome that you may have never felt before.

Chapter Ten

How Do I Look Forward to Each Day with My Child?

*"Change the way you see things,
and the things you see change."*
–Wayne Dyer

Each day is a fresh canvas on which you can paint a landscape, a bowl of fruit, people, abstract images, or anything else. You get to wake up, choose your mood, and step into your day, carrying the burdens from yesterday, or ditching them at the door. One of the greatest things I learned in therapy is that each day is a fresh start and that forgiving is important. I still use this "fresh start / forgive" idea to this day when I am speaking to Ethan, and that is a mantra I repeat, over and over again.

Every morning, I leave the past behind me, so I can stay present in how amazing this new day is. While I was writing this book, Ethan was staying with us, and he had a meltdown and broke my downstairs drawers in the bathroom. His emotions were bigger than he knew what to do with, and he ended up reacting in anger. Was I upset? No. Did I make him feel bad about it and bring it up later on another day? Of course not. Replaying what happened in the past creates a cycle of stuck that leaves your boots in the mud and you standing in them.

"Fresh start / forgive" opens you up to leaving yesterday behind, to creating space for amazing things to happen. Instead of bringing anger, resentment, guilt, or shame into the day, you can open your eyes to excitement, joy, and possibility. Don't worry if you feel like this is impossible right now. I found it so hard at first. I used to want Ethan to know how hurt, upset, and angry I was. I figured it would help him show more respect for me and how I was trying to help him. Unfortunately, it did not work that way. In truth, the more I let things go – focused on fresh starts and forgiving – the more he got upset with me, at first, because all the attention-seeking that used to get me riled up had no effect anymore.

Slowly but surely, he realized that he didn't have to throw things back in my face either, which felt way better. Instead of both of us trying to pull each other down all day, the house got calmer, less volatile, and more peaceful. That did not mean the behaviors went away, not at first, but there was more control over emotion, which felt way better than being on an emotional rollercoaster.

Mornings became my favorite part of the day. They became times to reflect, journal, and release my past. I spent hours putting down on paper all the things that had set up camp inside me but that I didn't like – issues with my parents, money, past boyfriends – everything made it onto the page. If it had caused me any hurt, I was going to write it down. I especially loved to write after my morning meditation (life gets real in those things).

Over time, I worked with my morning routine in order to get more out of each day. What could I do to make each day easier than the last? Less stressful. More about me. I woke up a little earlier to have some more space, more quiet to prepare for the what-ifs and maybes that could surface in the day. I started to hear and trust that I was not alone and there was something greater that was supporting me and keeping me safe. I couldn't remember how long it had been since I felt that way. Mornings were awesome.

Think about what your mornings look like right now. Do you wake up angry about yesterday, fuming over the messy kitchen, pissed off that you have to do everything and no one ever helps with anything unless you raise your voice? Do you have time for a coffee and some quiet time before you are being dragged in every direction by your partner and kids? Do feel like you are already rushing and you haven't even gone to work yet? Been there. Done it. I used to hate mornings. It meant I had to start all over and do it all again.

I am about to tell you what I do now, and you are going to think I'm crazy. I know you are, because a few years ago I would have found me to be crazy. These are the excuses I would have used to stop myself from having a morning routine:

"I don't have time for this. My sleep is way more important than getting up and doing some hokey pokey nonsense."

"This is all a load of bull crap. There is nothing that the Universe can help me with."

"I don't have enough imagination for this. I can barely make it through today, let alone think about tomorrow."

"It's a waste of time. This doesn't work."

"Save your breath. I don't believe it."

I have been here and played that record, listened to each one of those tracks on repeat. But here's the magic: *You don't believe until you do.* One day, it seems to click and things start to feel different and better.

I have practiced and tried so many morning routines, enough that I am going to skip over most of them and give you my golden nugget, the shining light of all awesomeness. Okay, okay, I'll stop.

This is what my morning routine looks like, and why:

1. **List three gratitudes** – Life cannot be so bad that you can't find three things you are grateful for each morning. If it is, then I suggest you look into finding more in-depth help from a professional. I'm not trying to sound harsh, but there is sunshine, clean sheets, your favorite song playing, the dishes being done. If nothing makes you smile or feel happy, I'm pro-medication to help. My list of three gratitudes wasn't pretty when I first started doing this. My husband recently started, and his list isn't great either. The important thing is that each morning you are thankful for what you have, even if it is simply coffee and matching socks!

2. **Do a visualization of the day** – Paint a picture in your mind of what you want your day to look like. Create some energy around what you would like to happen, then step into it. On Monday, I wrote that I was going to have a peaceful day. Things had been hectic on Sunday with Ethan. I worked with four clients on Monday, and at some point, each of them said they felt peaceful or at peace. Weird, but awesome. My visualization came true for me and even influenced others. You don't have to write a novel here – my vision is only a few lines that highlight what I'm doing that day and how I want the day to go. Today I wrote that I wanted to work with a particular someone, and guess what? I started working with them.

3. **Write some affirmations** – This one seems to upset some people. Affirmations may seem cheesy, but they work like a charm. I tell myself every day that "I am successful." I spent so much of my time being afraid of success, more so than failure, that I realized being successful was easier than fearing success, so I finally let it happen. Your affirmation can be about anything you want in life. The sky is the limit, so long as your mind can believe the affirmation you choose. Some

other affirmations are: "I love my body," "I am living an energetic life," "My soul mate is on his/her way," "I am doing a job I love," and "Money flows to me with ease." Don't sell yourself short here. I write at least seven affirmations each day. I would totally do more, but because I'm a nerd and seven is my lucky number, I stop there.

4. **Major purpose review** – Where are you setting your life GPS? Where are you headed and where do you want to go? Reviewing this helps you start your car and put it in drive to achieve that, metaphorically speaking. Right now, my major-purpose GPS is set to making a huge difference to the people reading this book (that's you). Your major purpose may be about wanting to quit your day job, find a soul mate, or simply "Be happy." Make your major purpose slightly uncomfortable, but also tangible and reachable. You want to be able to break it down and know that, with a little reach, you can make it happen. The most important thing is to identify a clear destination. Even if you make a wrong turn, your GPS will steer you back around and get you on the road to achieving it.

5. **Exercise** – This is when you get to play. This exercise might be dancing around the house, doing ten push ups against the bathroom counter before hopping in the shower (a personal favorite), going to the gym, stretching on your living room floor – anything that gets blood moving and gets your mind and body on the same page. There is no need to stick to what other people say exercise is. Choose movement that feels good for you, even if it's twerking to Miley Cyrus.

That morning routine might seem simple, but sometimes it's the simplest things that make the biggest differences. One of my clients told me she hadn't journaled for years, but when she followed the morning routine above, it gave her such a positive outlook for the day. She referred to it as giving her "the good feels."

Speaking of finding your major purpose, have you thought about what you want to do with the wide-open road before you? Knowing that you can choose your life can feel a little overwhelming, but exciting at the same time.

For almost a decade of my life, I had no idea what I wanted. I just went through the motions of living. You could say I had settled into a world that revolved around doing the same thing I had done the day before. Dreaming anything bigger felt scary. All I worried about was getting to bed without a disaster happening. I was not focused on creating the life I was put on Earth to find.

Did you know you can have a child who has mental health issues and still work on becoming the most amazing version of yourself? That you can do those at the same time? Yeah, me neither. I figured it out eventually, though, and I'm hoping you can, too, because it can change everything. It can change how you feel about yourself, how you feel about your days, and it can one hundred percent change how you feel about your child. I used to say that Ethan stopped me from having a life. Now I know he is one of the reasons I get to live the life of my dreams.

Just a warning. When you start to move into a space where you can see your dream and know it's there for you to reach out and grab, people around you will get pissed off. If they are stuck in their own life and can't seem to move forward, why should you? Have you ever told someone you were on a diet, or doing a cleanse, and they started to follow you around offering you cookies? This is like that. When you step into your light, there are going to be a ton of people, even ones you thought were your friends, who are going to try to pull you back. They are going to call you a bad mother, crazy, selfish, will tell you that you've changed (and not mean it in a good way), or that you are ignoring them. Keep moving. They don't see what you now see – that anything is possible.

This brings us to a very important part of the story – to an idea you may have heard about before, but not acknowledged in your life. It's the idea of boundaries. It's time to set some boundaries and stay true to them.

When I started to write this book, I told everyone and their uncle that from January to March I would be unavailable for gatherings of any kind, because I wanted to focus solely on my book and on coaching my clients. In January it was as though I became the most popular girl in high school. Everyone seemed to come out of the woodwork to test my ability to stay true to my decision. It was tough. I felt guilty, worried that I was losing friends, scared I was breaking bonds with people. Then I sat back and thought about how good it would feel to finally finish the book I've wanted to write since I was a little kid. All of a sudden, saying no became easier. I was writing a book, darn it, and nothing was going to stop me!

Once you set your GPS, you will find yourself wanting to only do the things that move you in the direction of your dream. If you turn onto a bunch of side streets and detours, it will take you so much longer to get where you want to be. Get firm on your direction, then stop making pit stops.

Chapter Eleven

But What If Things Get Worse?

"A belief is only a thought I keep thinking."
– Abraham Hicks

To tell you that things are going to be hunky dory and light as a feather from this chapter on would be a lie, so I won't. Life is funny that way. Every time I start to move in the direction of my dreams, so many things seem to come flailing at me, knocking me off my feet. For example, when I decided to write this book, things with Ethan went off the rails. Our relationship had been amazing for over a year. We hadn't fought, had enjoyed spending time together, and had been truly supportive of how each of us was moving forward in our lives. I was nearing the end of birthing a book about our relationship and how I had stepped out of the chaos. Ethan lived 45 minutes away, and when his apartment was broken into he came to live with us for a few weeks. It was terrible!

The first weekend, he wanted his friend to stay over for longer, and I said no. I could see the pattern of codependency beginning to form as Ethan repeatedly came into my bedroom to try to convince me to make a different decision. He even cried, telling me he would never see his friend again after that weekend. For a second, I thought about giving in. Then I remembered that I didn't have to. It was my house, we had routines, and I didn't need to explain to him why his friend couldn't come back to sleep over again on a Monday night.

The last weekend before Ethan moved back out seemed like another way the world tried to convince me I should give up my dream and go back to the way things were. Ethan was stressed from having no fixed address, and overwhelmed with having to deal with figuring out his work schedule while away in another city. His inability to deal with his emotions caused a major meltdown. I got a call from Ethan while I was at a restaurant with friends, and he told me that he didn't want to bother anymore and he should jump off a bridge.

The old me would have left my friends hanging, run home, and tried to soothe him. I would have changed my work schedule for the next day and given him whatever he needed. Instead, I asked if he wanted me to take him to the hospital, and asked what else I could do to make things easier for him. He didn't have an answer, so I stayed where I was. The next day, he got the keys to his new apartment, and things settled down.

Some people call these "tests," some call it "self-sabotage," and some say it's the Universe acting against them. Others believe, as I once did, that things happen to them to prevent them from having the life they want. No matter how we look at it, the part that's the real kicker is that resistance sucks. But it exists to move us forward.

Let me repeat that so it sinks in and permeates deep into your soul: Resistance exists to help us realize what it is we are meant to do in life. The more we feel resistance, the better the outcome will be. Resistance is here to tell us that something amazing is waiting for us on the other side.

When I filled out the application for the program I joined to write this book, I had a full-on panic attack. My hands were shaking, my teeth were quaking, and I had a blanket wrapped tightly around me. I kept having to take a break, because I could barely type. As waves of fear poured over me, I knew I was doing the right thing. There was no way there was that much kickback if the pay-off wasn't going to be amazing.

The fear continued for the first month I was in the program. Who was I to write a book? How was I going to help anyone? What if my family disowned me when they read it? Fear-based thoughts consumed me. Anxiety attacks made me want to hide from the world. I wasn't sure I had made the right decision, and I was scared out of my mind. But behind the fear, I knew I had to kill the safe, hidden Tamara in order to become the Tamara who wrote a book and helped more people. She didn't want to go down without a fight, so my body tried to shake her up and make her stay small.

My husband wrote an obituary when he wanted to move forward, to help with getting through the resistance. "On March 8th, at 1:18 p.m., the Jeff who was afraid of success and failure, was found dead at his place of business." He was ready to free himself to be seen, and to have his game apps get noticed. That meant he had to kill the Jeff who was scared, so he could become Jeff the successful game developer. I think all my positive mojo was beginning to rub off on him.

My client Holly was hit by serious resistance when she got ready to step into her light. Her mom was hospitalized twice. She found out her mom was a hoarder. Her brother told her his daughters had been sexually assaulted by someone. Her brother's car broke down. She got the flu. She went through a 24-hour electricity black-out. She had potentially gotten bit by a tick. And a family member died. All of that in one month. Yet, through it all, she also listed her first house as a real estate agent, even though it was with a co-realtor. And even though she felt the burden of having to do almost everything herself, the house sold. As she pushed through to becoming the Holly that kicks serious ass in her field, her old self was sending storms of uncertainty to keep her from moving forward, because her old self felt threatened.

How do we fight against resistance and step into our power anyway? Having help makes it easier. It helps to be around people who have stared the resistance demon in the eye and lived to tell the tale. I have been working with people to steer me in the right direction since I stepped out of being Ethan's mom full-time. I can't imagine having written this book without my coach, Angela Lauria at The Author Incubator, guiding me through my ups and downs. I had panic attacks, anxieties, imposter syndrome, fear, sinusitis, digestive problems, and my son move back in for a month. Through it all, I knew writing this book was what I wanted to do. Having Angela there to say what I was experiencing was normal helped me stay above the resistance.

Find someone you can share your journey with; someone who understands and doesn't make you feel bad. As you go through the process of becoming the you who is ready to find her purpose and passion, you deserve to be surrounded by people who are also doing the same thing and succeeding. If you feel that your friends or family are bringing you down, stop talking to them and keep going anyway. Find some pals who are journeying in the direction you want to go. This is a beautiful journey you are on. Sharing it with like-minded people is fun and helpful. I joined an online community right away when Ethan and I broke up. Watching and listening to others share their stories of strength and determination inspired me to keep working on myself.

In a group call with clients last night, Holly spoke up to say she was so thankful for having a safe place to share and talk without judgment. Remember that you don't have to seek approval from anyone as you move forward to find your joy, step into your power, and make your dreams come true. You can do it because it feels good, and because you are worth it. That doesn't make you a bad, selfish mother. On the contrary, it teaches your kids that they can strive to be anything they want to be, as well. They will watch you grow into your butterfly persona, and know they can soar, too.

Things may get worse before they get better, and your child may feel like you are pulling away from them. Breaking codependency may cause behaviors to heighten briefly as you step out of trying to fix everything and as you stop fanning every fire. Your kid may feel like you don't love them anymore and they may say that. Fortify your reserves and know that you are helping them find themselves by finding your own self. You are loving your child when you love yourself.

Once you start redefining who you are, the resistance will kick up, and you may want to use some hacks to keep yourself out of the chaos. It can be handy to prepare, in case the world loses its mind. A great way to stay ahead of the game is to have an emergency kit. On days when you want to give in, give up, and curl up in the fetal position, your emergency kit will help you remember that you are important and that how you feel matters. There is no right way to do one, but here are a couple ideas to get you started:

1. After reading this book, write out your feelings in the form of a letter. Write the suggestions that you tried out, which ones you loved, and what helped you stay true to yourself. Get right into it and detail out of your hopes, your thoughts, your perfect day – do all of that good stuff. Then put on some pretty lipstick, kiss the page, and tell yourself that you love yourself. When you have completed the letter, seal it in an envelope, address it to yourself, and put it away. On a day you don't know how you are going to make it through, open that letter

and read about how good you felt. Remind yourself that it is possible to have hope and love.

2. Buy a box and fill it with things you love. You might want to put a candle, a good book, some dark chocolate, a favorite DVD, bath salts, a gift card to a store you love – whatever. You can put in anything you love. When the day comes that you want to give up, run away, and leave your life, open the box and smile. You have permission to love the snot out of yourself. Ignore the world and spend some time with whatever's in the box.

Knowing your triggers is important. Knowing how to listen to your inner voice is crucial. Maintaining your ability to say no when crap hits the fan is life-saving. Don't let others decide for you what is best for you and for your family. Deciding for yourself saves you so much precious time and energy. No one knows what it's like to live with a child with mental illness, other than someone else who has lived with a child with mental illness.

When I spoke to my client Michelle this morning, she told me she felt paralyzed. Even though her nephew, who she raised, has moved out, she felt lost after eighteen years of raising him. Having the freedom to step into who she was put on this Earth to be was frightening. When every day is about chaos, the calm after the storm is eerie. She is so close to letting go of all the stress and pain, but every once in a while, the fear of moving forward takes over. It's like a giant hurricane, one that has held you in its grip for most of your life, spits you out, and you don't know where you are anymore when you look up.

The journey of letting go of the judgments of others, finding yourself amongst the chaos, and releasing from the guilt of being a terrible mom, is pure magic once you get in to the rhythm of it. Where once your life felt like it was going to open you up and swallow you whole, now it feels fresh and open to possibilities.

You may still think I'm full of hokey, and that's okay. You still got to this point in the book, so part of you wants to believe me. I can tell you that having worked with loads of moms, some of them just like you, it *is* possible. It's not just possible, it's happening. You do not need to stay stuck in fear. You can bust out into the dance of life, letting go of being solely responsible for everything and everyone, and lead a life that makes you smile from the moment you open your eyes. So throw your hands up in the air and wave them around like you just don't care. You are amazing, your life is wondrous, and everything you feel is important. Stand in your power, because you are worth fighting for!

Conclusion

"Today is a gift. That's why it's called the present."
–Unknown

Y ou made it! You read the book and now everything will be better.

If only it were that simple. It takes work, dedication, and a willingness to be your own badass self that makes life with your child get better.

It's time to become you, the person you have always wanted to be, free from the judgment of others. Imagine a world where you can discover all your secrets, like hidden treasure. Your past holds the treasure map, so now all you have to do is find the X and start digging.

This doesn't mean life won't come at you with all cylinders firing. There are times you will have a bad day or days, just like everyone else. It's how you deal with them that matters.

I would love for you to break free from the chaos and find your peace. Jump on over to www.mykidisdrivingmecrazy.com to find a three-part video series that covers, in detail, how to find yourself again, how to hear yourself – your own voice. It feels so amazing to know that what I have been through can help. It took me years to get here. I hope we can get you there faster!

Further Reading

Codependent No More – Melodie Beattie

The Universe Has Your Back – Gabrielle Bernstein

Money: A Love Story – Kate Northrup

Something More – Sarah Ban Breathnach

For information on the supplements Ethan and I use to feel good, hop on over to www.theenchantedfairy.usana.com

Acknowledgments

I don't think this book would have made it into the world if it weren't for my husband Jeff, who always knew it was in me. He is a man who not only decided to start dating me in the chaos, but stayed with me through the hard times, then married me and held me when I cried. I can't thank him enough for believing in me for the last five years. I am pretty sure he is surprised he survived, as well.

My son Ethan has been my greatest lesson and my greatest teacher, and if it weren't for him, this story wouldn't exist and I wouldn't be able to help others going through this. Although my years with Ethan were the hardest years of my life, they helped create the people we are today, and I am proud to say Ethan is becoming quite the man!

My other children – Siena, Claire, and Hayden – were so patient with me when I needed to focus on the book and not them. I am forever grateful that they saw the importance of this story, as well.

Thanks to The Author Incubator and Angela Lauria for making this a relatively painless process compared to trying to write the book on my own. Having her there, along with the other authors in transition, helped me become the Tamara who wrote and book and was ready to be seen. That was some hard shit to go through.

To the Morgan James Publishing team: Special thanks to David Hancock, CEO & Founder for believing in me and my message. To my Author Relations Manager, Gayle West, thanks for making the process seamless and easy. Many more thanks to everyone else, but especially Jim Howard, Bethany Marshall, and Nickcole Watkins.

For everyone else who helped me through the process – friends and family who gave me space, Grace, strangers who don't know they helped – you all mattered. Thank you.

About the Author

Tamara is a daughter and mother to mental illness. She has witnessed and healed from three suicide attempts by those closest to her – two by her mother, and one by her son.

Striving to bring wellness to the world, Tamara became a personal trainer and Healthy Eating and Weight-Loss Coach through *canfitpro* in 2007. Shortly after, her passion for helping others turned into teaching, and she became a *canfitpro* Pro Trainer, teaching courses to help others make an impact in the world.

During that time, her son, who suffers from oppositional defiance disorder, anxiety, and depression, exhibited suicidal tendencies and behavioral issues.

Tamara spent years going to therapy, for herself and with her son, learning how to balance living with mental health with having a strong sense of self.

In 2016, she became a life coach through the Certified Coaching Federation and created the program in this book to help others who are living with people with mental illness learn to separate themselves from the chaos, redefine who they are, and figure out what they want for their future.

Tamara has four kids, two cats, two dogs, and a loving husband. She is a huge nerd, loves New Kids on the Block and *Star Wars*, and spends most Friday and Saturday nights getting crazy with a good book.

Website: www.mykidisdrivingmecrazy.com

Thank You

I love each and every one of you who opened this book and committed to reading it from the introduction to the conclusion. You rock!

I've created a three-part video series that covers, in detail, ways you can manage living in a world where chaos and disorder is the daily menu. These videos give you ways to stay true to you, your heart, and your love for your child, without going absolutely crazy.

Jump on over to www.mykidisdrivingmecrazy.com

to access these fun, life-changing videos and have them delivered directly to your inbox.

Give yourself the joy of watching them over a fresh brewed coffee in the morning. I would love to be a part of your healing morning routine.

Morgan James
Speakers Group

↗ www.TheMorganJamesSpeakersGroup.com

We connect Morgan James published authors with live and online events and audiences who will benefit from their expertise.

Morgan James makes all of our titles available
through the Library for All Charity Organization.

www.LibraryForAll.org

in a way calculated to adulterate 'pure Socialism'; the Chancellor Hugh Gaitskell, Bevan's political rival, introduced prescription charges at the same time as he prepared for massive increases in Britain's military expenditures to meet the crisis of the Korean War.

Bevan had also been frustrated in his battle to build more houses – though the fact that he was given responsibility for this brief as Minister for Health must be regarded as an administrative mistake. Housing was one of the issues to which the voters – and the Party – attached most importance and the sheer scale of the problem demanded separate attention – logically at the Ministry of Local Government, since it was through the country's local authorities that the Government would have to act. In 1945 over 70 per cent of the nation's dwellings dated at least as far back as the nineteenth century.[31] During the war 200,000 houses were destroyed completely, 250,000 were rendered uninhabitable and another quarter of a million were severely damaged. In the election campaign, Labour 'had promised the earth' with Ernest Bevin talking about 'Five million homes in quick time'.[32] But the acute shortage of building materials and the money required to buy them made this an unlikely prospect.

To his credit, Bevan gave priority to rented public housing and insisted on 900 square feet of room-space per house, against the established standard of 750. He also increased the Treasury subsidy. But the building programme began very slowly. In the first year priority was given to repairs of damaged housing stock and the construction of 'temporary' accommodation (the 'prefabs' of which there were 125,000 by 1948). The squatter movement led by the Communist Party in London during 1946, involving as many as 50,000 people, is the best indication of how much was still to be done in a year when only 55,400 new homes were completed. The peak year for completions proved to be 1948 when over 227,000 were recorded; thereafter it fell back as balance of payments problems led to curbs on public investment. In total, 1,016,349 new houses were completed under Labour and a great many more were envisaged in the New Towns Act 1946. Still the Conservatives scored a great propaganda success when they were able to reach their electoral target of 300,000 completions in the first year of their return to government and no one would claim that Labour's housing record was a brilliant success.

The Mythology of a 'New Society'

But the Welfare State as a whole is another matter. Such was the scale of mythologising about the Attlee years that 'brilliant success' would rate as an understatement. Within a year of the Government's general election defeat, Anthony Crosland was arguing that 'Britain had in all essentials ceased to be a capitalist country'.[33] Tawney, drawing on Seebohm Rowntree's *Poverty and the Welfare State* (1951), was equally quick to link Labour's social legislation with the growth of economic equality and an alleged collapse in the percentage of people living in poverty.[34] By the mid-1950s Crosland was so convinced of the magnitude of Labour's success in narrowing the wealth and income differentials in British society that he pronounced further efforts in this direction a waste of energy; the case for equality must now rest, he insisted, on 'certain value or ethical judgements of a non-economic character' because the traditional egalitarian argument had become the victim of its own success.[35] In fact, the number of people living in poverty in the 1950s was to be measured in millions and was growing, as was the inequality of wealth distribution.[36] A 'moderate income equalization' did indeed take place in the 1940s but seemingly 'in association with the special pressures and policies of the war economy, [which] was petering out already before Labour left office in 1951'.[37] The myth that something more dramatic took place nevertheless lives on.[38]

Though the National Insurance Act of 1946 was supposed to guarantee a national minimum standard, benefits were

126

already falling behind the cost of living before the decade was out. In a context of inflation and rising real wages, the inequality between claimants and the employed would, of course, widen anyway. But it also has to be borne in mind that the subsistence income recommended by Beveridge was a matter of judgement, and his was both stringent and narrow, focusing on a range of notional necessities rather than the actual spending patterns of real people. He saw well enough that the subsistence minimum would have to change as the general standard of living changed. But there is reason to believe 'that the rates of benefits were too low to guarantee, even by Beveridge's own declared standards, security from want [and that] this initial inadequacy was aggravated by the developments of the post-war economy'.[39]

Critics on the Right

Sustained economic growth in the 1950s put paid to the argument that the Welfare State was an extravagance the nation could ill-afford, although Conservative critics such as Enoch Powell favoured ditching the universalist principle in favour of means testing as early as 1952. Later critiques of the Welfare State have no place in the present discussion – suffice to say that as public expenditure grew, the Welfare State became increasingly important as an instrument of mass manipulation and a site of bargaining between interest groups; when the post-war full-employment boom broke at the end of the 1960s, the problem of Britain's ailing economy was increasingly analysed in terms of this 'overloaded' corporatist state.[40] By the 1970s, the talk was of fiscal crisis and a crisis of legitimacy for an apparatus which much of the Left already found defective as an instrument for redistribution and democratic renewal.[41] For reasons that cannot be examined here, the New Right proved to be the main political beneficiary of these analyses while making new headway with reviving the 'politically necessary stereotypes' of old.

Unwin, London 1960, pp215-24; D. Rubinstein, *Socialism and the Labour Party; the Labour Left and Domestic Policy 1945-1950*, Labour Party Discussion Series No. 3, ILP Square One Publications, Leeds n.d., pp14-16; J. Brand, 'Faction as its Own Reward; Groups in the British Parliament 1945-1986', *Parliamentary Affairs; a Journal of Comparative Studies*, Vol. 2, No. 2, April 1989, p152; Schneer, *Labour's Conscience, cit.*, pp218, 222-4.

[57] For the Left's recognition of lack of public support for further nationalisation, and its declining importance as a political issue – 'Socialist Stocktaking IV – Nationalisation', *NS*, 13 November 1948; Cole, *Dream and Business, cit.*, pp203, 205; Cole, *Labour's Second Term, cit.*, p2; Crossman, 'Memorandum on Problems', *cit.*; Epstein, *op.cit.*, pp560-4, 573-4; Rubenstein, *op.cit.*, pp20, 23; Schneer, *Labour's Conscience, cit.*, pp97, 99-100.

[58] Wood, *op.cit.*, pp276-82; Tom Gittins, 'And You Chose Guns – Not Butter', *Daily Worker*, 5 June 1947; Konni Zilliacus, *I Choose Peace*, Penguin, Harmondsworth 1949, pp366-74, 437-8, 441-4; Zilliacus, *Why I Was Expelled, cit.*, p65; Mervyn Jones, 'As Reading Goes' *NS*, 14 January 1950.

[59] For the Labour Left's ideological divisions and their disruptive effect, see R. Crossman and George Wigg, 'Conscription', *NS*, 29 March 1947; 'Phineas', 'Parliament; Rebel Spirit', *NS*, 5 April 1947; K. Zilliacus, 'The Great Debate', *NS* (letter), 6 December 1947; Letters from Leonard Woolf and R. Crossman replying to Zilliacus, *NS*, 13 December 1947; Schneer, *Hopes Deferred, cit.*, pp213 and 218-21; Zilliacus, Why I was Expelled, pp18-21; Bill Jones, *The Russia Complex; The British Labour Party and the Soviet Union*, Manchester University Press, 1977, pp51-2, 56-61, 73; Jenkins, *op.cit.*, pp48-54; Schneer, *Labour's Conscience, cit.*, pp64-5, 75, 105-8, 118, 121-22, 129.

In particular, a story was developed to the effect that the 'illusions' of 1945 had created a 'dependency culture' or, as one critic would have us believe, 'a dank reality of a segregated, subliterate, unskilled, unhealthy, and institutionalised proletariat hanging on the nipple of state maternalism'.[42] According to this argument, a spirit of 'New Jerusalemism', itself a concoction of humanitarian and evangelical impulses, deflected the nation from the tasks of economic reconstruction in 1945 and saddled it with a growing welfare burden and relative decline. It is an argument which ignores the fact that social policy in Britain had long been influenced by hard-headed considerations of 'national efficiency' and the abatement of class conflict as well as the motivations exaggerated by Corelli Barnett.[43] Indeed the development of welfare states in most of the industrialised countries of western Europe in the decade after 1945 rather adds weight to such functionalist explanations because ideological and institutional factors necessarily varied from country to country.[44] The actual economic return on welfare investment must always be a matter for argument since there is no way it can be measured precisely. What is certain is that, by the late 1950s, Britain spent less on social security than all its major industrial rivals in Europe and most of the smaller ones.[45] It was not the Welfare State which sapped the British economy, but the fact that State obligations in respect of national development encroached so little on the ethos of market liberalism in this country.

Notes

[1] The argument that war is a great accelerator of the historical process is central to A. Marwick's *Britain in the Century of Total Wars*, Bodley Head, Oxford 1968, but the expectation that the Second World War would rapidly open up prospects for social and political advance on the home front was common property on the left in the war years.

[2] P. Addison, *The Road to 1945*, Quartet, London 1977, p15. See also A. Calder, *The People's War*, Cape, London 1969 and P.M.H. Bell, *John Bull*

and The Bear: British Public Opinion, Foreign Policy and the Soviet Union 1941-1945, Edward Arnold, London 1990.

[3] See S. Brooke, *Labour's War*, Clarendon Press, Oxford 1992, and T. Wildy, 'The Social and Economic Publicity and Propaganda of the Labour Governments of 1945-51', *Contemporary Record*, 6, 1, 1992.

[4] H. Perkin, *The Rise of Professional Society*, Routledge, London 1989, p415.

[5] T.H. Marshall, *Citizenship and Social Class*, Cambridge University Press, 1950.

[6] See J. Harris, 'Did British Workers Want The Welfare State?', in J. Winter (ed), *The Working Class in Modern British History*, Cambridge University Press, 1983, pp206-208.

[7] R. McKibbin, 'The Social Psychology of Unemployment in Inter-War Britain', in his *Ideologies of Class*, Oxford University Press, 1990, pp246-247.

[8] *Ibid*, p252.

[9] R. McKibbin, 'Class and Conventional Wisdom: The Conservative Party and the 'Public' in Inter-War Britain', in *Ideologies of Class, op.cit.*, p266.

[10] J. Harris, 'Social Planning in War-Time', in J.M. Winter (ed), *War and Economic Development*, Cambridge University Press, 1975, p240.

[11] See A. Marwick, 'The Labour Party and the Welfare State in Britain', *American Historical Review*, 73, 2, 1967, p385.

[12] J. Saville, 'The Welfare State: An Historical Approach', *New Reasoner*, Winter 1957-8, p21.

[13] J. Harris, 'Social Planning in War-Time', *op.cit.*, p248.

[14] J. Harris, 'Some Aspects of Social Policy in Britain During the Second World War', in W.J. Mommsen (ed), *The Emergence of the Welfare State in Britain and Germany*, Croom Helm, Beckenham 1981, p256.

[15] S. Brooke, *Labour's War, op.cit.*, pp164-165.

[16] J. Harris, 'Social Planning in War-Time', *op.cit.*, p244.

[17] J. Harris, 'Enterprise and the Welfare State: A Comparative Perspective', in T. Gourvish and A. O'Day (eds), *Britain Since 1945*, Macmillan, London 1991, p49.

[18] See J. Harris, *William Beveridge: A Biography*, Clarendon Press, Oxford 1977 and *ibid* pp49-50.

[19] See C. Barnett, *The Audit of War*, Macmillan, London 1986, pp201-233 and 276-304.

[20] C. Benn, 'Comprehensive School Reform and the 1945 Labour Government', *History Workshop Journal*, Autumn 1980, pp197-203.

[21] B. Vernon, *Ellen Wilkinson 1891-1947*, Croom Helm, Beckenham 1982, p226.

[22] See A. Wright, 'British Socialists and the British Constitution', *Parliamentary Affairs*, July 1990, pp326-327.

[23] See J. Callaghan, 'Fabian Socialism, Democracy and the State', in G. Duncan (ed), *Democracy and the Capitalist State*, Cambridge University Press, 1989, pp159-180.

[24] For example in S. Cripps, *Can Socialism Come By Constitutional Methods?*, Socialist League, London 1933.

[25] B. Pimlott, *Hugh Dalton*, Cape, London 1985, p398.

[26] K. Harris, *Attlee*, Weidenfeld and Nicholson, London 1982, p326.

[27] See S. Brooke, *Labour's War, op.cit.*, pp133-142 and A. Marwick, 'The Labour Party and the Welfare State', *op.cit.*, p399.

[28] S. Brooke, 'The Labour Party and the Second World War', in A. Gorst, L. Johnman and W. Scott Lucas (eds), *Contemporary British History: Politics and the Limits of Policy*, Pinter, London 1991, p5.

[29] Quoted in P. Hennessy, *Never Again: Britain 1945-1951*, Cape, London 1992, p132.

[30] A. Bevan, *In Place of Fear*, 1952 and Quartet, London 1978, p106 and pp114-115.

[31] A. Marwick, *British Society Since 1945*, Penguin, Harmondsworth 1982, p22.

[32] P. Hennessy, *op.cit.*, p169.

[33] C.A.R. Crosland, 'The Transition From Capitalism', in R.H.S. Crossman (ed), *New Fabian Essays*, Turnstile Press, London 1952, p43.

[34] Rowntree's study of York found only 3 per cent of the residents living in poverty in 1950 as against 31 per cent in 1936. See R.H. Tawney, 'British Socialism Today' (first published in *Socialist Commentary*, June 1952), in his *The Radical Tradition*, Penguin, Harmondsworth 1966, p179.

[35] C.A.R. Crosland, 'About Equality', *Encounter*, July 1956, p5.

[36] The evidence is reviewed in K. Coates and R. Silburn, *Poverty: The Forgotten Englishmen*, Penguin, Harmondsworth 1970, pp13-51.

[37] J. Westergaard and H. Resler, *Class in a Capitalist Society*, Penguin, Harmondsworth 1976, p47.

[38] For example Jay Winter, writing in 1983, asserted that 'it is well known … that a major redistribution of income levels took place in the period 1938-1948, thereby significantly reducing income inequality in this country'; see J. Winter, *The Working Class in Modern British History*, *op.cit.*, p233.

[39] K. Coates and R. Silburn, *op.cit.*, pp187-188.

[40] For example see, A. King, *Why Is Britain Becoming Harder To Govern?*, BBC Publication, London 1976.

[41] The argument that the middle class benefited more from certain Welfare State expenditures than the poor was put as early as 1959 by Brian Abel-Smith, but the full-blown analysis had to wait until J. Le Grand, *The Strategy of Equality: Redistribution and the Social Services*, Unwin Hyman, London 1982. Marxist writers did much to analyse the Welfare State in terms of bureaucratic management of conflict, fiscal crisis and legitimacy crisis. See, for example, C. Cockburn, *The Local State: Management of Cities and People*, Pluto Press, London 1977; P. Corrigan and P. Leonard, *Social Work Practice Under Capitalism*, Macmillan, London 1978; J. O'Connor, *The Fiscal Crisis of the State*, St Martin's Press, New York 1973; I. Gough, *The Political Economy of the Welfare State*, Macmillan,

London 1979; and J. Habermas, *Legitimation Crisis*, Heinemann, London 1976.

[42] C. Barnett, *op.cit.*, p304.

[43] See J.R. Hay, *The Origins of the Liberal Welfare Reforms 1906-1914*, Macmillan, London 1975, and his 'Employers and Social Policy in Britain: the Evolution of Welfare Legislation 1905-1914', *Social History*, 4, 1977.

[44] See G.V. Rimlinger, *Welfare Policy and Industrialisation in Europe, America and Russia*, John Wiley and Sons, New York 1971, and his 'Welfare Policy and Economic Development: A Comparative Historical Perspective', *Journal of Economic History*, 26, 1966.

[45] J. Kohl, 'Trends and Problems in Postwar Public Expenditure Development in Western Europe and North America', in P. Flora and A.J. Heidenheimer (eds), *The Development of Welfare States in Europe and America*, New Brunswick 1981, pp307-344.

An Historic Compromise: Labour and the Foundation of the National Health Service

Steve Iliffe

> It must be clear, however, to everybody in the Labour Movement that we are not going to obtain from the National Health Service the best results possible except by the utmost vigilance on the part of the whole socialist, co-operative and trades union movement.
>
> Aneurin Bevan, *Tribune*, 5 July 1948

In August 1990 nurses and ancillary staff at a London teaching hospital with perhaps the best record of scientific research of any medical institution in Britain, began an indefinite strike. Several hundred staff picketed half of the hospital's twenty entrances on their first day of action, collecting signatures for a protest petition and prompting a cacophony of supportive toots from passing motorists. Their aim was to publicise the possible loss of services to the public following plans to rationalise London's hospitals.[1]

By the end of the first week only twenty or so staff remained on strike, but the union organiser was unable to say how long he thought the action would continue. Hospital managers claimed patient services were unaffected, that the great majority of the hospital's 1500 staff were at work, and that additional emergency staffing had not been needed. A few days after the start of the strike all non-urgent surgery for local residents was postponed because the hospital had fulfilled its contract to the local Health Authority, and had, in effect, run out of money.

How could this happen in a health service once proclaimed as the envy of the civilised world? What had happened to the NHS launched in the summer of 1948 with such high hopes, and which had been second only to the monarchy in popularity for most of the post-war period?

Bad government by ideological enemies of the National Health Service is only part of the answer. To blame all that has happened to the NHS on Tory malevolence is like blaming food poisoning on salmonella, and not asking who has abandoned hygiene, and why? The origins of the present problems of the health service lie in its conception and birth, and the features of current medico-political conflicts stem from the political game begun in 1948.

The Players

What was the National Health Service, when it was founded? Beneath the rhetoric of a civilised approach to medical care, it was many things to many people. For some civil servants it was a solution to administrative chaos in pre-war medical services, and an end to unsatisfactory compromises and half-solutions to problems of reform. To some working in the voluntary hospitals it was an end to their economic difficulties. To those working people who already had access to free general practitioner care, it meant free access to specialist medicine. To the middle class and to working people not on 'the Panel' it meant access to free general practitioner services, for the first time. For the tiny group of specialists it promised a strategy for modern, hospital-based medical practice, without detriment to their income or power. To the medical profession as a whole it signalled a compromise reached with a fearsome Labour adversary, and the avoidance of local government control of medical care. And to the Left it meant, at best a half-way house to a locally-run health service based on a network of health centres, and at worst a compromise in which too much had been conceded to too many powerful, conservative interests.

When Labour won the 1945 General Election, some of the most ardent advocates of a comprehensive National Health Service, staffed by salaried professionals, were to be found in Whitehall. This radicalism of key figures in the Civil Service converged with that of the Socialist Medical Association.[2] Professional civil servants like John Maude had become convinced of the need for a health service that met all needs, without the stigma of the Poor Law, and saw medicine as an honourable profession that fulfilled its social responsibilities without recourse to commerce. Market forces were seen as the cause of inequality in access to care and had nothing to contribute to reforming medical services; doctors should be paid salaries, and those in the public service should eschew private practice altogether.

The failure of reform in the inter-war period was a stimulus to these socially responsible civil servants. In 1911 the National Insurance Act had transformed medical care in the UK, extending free GP care ('the Panel') from the five million skilled artisans who were members of friendly societies to fifteen million workers, nearly one third of the nation.[3] Subsequent reform was slow, and a pluralistic system of provision developed, with services provided by 'the Panel', local government, charitable ('voluntary') hospitals and private doctors.

At the end of the First World War, a working-class family could receive medical care from as many as nine different doctors working under five different organisations.[4] The working man would see his panel doctor for all illnesses other

134

than tuberculosis. His wife, if she were separately insured, would see the same panel doctor for her illnesses, except for tuberculosis and problems in pregnancy and child-birth. If she were not insured she could consult a private doctor if she could afford it, a parish doctor (provided under Poor Law regulations) or a doctor from a medical charity if she could not. During pregnancy she could use the municipal maternity service, which also provided child health services for infants and children up to school age. Once the children were at school, a schools medical officer would attend to 'school diseases' (mainly infections and under-nutrition), whilst a private doctor would be called if the children were too ill to go to school. Between leaving school (at twelve or fourteen) and sixteen years of age the children would be seen by the private doctor, but after their sixteenth birthdays they could join the same doctor's panel.

Separate administrative structures existed to run each type of service, with little or no attempt at co-ordination. Whenever change was sought, the conflicting interests of different administrative structures, different groups in the population and different currents of thought within medicine itself formed changing alliances to promote or resist each new scheme. Some changes occurred, nonetheless. Maternity care was greatly improved, although painfully slowly, through the expansion of municipal services, but the overall experience of reformers in the inter-war years was one of frustration.

There was little solace in the development of Britain's hospitals. The Ministry of Health, founded in 1919, had little knowledge of the extent of hospital development, and less influence. Municipal hospitals developed without central interference, teaching hospitals received some State funds, channelled through the University Grants Committee, not the Ministry, and voluntary hospitals kept at arms length from government involvement, except for contracts with local government to provide TB, cancer and sexually transmitted disease services.[5] This separation of Ministry and hospitals came to an end only in 1938, when the financial problems of

London's teaching hospitals prompted a request for State help. Arguments about the source of funding were resolved by the creation in May 1939 of an Emergency Medical Service (EMS), within which voluntary, teaching and municipal hospitals were co-ordinated and supported. The success of the wartime EMS strengthened the enthusiasm of reformers within the Ministry for a centralised health service.

Organised Labour was a key player in the war of attrition that characterised the reform process between the wars. Whilst working people had increasingly been able to see the Panel, so that nearly half the population was covered by 1938, access to specialist medicine was much less satisfactory. Panel members could get some free or cheap treatment, at the price of long waits in the outpatient clinics of the voluntary hospitals, but easy access depended on payment. Expert assistance in a matter that concerned the unions, fighting compensation cases where workers' health had been damaged by their jobs, also came from specialists, and the creation of the EMS had increased access to consultants.[6] When the trade union movement chose its positions in the debates around a National Health Service, these preoccupations influenced its choice of alliances and its objectives.

For the middle classes, excluded from the Panel system and reliant upon private medicine, the growth of medicine's effectiveness meant an increase in personal expenditure whenever illness affected them. The financial problems encountered by the London teaching hospitals were mirrored in the household budgets of affluent homes, making the middle classes increasingly interested in State subsidies for medical care. Whilst under the NHS the middle classes had to accept paying into the system through National Insurance, they were to receive in services more than half as much again as they paid in premiums.[7] They too began to make political choices and accept new alliances, in a gamble that paid off well, for the post-war expansion and affluence of these classes was greatly enhanced by free education for their children and free medical care for all.

The specialists who were the object of so much interest were a tiny group largely reliant on private practice, yet also at the forefront of medical development through their tradition of honorary work in the voluntary hospitals. The Depression may have done something to their private practice income, and their increasing importance in the voluntary hospitals had prompted a desire for remuneration from this source, thus contributing to the financial problems of the voluntary sector.

Medicine was undergoing great change and the first signs of pharmacological revolution were visible. Medical expertise was needed, in greater quantities than before, and the existing system of isolated centres of excellence staffed by consultants and larger numbers of small cottage hospitals staffed mainly by GPs with limited skills, was an insufficient basis for the next step in the modernisation of medical practice. Consultants had much to gain, therefore, from increased funding of the hospital network, and at a crucial stage in the foundation of the NHS they were to trade their influence over the medical profession for favourable terms within the new health service.

The political changes within British society presented the medical profession with a significant new challenge to add to its traditional struggle with the spectre of local government control. The Depression and the Second World War had generated a shift to the left that exacerbated the medical profession's anxiety about its power to determine how medical care would develop. This concern with professional supremacy was not an idiosyncrasy of Britain, but its solution was peculiarly British. In pre-war Germany the medical profession had come to an agreement with the Nazi government to exclude trade union influence from the German social insurance programme,[8] and in the Soviet Union the State had constructed a centralised medical service on the ruins of pre-Bolshevik professional organisations.[9] In Britain the profession had no choice but to seek a compromise with Labour that preserved as much of its autonomy as possible whilst extracting as many benefits from the new order as feasible.

The NHS is often seen as a socialist institution because of its foundation by the 1945-50 Labour government, and because of the long history of campaigning for a national health service on the Left.[10] However its dominant characteristics have arisen from the compromises required to create it, which allowed socialists to see it either as an incomplete institution needing democratisation as its finalising touch, or as a flawed structure all too open to distortion by the Right.

The Game

These were the players, but what was the game? On the Left, the Socialist Medical Association wanted to create a municipal health service based on health centres. On the Right, the British Medical Association wanted no erosion of the autonomy of its principal membership group, general practitioners, and no loss of freedom for its consultant members (and to a lesser extent its GPs) to practice privately. The Government faced a war, a history of thwarted reform and a restive population wanting social change as a reward for wartime effort and as an irreversible escape from the social and personal consequences of the Depression. Medicine was approaching a turning point in its scientific content and its effectiveness, with the first antibiotics appearing as heralds of the pharmacological revolution. And there had been a fiscal and skilled manpower crisis in the centres of excellence, the London teaching hospitals, which would be needed to lead the scientific revolution.

The pluralistic, interest-group politics of the inter-war years were inappropriate to this new situation, where substantial and rapid change was needed. Not only did the political situation demand determined leadership, but it also needed a new vision. Some of the leadership existed within the Civil Service, in the form of socially-responsible officials with much knowledge of medical care and much experience of the Byzantine world of medical politics. More was to appear in the shape of a passionate and pugilistic Minister of Health, Aneurin Bevan, who was considered awkward enough by his own side to make a suitably combative midwife for the NHS.

The new vision was one of a nationalised hospital network that brought high quality medicine and surgery to the whole country, replacing the mediocre service provided by GPs in the cottage hospitals. Free access for all to general practice, dentistry and opthalmic services was an additional benefit that was much valued by people at the time, but it was not intended as the primary long-term gain for the population. The mechanisms for bringing about the central change, the nationalisation of the hospitals, had been put in place with the formation of the EMS in 1939.

The Left's perspective – an NHS based on municipal health centres – failed to materialise for two inter-related reasons. It would have required such a degree of submission to local control from the very profession that was to play a crucial role in building the new health service, that Bevan and the Cabinet could not face the battle. And it reflected the conservatism of even the most forward-looking section of the profession, those in the SMA, which accepted as given the then dominance of general practice, even though the evidence was against GPs being the best group to initiate change, absorb the new medical science, and promote new services. Forty years later the potential for redeveloping the health service around primary care services based in the community remains slight, despite the efforts of utopian advocates like Julian Tudor Hart.[11]

Hospital medicine was chosen as the leading force in the new health service, and specialists were its champions. Not only could they deploy modern science effectively, but they could also swing the doubters within the profession behind – or at least out of the way of – the 1948 NHS Act. Bevan, it is said, 'stuffed the consultants mouths with gold' by allowing them part-time employment in the NHS, scope for private practice, professional control over the 'merit award' bonuses and a great deal of control over the enlarged hospital network, in return for their breaking ranks with the GPs, who were more hostile to the plans for the NHS. This colourful description makes the concession look much more generous than it really was.[12] The part-time contracts and merit awards affected about four thousand consultants, mostly in the Home Counties, who had a flat-rate salary from the NHS and then competed for private income amongst themselves. Since the numbers of consultants in that enviable position could be controlled, the NHS gained a source of political support as well as of technical expertise at a price lower than expected when full-time salaries for all were being considered by the Ministry of Health.

For the Left this outcome could be seen as a necessary expedient, one step on the road to a truly socialist health service, and no doubt the Labour Treasury Minister encouraged this view. In retrospect it reflects those typical NHS characteristics, the pursuit of services on the cheap and the leaving of professional power largely untouched. The NHS was to pay for this early under-investment forty years later, when consultant numbers had more than doubled, and half of the income of a London specialist came from private practice.[13]

The Result

There is no doubt that the NHS relieved the discomfort or distress of millions of citizens, offering better quality dental and opthalmic care than most had ever experienced, spreading accessible specialist medical services across the country, and dealing with a backlog of medical problems (especially in areas such as gynaecological surgery) that would otherwise have remained neglected. For the first time, citizens could be secure in the knowledge that they would receive modern medical treatment if they became ill, without having to pay for it personally.

The medical profession was able to expand inside the new NHS, and other professions like physiotherapy, clinical psychology, and radiology were able to emerge. New technology brought large laboratories able to do more investigations, eventually on a mass-production basis, and new types of scientific worker entered the NHS. The wider economy responded to the demand for both new pharmaceutical preparations and for new equipment, making the NHS into an important stimulant to post-war recovery.

It is hardly surprising that the NHS was, and still is, popular, and that the social alliance that created it held together for decades. Early Conservative efforts to attack the NHS on the grounds that its costs were rising too fast were defeated with the publication of the Guillebaud report on NHS costs in 1956, although this defeat did not inhibit successive Conservative governments from holding down NHS expenditure throughout the 1950s. Nevertheless, the social alliance for the NHS was strong enough to influence Conservatism, so that the modernisation of the health service (through an ambitious hospital-building programme) began in 1962, two years before the Conservatives were removed from office by a Labour Party purporting to represent modernisation.

The benefits that the NHS brought to Britain are clear. Less apparent, at least on the Left, are the losses that Britain experienced by evolving its health service in the particular form that the NHS took towards the end of the 1940s. Forty-five years later we are feeling those losses, as another round of Tory governments moves the NHS into the marketplace with astonishingly little resistance from the political opposition, the trade union movement and the public.

Bevan's legacy contained a balance of power between capital, professionals and the people, and a centralised structure for the NHS that together epitomise the weakness of British Socialism. In 1948 it was clear that the revolution in modern medicine was led by scientists and doctors, with most believing that hospitals were their natural bases. These new hospitals were not like the old cottage hospitals, held together by local benefactors and by flag days, with beds donated in memory of local notables or by subscription from the miners' lodge or the trades council. They were the factories of the brave new medical world, run by the socially-responsible professional men so much desired by Whitehall's better civil servants. In creating the NHS, Labour created a nationalised industry with its own corporate command structure and a governing body of sorts, the Ministry of Health, far detached from the lives of the ill and from public influence too.

Like other nationalised industries, the NHS was only nominally owned by the people of Britain. There was no effective way in which citizens could influence its development without recourse to campaign politics. A trickle of local government representation on NHS management bodies was halted in 1974, at the beginning of a phase of unending managerial reforms. Opportunities for trade unions to influence the NHS indirectly through Community Health Councils (established in the same round of reforms) were rarely taken. Change from 'outside' the NHS did occur, but this was uncommon and difficult. Organisations of parents eventually transformed the care of ill children in hospital, from being as physically spartan and emotionally brutal as a public school regime, to being child- and family-friendly. Women's pressure groups did something to slow down the indiscriminate and dogmatic appliance of new technology by inexperienced and, arguably, misogynist obstetricians in the 1970s, although there is still work to do in this area.

These were the exceptions. For the most part medical care was something provided for people by experts, so that left-wing political activists in the 1970s could be heard arguing for a 'true health service', not a 'sickness service', as if 'health' was a thing that could be delivered to people like pizzas, or the daily paper, rather than a state of being shaped by politics and economics. This perception of health as the product of experts' actions has had more serious consequences, for it turns medical care and health into marketable commodities, just as the medical profession has always wanted. When the politics was taken out of the NHS by the foundation of a health service run by quangos, the social origins of illness and health, and the long history of popular struggle for better health and better medical care began to be erased from political consciousness.

The 1945-50 Labour government wanted to put things right for those who had suffered during the Depression, and who had sacrificed so much during the war. The NHS was perhaps its finest achievement, but it was built as an institution that did things for and to people, not with them. That was not entirely the fault of the Government, nor of Bevan himself, for circumstances channelled political thinking and practice in the direction of a centrally organised industry nominally under state control, but actually driven from day-to-day by the medical profession. By taking the NHS out of politics, and in particular out of local government politics, Bevan and the Labour government lifted a weight off the back of the trade union movement, which had had to struggle for decades to achieve improved medical care for working people. And it greatly relieved the medical profession, which did not want to be controlled by anyone, least of all working-class organisations and potentially querulous councils.

The relief experienced by the medical profession at its deliverance from control was profound, and allowed the burgeoning of hospital medicine which transformed the quality of life of thousands of people with serious illnesses. Modernisation even reached general practitioners (GPs), in the end, although further reform was needed in 1966 to achieve this. The profession's stand on its autonomy had a lasting consequence in general practice, which began to appear at the end of the 1980s. GPs were brought into contract with the NHS, but have never been employed by it.

In 1948 Britain's GPs were enrolled in a public sector franchise network, and the subsequent development of general practice from solo lock-up shop to group practice in medical centres has demonstrated how effective franchising can be as a system. By providing their own buildings and absorbing some staff costs themselves, GPs have also demonstrated how cheap franchising can be for the government. This lesson was not lost on Thatcher's government, which has in effect moved hospitals onto a franchise basis by creating Hospital Trusts and a so-called internal market in the NHS.

Aftermath

The political and economic problems apparently resolved in 1948 resurfaced forty years later, but with different players in a changed game. Bevan's injunction to be vigilant in defence of the NHS may have sounded wise, but the health service had been built outside public control in a society where vigilance was more easily expressed by individuals, for themselves, than by the collective, for itself. Had the NHS not been constructed on the cheap, and had the British economy not continued its long-term decline despite the post-war boom, the health service might not have experienced its current protracted crisis, with the public that uses it relegated to walk-on roles in demonstrations whilst the staff who run it oscillate between gesture politics and demoralisation.

None of this diminishes the achievement of the post-war Labour government in creating the NHS, nor does recent history suggest that any alternative system would have had greater durability. The National Health Service was an expression of progressive modernisation but not the pinnacle of civilisation that its uncritical adherents sometimes think. As it is forced into a market framework, the political issues of under-funding and public powerlessness long buried in the former centralised structure of the NHS, are returning to the public domain, where they belong.

Notes

[1] L. Beecham, 'NHS Internal Market Leads to Nurses' Strike', *British Medical Journal* 1993; 307:523.

[2] F. Honigsbaum, *Health, Happiness & Security: the Creation of the National Health Service*, Routledge, London 1989, p49.

[3] *Ibid.*,p4.

[4] S. Iliffe, *The NHS – a Picture of Health?*, Lawrence & Wishart, London 1983, p20-21.

[5] F. Honigsbaum, *op.cit.*, p15.

[6] F. Honigsbaum, *The Division in British Medicine*, Kogan Page, London 1979, p250.

[7] P. Baldwin, *The Politics of Social Solidarity: Class Bases of the European Welfare State 1875-1975*, Cambridge University Press, 1990, p121.

[8] M. Moran & B. Wood, *States, Regulation and the Medical Profession*, Open University Press, Milton Keynes 1993, p44.

[9] M. Ryan, *The Organisation of Soviet Medical Care*, Basil Blackwell & Martin Robertson, Oxford & London 1978.

[10] D. Stark Murray, *Why a National Health Service?*, Pemberton, London 1971, chapters 3-5.

[11] J. Tudor Hart, *A New Kind of Doctor*, Merlin Press, London 1988.

[12] C. Webster, *Aneurin Bevan on the NHS*, Wellcome Unit for the History of Medicine, University of Oxford, 1991, p220-22.

[13] P. Martin, 'London's Health Services', *Health Matters* 10, 1992, p12-13.

Housing the People

Alison Ravetz

I visualise England, Scotland and Wales as a carefully planned pattern of garden land, farm land, well defined and sharply limited industrial areas ... The homes of the workers of all kinds should be away from pits and factories in prettily laid-out garden cities within which there should be all the conveniences which modern science can give. I hate the idea which many people hold that working people do not desire decent homes and are content with what is given them ... My garden city will have all kinds of labour-saving appliances for the home, restaurants for the supply of all kinds of food, laundries and baths.

George Lansbury, *My England*, Selwyn & Blount, London, n.d. (1930s).

The Promise of 1945

The six years of war, upheaval and suffering were, for many, made worthwhile by the feeling that all were fighting together for a better society. The wartime government had intervened in some of the most intimate areas of life: the black-out, diet, cooking, 'make do and mend' – even the private conversations that 'cost lives'. Much propaganda had been directed at the housewife: 'she was the one whom all the exhortations were aimed at'.[1] This was the more possible because of the emergence of a new-style, suburban housewife between the wars: typically a woman with only one or two children, interested in getting the most out of her household equipment and keen on budgeting. The State now needed her co-operation, and, unless she was actively child-bearing or rearing, she was also required, with other women, to maintain war production and the voluntary welfare services.

Housing was one of the stress points of war. London and

146

other big cities lost 20 per cent or more of their pre-war numbers, while towns that were centres of defence industries, became seriously overcrowded. Homes previously under-occupied became full to bursting. Nearly three million families had no choice but to go on living in houses that were already condemned or due to be condemned as unfit in 1939, or in bomb-damaged houses with only first-aid repairs. At the end of the war around 6 per cent of the pre-war stock of houses had been destroyed or seriously damaged, or had been requisitioned. Meanwhile there was a pent-up housing demand due to a rising birth rate which shot up a third above its pre-war level. The general turbulence of wartime life brought with it a strange paradox: although its co-operation, high morale and enforced communality brought a common wish to 'win the peace' as we had won the war, the main goal of this peace was self-containedness and the chance to rebuild family relationships in privacy.

People who were adult at this time had memories of housing going back long before the war. Even Nye Bevan, at forty-eight the youngest member of a rather elderly Cabinet, had been old enough to follow all the problems, controversies and policies for housing between the wars. In 1918 the vast majority of people of all classes lived in landlord-owned houses, many of them dating from the early stages of the industrial revolution and many with two or more families in a house intended for only one. Up until 1939 there was a continuing and clear association between bad housing and mortality and disease, as well as startling class differences in life expectancy and infant death rates, between outer and inner wards of cities. There was also a deeply engrained loathing of private landlords and a habitual warfare between them and tenants that sometimes broke out in organised militancy, as on 'red' Clydeside in 1915 and in the tenants' movements of the 1930s.

Many landlords – or, as was often the case, landladies – were not socially far removed from their tenants, for the majority of houses had been passed down through families.

But ultimately the interests of owners and tenants could not be reconciled. The Rent and Mortgage Interest Restrictions Act of 1915, which pegged rents to 1914 levels, remained in force for older houses for much or all of the inter-war period, and in 1939 rents were again frozen. Thus, despite some provision for raising rents after repairs, landlords had little incentive to keep their property in good condition. The consequence for tenants was that their homes became increasingly dilapidated, while the pegging of rents was a disincentive for moving. With the shrinkage of this stock of older houses through the slum clearances of the 1930s, private rentals were both of low standard and hard to get, often subject to extortionate levies of 'key money' in pressure areas. The tenure consequently lost what had always been considered its main advantage: flexibility and freedom of movement for people who were relatively poor or whose financial position was subject to sudden fluctuations.

As well as a collective memory there was a common vision for a future, portrayed in the media and endlessly discussed among servicemen and women, among housewives, even between those sheltering in air-raid shelters. In this vision the homes of the future probably played the dominant part. Mass Observation's *Enquiry into People's Homes*[2] was based on in-depth surveys of eleven different places as well as other material drawn from different parts of England and Wales. The Town and Country Planning Association and *Daily Mail* Ideal Home Exhibition were both able to report on attitude surveys among civilians and the armed forces, while the 1946 *Housing Digest*, put together for the Electrical Association for Women[3], compiled comments from no less than thirty-four professional, commercial, press, political, scientific, religious and women's organisations, as well as twenty-three government reports, all between 1941-45. It was, therefore, legitimate for the Dudley Report[4], which in 1944 set new official guidelines for post-war public housing, to be confident about the expectations and standards that would need to be met.

All this conveyed an impression that people would indeed have a real choice of homes after the war – and in view of the huge successes of a centralised wartime State this was not perhaps naive. People queued to buy the Beveridge Report when it appeared in 1942 and, despite its dry insistence on facts, this displayed an almost mystic quality in its description of five great social 'Evils' to be overcome. The unhealthy, decaying and badly planned homes and neighbourhoods were represented as 'Squalor'.

This, then, was the context in which the Labour Party promised to use every resource, including modern building technology and a new Ministry of Housing and Planning, to produce a good home in a well planned environment for every family in need.[5] Virtually every candidate in the General Election raised housing as a key issue: to judge from their speeches, the housing problem was 'acute in every town or rural area in Great Britain'.[6] The issue may well have made a large contribution to Labour's landslide victory, particularly since first-time voters included many women and also ex-service people, who were reputedly angry about the housing shortage that would face them on their return to civilian life.

The Legacy of Housing Policy

The new Government, however, did not come up with any greatly innovatory housing policy – not even, at first, to the extent of fulfilling its pledge to put housing into a new ministry with planning. Bevan, as Minister of Health, included housing in his portfolio, as had been the case with the first such Minister, Christopher Addison, in 1919, but planning was assigned its own Ministry of Town and Country Planning. In a remark since noted many times by historians, Bevan claimed to spend five minutes a week on housing. This did not reflect his real level of concern for the issue, about which he felt deeply, but there is no doubt that the task of setting up the National Health Service took precedence, or that the administrative load of both health and housing together was more than was reasonable for one man to bear.

Besides rent control and slum clearance the main housing function of local authorities was to build new dwellings for the needs of the working classes. This had already had behind it a long controversy and struggle when Addison instituted subsidised housing in 1919. His Act of that year embodied a daring if not dangerous idea: that public money should be used to give working-class tenants access to the most advanced modern housing of its day: low-density, suburban 'cottages' on planned, garden-city style estates.

The two wings of housing policy were often presented as polarities, the Tories favouring that of action against insanitary houses and Labour that of building new, ideal, council estates. In many respects the essence of Tory policy was to draw a bottom line below which no one should be permitted to fall, in the interest of public health. The essence of Labour policy was to set an ideal standard and to raise everyone to this. In practice, however, matters were more complex. From 1919 onwards, both parties had subscribed to a mixed system of public and private housing, with a good deal of confusion as to what the exact role of the public sector should be. At a national level Conservative governments continued the public subsidy, though targeting it in the first place at private enterprise, to encourage entrepreneurs to take up their old role of providing working-class housing for rent. On the other hand, the 1924 Labour government was prepared to let standards fall to achieve higher numbers. At the local level a Labour council might pursue either a more, or less, 'sanitary' policy, so that it was possible for an astute London county councillor to admit that, in practice, there might be little difference between one party and another.[7]

Bevan's Vision and Practice

Underlying these overlaps were a number of real dilemmas of policy and practice which, by 1945, had resulted in a large body of research and debate. Whether or not the new minister was aware of this, he showed little sign in his policy-making. Bevan's first principle was that housing should not be a commodity to be bought and sold for profit. His vision of the future council estate was of a mixed-class community, living in harmony as he supposed the traditional English village to have done. To this end he took the symbolic step, in the 1949 Housing Act, of removing the condition dating back to its origins, that council housing should be exclusively for members of the working class. Important as this was symbolically, it made little difference in practice, since in the acute post-war shortage councils allocated according to priority need, which naturally discriminated in favour of poorer and local people. Bevan appeared to see no contradiction in this, doubtless because it would have seemed justified in the short term. In the longer term, when there would be enough public housing for all, housing authorities would be spared the necessity of discriminating between one applicant and another.

Bevan was also dominated by the idea that before the war the only way for a working-class family to get a decent house was either to live in a declared slum (and so be rehoused) or to buy their own home. This was not in fact always true because there were many good houses, old and newly built, for rent; but it did hold good for large numbers who rented from private landlords. He therefore fought, and won, a battle with the Chancellor, Hugh Dalton, to hold council rents down to ten shillings (50p) rather than the twelve shillings (60p) demanded by the Treasury. The most crucial thing, however, was the supply of new houses, not only to satisfy demand but to redeem Labour's pledges to its electorate. The problems of the post-war economy, in particular serious shortages of building materials and skilled labour, permitted Bevan to divert virtually all the housing construction that did take place into the public rather than the private sector. Licences were required for any private building and restrictions placed on resale. Such odd private houses as were built at this time were often constructed in stages, as licences and materials became available. Eventually a ratio of five public to one private dwelling was achieved.

The first post-war Housing Act to be passed, in 1946, increased the subsidy for council houses and gave a special subsidy for flats. It also extended controls on private landlords by bringing furnished accommodation and new lets within rent control and setting up rent tribunals. But the most important Housing Act of the Labour administration was that of 1949, which confirmed all existing strands of policy for clearance, relief of overcrowding and the building of new stock by local authorities. A number of innovations reflected Bevan's peculiarly idealistic vision. They included improvement grants for older property, powers to build hostels with subsidy, to provide board and laundry facilities, and to sell (in addition to merely hiring out) furniture for the new dwellings. For all these activities councils had the right – indeed, requirement – to borrow at low rates of interest ($2\frac{1}{2}$ per cent at this time) from the Public Works Loan Board.

All these clauses demonstrated the confidence of the Labour government in public housing as a permanent and universal service; but to put this in the context of its time, the Act received a welcome from all parties in the House, with few qualifications. Much of the debate concerned whether or not tied cottages should be excluded from improvement grants, Bevan being sure that they should, so that farmers would be compelled to convert them into normal tenancies. It was Jennie Lee who voiced great doubts about the whole principle of improvement grants on the grounds that, unlike the subsidy for new council houses, they would not necessarily benefit the neediest.

The New Towns

The Housing Acts alone do not convey the full breadth of the Government's vision for housing at this time. The older policies, together with new additions, were given an added weight by being integrated with town and country planning. The historical roots of such planning lay in a tradition of model industrial villages dating back to the early part of the nineteenth century, and latterly promulgated in the settlements founded by William Lever, George Cadbury and Joseph Rowntree. These were eminent figures in the turn-of-the-century garden city movement, which in turn gave rise to a campaign for town and country planning. This was supported not only by architects and planners and by politicians of the centre and left, by churches, women's organisations and amenity groups of all kinds. One particular strand of the campaign was for the State to fund a hundred new towns for five million people, so allowing a properly planned dispersal of urban populations, in contrast with the unplanned suburban sprawl that was defacing the countryside. The Leader of London Council, Herbert Morrison (who as a conscientious objector in the First World War had worked in a market garden in the Garden City of Letchworth) paved the way for this by creating a 'Green Belt' around London. His former Housing Chairman, Lewis Silkin, as the first Minister of Town and Country Planning in 1947, presided over the beginning of the Government's new towns programme.

Throughout society there was little if any disagreement about the ideal of containing existing towns and cities, with new growth taking place in satellite towns or garden cities. There existed countless wartime blueprints for reshaping existing urban settlements after the war into neatly divided industrial, commercial, administrative and residential areas. What was new was the power to implement this radical restructuring. Several major acts of Parliament, on the distribution of industry, the creation of new towns and

153

national parks, made a significant contribution; but underpinning all this was the 1947 Town and Country Planning Act. This governed all land use, including housing, by the revolutionary device of nationalising the right of property owners to develop their land as they saw fit. This was done with a once-for-all compensation scheme which, in the event, proved difficult to administer and was unfair and unpopular, so that it contributed not a little to the eventual return to power of the Conservatives. It was also accompanied by a drastic 100 per cent tax on the profits of development which, had it worked, would have made the whole business of private property development redundant. This also proved unworkable and, not surprisingly, was targeted for anulment by the Conservatives some years before they returned to power. Even so, the 1947 Act laid the foundation of the planning system for the second half of this century. In particular, it ensured that the numerous visionary wartime plans were succeeded by statutory development plans which covered the entire country. These shared the same philosophy of making a clean sweep of all that was bad in the old environment and replacing it with a new one that was modern, efficient, and scientifically worked out. It was into this comprehensive approach, fit if not for a classless then for an all-class society, that Labour's housing policy fitted.

The Best for the People

The final dimension of this policy was Bevan's idealism regarding housing standards. He had the garden city tradition of cottage-style houses, adapted for council estates by the Tudor Walters Report in 1918,[8] and the surveys and anticipations of the war years to draw upon. Above all he followed the recommendations of the Dudley Report of 1944, which were closely based on the reported performance of council dwellings and estates since Tudor Walters, with further evidence given by over fifty non-government organisations. Not many of these could be termed working-class, but Bevan could be confident that, had working-class people been directly consulted, as in the wartime surveys, the conclusions reached would not have been any different.

The Dudley Report aimed at new standards both for dwellings and estates. Floor areas of houses were increased and houses for five or more people provided with downstairs cloakrooms and utility rooms. The old-fashioned parlour, which had already been sacrificed in pre-war economies, was now replaced by a 'through' lounge accompanied by a dining recess or a dining kitchen: a device copied in the private sector when it started building again. These early post-war houses were among the best that councils ever built and, despite widespread criticism of extravagance, not least from his Cabinet colleagues, Bevan stuck staunchly to his principles, saying 'while we shall be judged for a year or two by the *number* of houses we build ... we shall be judged in ten years' time by the *type* of houses we build'.[9] In the new towns, with their special resources and the best of professional design, it was possible for public housing to reach even higher standards. But the first batch of new towns had hardly taken shape by 1951, when only a few thousand houses had been completed, many of them occupied by their own building workers.

The main recommendation for estates in the Dudley Report was that they should no longer be planned with only one or two different house types for families, but should be complete neighbourhoods catering for social diversity, with flats and maisonettes as well as houses. Even estates that for reasons of density consisted mainly of blocks of flats had their subsidies slanted so that some houses could be included. Council housing was now to cater also for the elderly, in bungalows, flats or hostels, which might also include some single working people. Only the more progressive authorities had built for the elderly before the war, using slum clearance subsidies, but now there was a new annual subsidy of £5 per room for old people's accommodation, whether purpose-built or converted.

The assumption of responsibility for older people's housing needs marks a milestone in welfare. Until 1948, unless they were displaced by slum clearance, any older people who could not look after their own housing needs went to Public Assistance Committee institutions which had been created, in 1929, from workhouses of the nineteenth-century Poor Law. In many respects these retained the repressive regimes of workhouses, denying inmates privacy (even in bathrooms and lavatories) or the right to personal possessions and clothing. Under the National Health Service Act of 1948, such institutions were allocated either to the National Health Service for use as hospitals or to local authorities for residential homes. From that time councils began to build or convert their own homes but, in addition, they used their powers under the 1949 Housing Act to build early forms of sheltered housing, with wardens and common lounges. These schemes became part of the new mixed estates, and the erstwhile paupers, now with pensions of their own as of right, paid their own way as independent citizens.

The Festival and the Prefabs

All that was most advanced in design at this time was encapsulated in the 'living architecture' exhibition at Lansbury, East London, for the 1951 Festival of Britain. Designed in London County Council's Architects' Department, which still counted followers of William Morris among its staff, Lansbury was defined as a 'comprehensive development area' and a new neighbourhood under the 1943 County of London Plan. It was described as 'a small town within a town', so designed as to maintain or recreate the three old 'communities' of Poplar, Stepney and Bow. It contained houses, flats, maisonettes, a retirement home and flats for older people, for a population of around 1500. It also contained shops, an open air market, pubs, churches, a park, a school and nursery school. For Festival visitors it had a Building Research Pavilion, a café (the 'Rosie Lee') and *Gremlin Grange*, a life-size mock-up of a conventional, three-bedroom, spec-built 'semi' which was intended as an object lesson in all the building defects associated with the private house builder. This reflected the Labour Party's prejudices towards private housing: as its own Speakers' Handbook remarked, with some gusto, 'Jerry built them, Jerry blitzed them'.[10] It was not that accurate an observation, for in spite of some flagrant cases of jerry-building, the suburban stock of the 1930s, if reasonably maintained, proved uncommonly long-lasting.

Bevan also proved to have a wrong view of the 'prefabs', a programme for 150,000 people which he inherited from the wartime government. Fabricated in redundant aircraft factories as emergency houses with an intended life of not more than ten years, these were transported to sites and erected as supposedly cheap substitutes for permanent houses. Bevan described them as rabbit hutches, and in fact they had some serious drawbacks of which condensation was the worst. They were also far from cheap. But they proved to be one of the most popular of all twentieth-century dwelling types, public or private, and many have remained in use, with improvements and often purchased by their tenants, to the present day.

In another respect Bevan's design ideas were advanced for his time. This was his willingness to give special grants for environmentally sensitive areas. He had an unusually sympathetic view that older houses were capable of being brought up to a modern standard. He found them often to have 'a much more pleasant personality than the new house … They have grown up organically, they have been adapted and changed to the needs of each generation. They are often much more pleasant places in which to live.'[11]

Bevan, however, was not the only one to shape the Labour government's housing policy. Unlike Addison before him, he stayed in post during Treasury-induced cuts in his programme, including cuts in his cherished design standards; but finally he resigned from the Cabinet on the issue of prescription charges in the Health Service, whereupon responsibility for housing, now in a newly constituted Ministry of Housing and Local Government, was taken over by Hugh Dalton. Dalton is credited with injecting new life into a tired housing programme, so preventing it from being an electoral albatross in the 1950 and 1951 General Elections.

Hopes Deferred

By this time its housing record was not something of which Labour felt particularly proud. From the beginning, Attlee and other members of the Cabinet had been critical of the slow progress made. The Prime Minister's economic adviser, Douglas Jay, attacked Bevan for relying too much on local councils – a criticism endorsed by Addison, as elder statesman and Labour leader in the House of Lords. Attlee personally intervened to boost house production, first by a special Cabinet Committee presided over by himself, and later by creating a Housing Production Executive. There was much political capital to be made out of mounting numbers of half-finished houses, and while in 1948 Bevan could stoutly claim to have passed the target of three quarters of a million new houses set by the previous Government, it was clear that this figure had been a serious underestimate of needs. The peak of production came in that year when 227,000 houses were completed, but after that, yearly totals declined to less than 200,000. Labour's General Election manifesto of 1950 was brief and almost platitudinous on the subject of housing, which was however the dominant theme of all Conservative election addresses. In the General Election of the following year Labour's manifesto let housing slip almost to bottom place, remarking that it intended to maintain production at 200,000 units a year and to raise this as soon as possible. The

Conservatives, on the other hand, called housing 'the first of the social services' and promised 300,000 houses a year, a target that Harold Macmillan, as Housing Minister, reached in 1953.

Frustration with the slow rate of building flared up in the squatters' movement in the summer of 1946. This began among ex-servicemen and others desperate for homes, by a spontaneous invasion of a disused military camp in Scunthorpe, and spread rapidly to many parts of the country. By the autumn over a thousand camps had been invaded and occupied by more than forty thousand families. Other empty buildings such as hotels and schools were also squatted, and by September of that year a series of squats began in London with the occupation of a vacant block of luxury flats. These had been derequisitioned and offered by the Government to Kensington Borough Council for temporary housing, but the offer had been declined. Hundreds of homeless or badly housed Londoners, ex-servicemen prominent among them, took part in these occupations, in which a number of Communist councillors took a leading role.

The squatters received considerable public help in connecting water, gas and electricity and supplying food and necessities; but after initial tolerance the police turned hostile and laid siege in such a fashion that extraordinary feats were required to bring in supplies and enable squatters and their friends to enter and leave. The former, with true wartime spirit, organised communal catering, childcare, discussion groups. For some it was a never-to-be-forgotten experience, and the Communist Party gained a number of members through it.[12] The Government's reaction was predominantly one of fright. Bevan accused the squatters of jumping the housing queue and demanded that the councils concerned should cut off gas and electricity supplies. Eventually, five Communist councillor leaders were brought to trial for criminal conspiracy to trespass (and bound over) while they had in fact led an orderly retreat from the occupied buildings, satisfied that they had successfully jolted the Government into action. After first being moved to temporary rest centres, many of the former squatters were eventually rehoused. Throughout the country as a whole over seven hundred military camps were handed over to local councils. In some cases tenants, including original squatters, remained in them for years, and a few of the camps were gradually converted into permanent council estates.

In the judgment of one historian, Labour's housing achievements in six years of government reflected that 'mosaic of reform and conservatism' that one comes to expect of the Welfare State.[13] The programme for housing confirmed and reinforced the mainstream policies developed in the inter-war years, establishing council housing as something accepted by a broad cross-section, including 'Butskellite' Tories and Labour alike, until the Thatcher revolution put an end to this consensus, in housing as in all fields of social welfare. As the landlord-owned sector dwindled almost to vanishing point, council-provided, rented housing became for the majority the only effective alternative to owner occupation, thus making Britain into a society of 'two estates', of which owner occupation was by far the more favoured.

This was not what Bevan had intended. His vision was for public renting to become virtually universal, ultimately including municipalised, older housing taken over from landlords, and even tolerating a limited amount of home ownership, so long as this was merely 'an extension and expression of the personality of the owner.'[14] But the realisation of the vision was crucially dependent on producing a sufficient quantity of houses fast enough to swamp, as it were, the existing system. Without this, council housing was doomed to go on operating in conditions of shortage and consequently invidious discrimination between different categories of housing need. It was a situation that, as Bevan himself remarked, was exacerbated by the very success of the Welfare State, which enabled more people than ever before to afford, and hence to apply for, a council tenancy. Even

160

Macmillan's increased production in the 1950s could not satisfy demand; nor did Labour's approach to private renting do anything to promote a planned and co-ordinated transformation of the housing system as a whole.[15]

Hence Labour's housing policy was only partially redistributive, although it may be supposed that it did more to promote social equity than a Conservative government of this time would have done. The bias to high quality family housing and the scant attention paid to the landlord-owned sector resulted, eventually, in a critical situation amongst certain social minorities who found the stock of housing available to them shrinking. The weight placed on local councils as housing authorities – as developers, owners and managers – turned them, for several decades, into virtually unchallengeable landlords: a situation that goes far to explain their less fortunate design decisions and management styles.

It would, of course, have been hard for a Labour politician, or indeed anyone, to have foreseen all this in the 1940s. The fact remains that the Government's single-minded vision ruled out any alternative policies for producing and managing affordable housing. It is true that Labour paid lip service to housing associations as alternative housing agencies, including them in its improvement grant provisions, for instance, but little resulted from this until the Harold Wilson years in the 1960s. Still more overlooked were housing co-operatives and self-build societies, one type of which, the co-partnership housing societies, had made a significant contribution to the garden city movement. There had also been some previous experience of estate management by co-operative retail societies. The rejection of a co-operative channel for housing, or of subsidising any other potential agencies such as trade unions, with the absence of any subsidy for private rented housing after 1939, gave the British housing system a distinctive, monolithic quality that set it apart from virtually all other European housing systems. Labour's housing achievement in the crucial post-war years must be characterised as utopian rather than revolutionary: one that

161

befitted a centralised, collectivist, expertly advised and caring, but ultimately paternalistic, State.

Notes

[1] Peter Lewis, *A People's War*, Thames Methuen, London 1986, p175.

[2] Mass Observation, *An Enquiry into People's Homes*, Advertising Service Guild, London March 1943.

[3] Electrical Association for Women, *Housing Digest: an analysis of housing reports 1941-1945*, Art & Educational Publishers, London & Glasgow 1946.

[4] Dudley Report, *Design of Dwellings: Report of Central Housing Advisory Committee*, HMSO, London 1944.

[5] F.W.S. Craig, *British General Election Manifestoes 1918-1966*, Macmillan, London 1975.

[6] R.B. McCallum and Alison Readman, *The British General Election of 1945*, Cumberlege and Oxford University Press, London 1947, p4.

[7] Andrew Saint (ed), *Politics and the People of London: the London County Council 1889-1965*, Hambledon Press, London 1989, ch7: Helen Jones: 'Conservatives and the LCC after the War'.

[8] Tudor Walters Report, *Report of the Committee ... to consider questions of building construction in connection with the provisions of dwellings for the working classes*, Cd.9191, HMSO, London 1918.

[9] Michael Foot, *Aneurin Bevan: a Biography, Volume 2: 1945-1960*, Davis Poynter, London 1973, p82.

[10] Labour Party, *Speakers' Handbook, 1949-50*, p371.

[11] Hansard, *Parliamentary Debates* (second reading of 1949 Housing Bill), Vol. 462, 16 March 1949, col.2130.

[12] Noreen Branson (ed), *London Squatters 1946*, Proceedings of Conference of Communist Party History Group, Pamphlet 80, May 1984.

[13] Kenneth O. Morgan, *Labour in Power 1945-1951*, Oxford University Press, Oxford 1984, p179.

[14] Labour Party *op.cit.* p358.

[15] David H. McKay and Andrew W. Cox, *The Politics of Urban Change*, Croom Helm, Beckenham 1979, pp120-1.

Equality of Opportunity?: The Labour Government and Schools

Douglas Bourn

> The next Labour government must take the challenge up. It must make clear from the start that it does not merely intend to offer somewhat better educational opportunities to the children of the workers, but that it stands for complete educational equality and for the final abolition of the system under which the quality of education offered children has depended upon the income or social position of their parents.
>
> R.H.Tawney, in *Labour and Education*,
> The Labour Party, 1934

The Labour Party had long stood for educational reform as a path to a more equitable and democratic society. It had close links with progressive educational thinkers[1]. So it was surprising that its 1945 policy statement *Let Us Face the Future* contained only one proposal for educational reform – that the school-leaving age should be raised to sixteen as soon as possible. The Labour government, in the event, did not even deliver on this.

Labour believed that its educational aims had been achieved with the passing of the Coalition government's Education Act in 1944, to which many of its educationalists had made a major contribution. The Act's provision for free grammar school education for all children with the necessary qualifications was accepted as meaning that working-class children now had the same chance of mounting the educational ladder as middle-class children. Working-class Labour leaders, such as Ernest Bevin, who had themselves been deprived of such a chance, saw grammar schools as the goal for the children of working-class families.[2] Once in office the Government found that educational improvements, which needed large funds, were restricted by the problems of the economy. Nor were either of the Labour Ministers of Education, Ellen Wilkinson (1945-47) and George Tomlinson (1947-51), willing to stand up to their civil servants who were anxious to preserve the grammar school tradition and feared radical change.[3]

The Government and the Labour Party retreated into pragmatic administration of existing legislation, no longer seeing the development of new ideas and policies as their concern. The great commitment to educational reform and social justice lay in the past.

1944 Education Act

Labour's lack of foresight and its complacency about the 1944 Act have been blamed for the inequalities in the secondary school system of the 1950s and 1960s.[4] Whilst recognising that an opportunity was lost, I will argue that the conditions did not exist within the Government, or the educational service, for further advance to take place. The educational and political climate changed, and while there were those who called for reforms, the teaching profession and many educational thinkers became increasingly conservative about secondary education, while the Labour Party itself was divided and no longer had the heart for educational reform.[5] So, whilst we should not be uncritical of a government which, far from advancing educational thinking, played a negative role, a more constructive approach would be an assessment of its implementation of the 1944 Act, which it saw in 1945 as its main task.[6]

The central feature of the Act was to replace the socially divisive 'elementary' and 'secondary' schools by three progressive stages of primary, secondary and further education, under the responsibility of local education authorities. Primary and secondary education were to be provided in separate schools, in contrast to the past, when many elementary schools had continued to provide schooling for non-scholarship children to fourteen. The Act also recognised the need for provision for children under five years of age through nursery schools or nursery classes in other schools, as well as the need for special provision for children with disabilities, either through special schools or specialist teaching. Local authorities were also obliged to provide free medical treatment, and free milk and meals were to become a feature of school life until the 1970s.[7] Central to the Act was the creation of a new partnership between central and local government. The Minister for Education had increased powers, charged with the duty of securing the effective execution by local education authorities of the national educational policy. In theory, the authorities were responsible for their own systems but in practice they would look to government for guidance and had to obtain its approval in order to implement their recommendations.[8]

The new Ministry was therefore faced with considerable challenges. The war had left much of the school system in disarray. Many school buildings needed to be substantially re-built or refurbished. There was severe shortage of teachers. Local authorities would have to change their roles towards education and the school system. Education was moreover no longer seen as the preserve of the élite; the needs of the average child were expected to be tackled first.[9]

When Labour won the election it was expected that Chuter Ede, who had been Parliamentary Secretary to the Board of Education during the war, would be the new Minister of

Education. But Attlee told him, 'he had something more important in store'; it was the Home Office.[10] To the surprise of many educationalists and politicians, Attlee appointed Ellen Wilkinson. She had been Herbert Morrison's Parliamentary Secretary during the wartime Coalition government and was known for having led the Jarrow March of 1936. She had a reputation as a 'fiery left-winger', from a working class background who had to fight her own way through to university.[11] Although she had not played a leading role in the Party's discussions on education between the wars, she was well known for her commitment to reform, and specifically asked Attlee to be considered for the post. During the last year of the war, she was chair of the Party's National Executive Committee, and by 1945 was seen to be part of the mainstream of the Parliamentary Party despite her 'left-wing' background.[12]

D.R. Hardman, a Cambridge man, primarily interested in higher education, became her Parliamentary Secretary, and H.D. Hughes, later Principal of Ruskin College, her Parliamentary Private Secretary. There may have been a degree of naivety on her part as to the role of senior civil servants, whose views she accepted, and she was ill for the last few months of her ministry, but there is evidence to suggest that she was a persistent and probing questioner who kept her advisers on their toes. Ellen Wilkinson was conscious of the need to have support from key specialists, but her attempts to develop a Standing Committee to discuss policy matters never really got off the ground. It met infrequently and eventually disappeared as day-to-day measures preoccupied the Ministry.[13] This was a serious failure because she lost touch with those key figures in the Party who had played such an important role in developing a new consensus on educational reform during the war.

Her immediate tasks were to provide local authorities with the resources for an emergency building programme and to raise the teaching force by 50 per cent within two years. The building programme was partially successful, although increasing economic problems meant that the main beneficiaries were those living in the new suburbs and housing estates. Older school buildings had to make do with short term prefabricated additions or, in some cases, no improvements at all.[14] The initial targets in the teacher training programme were achieved, in part because a large number of the trainees had been involved in educational work in some form during the war. The programme, however, re-inforced existing divisions. The vast majority of emergency trained teachers found employment in the new secondary moderns or in the primary sector, not in the grammar schools. Several authorities took the view that the primary sector was best served by women teachers who had themselves been educated in secondary modern schools.

What Sort of Secondary Schools?

The Act had left the door open as to the future nature of secondary schooling. From the 1926 Hadow Report to the Spens Report of 1938 and the Norwood Committee of 1942, the dominant view was that there should be three types of secondary schooling, linked to different and 'innate' abilities and that, above all, the grammar school tradition should be preserved. The Labour Party in its policy documents had supported this approach, but there was growing support, led by Labour teachers, for the idea of a single, or multilateral school.[15] The Labour Party Conferences of 1942 and 1945 supported this idea.[16] But more radical ideas were emerging within the Party during the war. The multilateral idea had accepted the view of innate differences in children as it meant in practice three schools under one roof. In contrast, the Party's Advisory Committee in 1943, influenced by the ideas of Labour teachers, began to talk about a common curriculum to age thirteen with the emphasis on equal opportunities for all children to progress and develop their abilities at their own rate.[17]

It is from this point that we can talk of the principle of the 'comprehensive school.' There is little evidence that Labour politicians or educationalists either fully understood or supported these ideas. R.H. Tawney and G.D.H. Cole, influential figures both during and after the war, continued to support different types of schools, though Cole did say that the school should be equally reputable so that a boy or girl could easily shift from one to another.[18]

Although the Labour Party may have had a policy of promoting the development of single secondary schools in 1945, there had been no internal Party discussion as to what this meant. The leading advocates of the comprehensive idea were the National Association of Labour Teachers (NALT), which had the support of MPs, W.G. Cove, Leah Manning and Margaret Herbison and educationalists such as G.C.T. Giles, ex-President of the National Union of Teachers (NUT) who in the *New School Tie*, called for a new secondary system, based on a core curriculum to thirteen, with differentiation thereafter on specialisation, but not ability.[19] NALT developed these ideas in 1946, defining the purpose of the comprehensive school as a liberal education, ministering to three main types of interest: cultural for the enrichment of personal leisure, vocational in preparation for the successful gaining of a livelihood and civic to prepare for responsible participation in the duties of citizenship.[20] NALT lobbied Transport House, the Labour Party headquarters, for a clear policy but the Party was recommending to local authorities that they should not support the development of comprehensive schools. The Fabian Society, very influential at Transport House was known to be a strong supporter of the tripartite model.[21]

That there was no consensus in the Party can be seen from the discussions at the 1946 Annual Conference. Delegates objected to the tripartite system because it conflicted with multilateralism, but at the same time criticised ministers for limiting the number of grammar school places in a way which could deprive working-class children of their now legally recognised opportunities.[22] There were three contradictory themes within the Party. The defenders of the tripartite system, aiming to defend working-class opportunities, were the dominant group amongst MPS and included Ellen Wilkinson, Herbert Morrison and Creech-Jones. Chuter Ede reflected the middle way of experimenting with multilateral schools, while accepting the basic tripartite principle, while a grouping of Labour teachers and Socialists, some inside and some outside the Party, led the call for comprehensive schools.

The Labour government neither gave leadership to promote a new concept of secondary schooling, nor encouraged experimentation with multilateral schools. Up to its dying days it resisted experimentation, except in a few isolated areas like Anglesey, or where there was a strong local pressure, as in the West Riding, London and Middlesex[23]. The Ministry, despite the openness of the Act, went on the offensive against comprehensive schools and multilateralism, and gave clear guidelines for a tripartite system of grammar, technical and modern secondary schools.

Even before Ellen Wilkinson took office in 1945, the consultation process with local authorities had begun with the pamphlet *The Nation's Schools* whose main thesis was that secondary education should be of a tripartite character. It was scathing of the multilateral school and stated that the new secondary (modern) schools should be conceived as schools for working-class children 'whose future employment will not demand any measure of technical skill knowledge'.[24]

The pamphlet was attacked by educationalists for its defence of the status quo.[25] It was later withdrawn, but its main features were incorporated in Ministry circulars and pamphlets produced over the next five years; for example, Circular 73 entitled 'Organisation of Secondary Education', published in December 1945, recommended that 70 to 75 per cent of places should go to 'modern', the remaining 25 to 30 per cent being to grammar and technical schools. It did, however, note that the Ministry was prepared to consider schemes for bilateral or multilateral schools, but there was a clear recommendation to authorities to propose a tripartite system.[26]

At the 1946 Labour Party Conference, W.G. Cove MP, a leading advocate of comprehensive schools and key figure in the NALT, succeeded in winning unanimous support for a resolution demanding the withdrawal of *The Nation's Schools* despite protests from Ellen Wilkinson.[27] It was one of only five occasions on which the National Executive Committee was defeated at Conference during the six years of the Labour administration.

Ellen Wilkinson in her public comments on the future of secondary schooling emphasised the defence of grammar schools, saying it would be folly to injure them, and criticising those who said that to have the three types of schooling was an incorrect social philosophy.[28] To her, the abolition of fees had ensured entry on merit. Her starting point was providing opportunities for working-class children. Although a number of local authorities did consider developing multilateral schools, the Ministry, in further circulars in 1947, re-emphasised the value of the tripartite system and criticised single schools.[29] Its policy was helped by a growing change of opinion within the teaching profession. Teachers in grammar schools feared that the development of multilateral schools would undermine the quality of secondary schooling. The teaching unions had been supporters of the concept of a single secondary school before the war, but of 'types of schooling under one roof' rather than of the comprehensive principle. The secondary school teachers, in their acceptance of the multi-bias school, had hoped to see their own 'secondary standards' spread, but they now feared the loss of those standards through a domination of the modern over the grammar school stream.[30]

On 6 February 1947, Ellen Wilkinson died. She had fought long and hard in Cabinet for educational reform. Her greatest achievement was undoubtedly the raising of the school leaving age to fifteen years. Some in the Cabinet said that this should be delayed because it would lead to a direct loss to the national labour force. 'No educational grounds,' she argued, 'could justify the delay.' With support from Ede and Morrison, she secured Cabinet approval.[31]

Her successor, George Tomlinson, was a different kind of Labour politician. A former weaver, trade union organiser and local councillor, Tomlinson was viewed as 'solid' and 'reliable' by Attlee. He had been a member of the Party's Education Advisory Committee and would be more conciliatory to local authorities and educationalists than Wilkinson. He was a negotiator, less assertive than his predecessor, but no less effective in ensuring that gains achieved over the previous two years were maintained. Like Wilkinson, he defended the tripartite system because it offered opportunities for working-class children.[32]

Ministry policy remained the same although there were some concessions to local authority requests for common secondary schools, but only in rural areas and where the school was a multilateral, rather than a comprehensive school with a six or seven entry form. Pressure grew inside the Labour Party for the 'rapid development of a common secondary school'.[33] At long last the NEC, in 1949, convened an ad hoc group to resolve the comprehensive issue. NALT played a leading role in the group, with Alice Bacon, also an NEC member and MP, as the chief advocate for comprehensive schools. The outcome of their discussions appeared in a new pamphlet on secondary education, published in 1951, saying that the tripartite system did not promote equality of opportunity and was therefore out of tune 'with the aspirations of socialism'. The comprehensive school was seen as the answer to overcoming these injustices, giving children a general education and opportunities to develop their own specialist interests free from any organisational constraints.[34]

Tomlinson remained unmoved and argued that there was no mass support for comprehensive schools.[35] In criticising the plan put forward by Middlesex, he said that all children were not alike either in their aptitude or in their standards of ability. His views had support from two distinct quarters. There was a fear among young middle-class families, many of whom had voted Labour in 1945 for the first time, that the grammar school tradition would be undermined, and there was still strong support from sections of the Labour Movement for the scholarship system.[36] Tomlinson felt safe in his views because, despite the protestations of conferences, he had the support of Cabinet colleagues and there was no groundswell of support for change from either the educational sector or trade unions.

The Party never resolved these differences during the lifetime of the Government. It was noticeable that during these years no more than half a dozen Labour MPs came out in full support of comprehensive schools.

Perpetuating Inequality

There were probably three general reasons for the continued conservatism within the Party. It moved to the right in the late 1940s. Radical ideas on education were linked to the left of the Party and the now despised and isolated Communists, reflecting the Cold War climate. Defending existing institutions and standards became the vocabulary of the time. Also, with the view that the main task was achieved with the 1944 Act, Labour leaders tended to view education as the terrain of 'experts', no longer as a political issue. Consequently, educational ideas which defended the status quo and looked to innate differences in children's ability through intelligence testing became accepted.[37] Finally there was a lack of clarity and understanding as to what was now understood by terms like 'equality' and 'equality of opportunity'. 'Equality' was viewed as a dirty word, linked to Communism and a levelling down of skills and abilities.[38] Support for the 1944 Act had come from all sections of the Labour Movement because they saw it as based on the principles of equality of opportunity and parity of all second-ary schools.

Inequality was further perpetuated by the Government's failure to tackle direct grant grammar schools and public schools. Ellen Wilkinson did refuse sixty direct grant schools admission to the new system and regulations, but did not fulfil the hope of many in the Party that all places to these schools would be free. Public schools remained even more untouched, despite protestations from NALT and the Workers' Education Association (WEA). 'I do not think the time has come when the "nationalisation" of these schools would be worth the very considerable opposition which any such proposals would create,' Tomlinson told a Party sub-committee in 1948.[39] He went even further, later in his Ministry, by reassuring the Incorporated Association of Preparatory Schools that the Education Act recognised a place for independent schools and that 'the latest government statement of educational policy made no suggestion of absorbing them into the state system.'[40]

The Government also failed to fulfil the Act's proposals on nursery education. Nursery schools were expected to be part of local authority development plans, but within a year of the Government taking office, the Ministry of Health ceased paying 100 per cent grants for new day nurseries. The 1948 Education (Miscellaneous Provisions) Act defined the statu-tory age of admission to infant schools as five years of age, effectively frustrating the aims of the Act. Discretion was still permitted, but the nursery-infant stage as the first stage in the education process was no longer recognised. Financial reasons were given for the changes in policy, but the lack of protests to the retraction reflect a changing mood towards women's role in the home and family based childcare.[41] By 1947, however, the Government was pleading with women to go into industry and other paid work to help with the rebuilding of the economy. By 1951 there were as many women in paid work as there had been during the war. The lack of progress on nursery education is therefore even more surprising.

In the 1950s advancement for working-class children

became restricted by the vision of secondary modern schools as the schools for them. The Labour government did secure some advances – the raising of the school-leaving age was important. The teacher training programme and the emergency building programme in the early years of the administration secured at least an extension of provision. There was also a noticeable outpouring of pamphlets on teaching methods which became a source for liberal initiatives in the classroom in the following decades.[42]

The Government, however, failed to tackle issues that had been deliberately fudged during the war and by the 1944 Act. The public schools, remained untouched. The wartime concern over voluntary religious-based schools was not resolved. The divisions within the education system therefore remained. G.C.T. Giles had hoped that the 1944 Act would provide a thorough recasting of the education system and 'give expression to a modern democratic outlook,' but his high expectations soon went as the Government retreated within the existing system and structures.[43]

These failures reflected some of the contradictions in the Party in government. Was it the role of the Government to shift power and class relations fundamentally, to challenge and remove inequalities which existed, or to mediate between them? Was it the role of the Government to give a new vision and ideology or merely manage within existing ideas and value systems?' The Government in the end flowed with the tide created by others and left a legacy of continuing divisions and inequality, of pragmatism and capitulation to the views of educational establishment.

Notes

[1] See D. Bourn, *The Development of Labour Party Ideas on Education, with special reference to the period 1918-44*. Unpublished Phd thesis, Keele University 1978; R. Barker, *Education and Politics*, Oxford University Press, London 1972; M. Parkinson, *The Labour Party and the Organisation of Secondary Education*, Routledge, London 1970; B. Simon,

Politics of Educational Reform 1920-1940, Lawrence & Wishart, London 1974 and *Education and the Social Order 1940-1990*, Lawrence & Wishart, London 1991; P.H.J.H. Gosden, *Education in the Second World War*, Methuen, London 1976.

[2] See e.g. A. Bullock, *Life and Times of Ernest Bevin, Volume One*, Heinemann, London 1960, pp123-30; F. Blackburn, *George Tomlinson*, Heinemann, London 1954, pp164-70.

[3] D.W. Dean, 'Planning for a Post-War Generation: Ellen Wilkinson and George Tomlinson at the Ministry of Education 1945-51', in *History of Education* 1986, Volume 15, Number 2, pp95-117.

[4] See especially M. Locke, *Power and Politics in the School System*, Routledge, London 1974; I.G.K. Fenwick, *The Comprehensive School 1944-1970*, Methuen, London 1976; H. Silver, *Education and the Social Condition*, Methuen, London 1980; R. Pedley, *The Comprehensive School*, Penguin, Harmondsworth, London 1969.

[5] These points are discussed in more detail in R. Lowe, *Education in the Post-War Years*, Routledge, London 1988, chapters 1-3.

[6] See N. Middleton & S. Weitzman, *A Place for Everyone*, Gollancz, London 1976, chapters IX-X; P.H.J.H. Gosden, *op.cit.*

[7] G.C.T. Giles, *The New School Tie*, Pilot, London 1945; B. Simon, 1991, *op.cit.*

[8] On the impact of local authorities, see Fenwick, *op.cit.*, chapters 1-3.

[9] Giles, *op.cit.*, p15.

[10] *Ede Diaries*, Volume 7, p26, 28.7.45. British Library, unpublished.

[11] *Labour Party Annual Conference Report 1946*, p189. See also *New Statesman*, 18 August 1945 for her views on education.

[12] Ellen Wilkinson's contribution to education has been the subject of considerable debate in recent years. Her biographer B. Vernon, *Ellen Wilkinson*, Croom Helm, Beckenham 1982, takes a broadly sympathetic approach as does A. Percival, 'The Death of Red Ellen', *Times Educational Supplement*, 15 November 1974. There was a major debate in *History Workshop Journal*, (HWJ) on her work with Hughes defending her record and Rubinstein criticising her. H.D. Hughes, 'In defence of Ellen Wilkinson', D. Rubinstein, 'Ellen Wilkinson Re-Considered', *HWJ* Number 7, 1979; D. Reid. 'Ellen Wilkinson' *HWJ* Number 8, 1979; C. Benn, 'Comprehensive School reform and the 1945 Labour Government', *HWJ* Number 10, 1980.

[13] Her Permanent Secretary defended her at the time and this is re-inforced in his memoirs. J. Radcliffe Maud, *Experiences of An Optimist*, Hamish Hamilton, London 1981.

[14] Middleton & Weitzman, *op.cit.*, pp316-327.

[15] D. Rubinstein & B. Simon, *The Evolution of the Comprehensive School 1926-1972*, Routledge, London 1973, pp15-16; D. Bourn, *op.cit.*

[16] *Labour Party Annual Conference Report 1943*, p141; *1945*, p126.

[17] *Labour Party Archives: Labour Party Education Sub-Committee*: L.G. Memo 187, 'Spens Report & Multilateral School'; R.D.R. 88 – Alice Bacon,

'Secondary Schools'; R.D.R. 107 – Lady Shena Simon, 'Multilateral schools'; R.D.R. 167 – H. Shearman, 'New Secondary Schools'; D. Bourn, *op.cit.*, pp340-348. NALT had raised the idea of a common secondary curriculum from thirteen years of age in their pamphlet criticising the Spens Report published just before the outbreak of war, *Social Justice and Public Education*, 1939.

[18] D. Bourn, *op.cit.*, p348; G.D.H. Cole, *Great Britain in the Post War World*, Gollancz, London 1942, pp128-9; Cole did later change his views as can be seen by his essay, 'Education – A Socialist View', *Year Book of Education 1952*, Evans, London 1952.

[19] Giles, *op.cit.*

[20] L. Manning, *A Life for Education*, Gollancz, London 1970; NALT, *The Comprehensive School, 1947*, pp14-16.

[21] C. Benn, *op.cit.*, pp200-1.

[22] B. Simon, 1991, *op.cit.*, pp107-8, 129-31.

[23] Fenwick, *op.cit.*, chapter 3.

[24] B. Simon, 1991, *op.cit.*, pp102-5.

[25] G.C.T. Giles, 'Secondary Education for All, *TES*, 26 May 1945; H. Dent re-inforced this view in a leader in *TES*, 15 July 1945.

[26] See B. Simon, 1991, *op.cit.*, p108.

[27] *Labour Party Annual Conference Report 1946*, pp189-95.

[28] *Education*, 2 October 1945.

[29] These local authorities including Reading, Oldham, Southend, London, Middlesex and the West Riding. Circular 144 'New Organisation of Secondary Education', June 1947; 'New Secondary Education' pamphlet, 1947.

[30] O. Banks, *Parity and Prestige in English Secondary Education*, Routledge, London 1955, pp142-4; Fenwick, *op.cit.*, pp47-51.

[31] Quoted in B. Simon, 1991, *op.cit.*, p99.

[32] F. Blackburn, *op.cit.*, pp169-70.

[33] *Labour Party Annual Conference Report 1950*.

[34] *Policy for Secondary Education*, 1951 p9, C. Burn, *op.cit.*, p201.

[35] *Labour Party Annual Conference Report 1950*, pp92-3; R. Barker, *op.cit.*, p92.

[36] B. Simon, 1991, *op.cit.*, pp121-5.

[37] These points were discussed further in the early 1950s by Brian Simon in his work on intelligence testing. See his *Intelligence, Psychology and Education* Lawrence & Wishart, London 1971, which includes his seminal essay on intelligence testing and comprehensive schools, first published in 1953.

[38] On the wider questions of equality of opportunity and Labour Party thinking, see R. Johnson, *et al*, *Unpopular Education*, Hutchinson, London 1981.

[39] *Labour Party Archives*, R.D.M. 180, Memo by Minister of Education for Social Services Sub-Committee.

[40] *TES*, 15 September 1950. Tomlinsons' support for public schools had

also been influenced by his visit to Eton College a couple of years earlier; F. Blackburn, *op.cit.*, pp6-8.

[41] N. Whitbread, *The Evolution of the Nursery-Infant School*, Routledge, London 1972, pp110-111.

[42] See Weitzman and Middleton, *op.cit.*, pp31-2 who refer particularly to 'Story of a School' published in 1947 which showed what was possible with an archaic building in the introduction of liberal methods.

[43] Giles, *op.cit.*, p111.

Part 3 – A People's Culture?

The Government, the People and the Festival

Alan Sinfield

We're proud to say
In every way
We're ordinary folk,
But please to observe
We still preserve
Our sturdy hearts of oak.
Although as servants of the state
We may have been coerced,
As we've been told to celebrate
We'll celebrate or burst.
Though while we brag
Our shoulders sag
Beneath a heavy yoke
We all get terribly heated
If it's treated
As a joke. so:

Don't make fun of the Festival ...[1]

This was Noel Coward's song in the Lyric Revue, 1951. Evidently he does not approve of the Festival of Britain, and he suggests that 'we' – British people – do not either. But who is he speaking for? The contest here is about the whole concept of Britishness and of the place of culture within it.

181

A People's Culture

The war ethos – for my generation 'the war' means the one of 1939-45 – was unprecedentedly egalitarian and progressive. The typical wartime film included a reflective moment where someone asks 'What are we fighting for?' and the reply is something like 'To create a world fit to live in'. It was widely agreed that there could be no return to the conditions that many people had suffered before. The war inspired idealistic plans for the future. For instance, the 1941 book *A People's Runnymede*, by Robert J. Scrutton, demanded a People's Common Law Parliament; the idea was

> not merely to rebuild a city but to raise a new political, economic, and social order from the dust of the old. ... When this war is over hundreds and thousands of engineers, teachers, architects, and scientists thrown out of the forces will be looking for work. This talent must not be wasted. Plans and maps must be prepared for rebuilding London and other great cities, and for garden-cities throughout the country. They must be given to our young architects with the instruction – build beautiful and healthy cities for the people.[2]

In this context, the traditional leisure-class tone of 'good' culture – the *posh* tone, I was brought up to say – was something of an embarrassment, even an anachronism. Some people envisaged alternatives. Herbert Read welcomed the idea of proletarian art in a little book published in 1941, called *To Hell with Culture*. He saw 'culture' and its specialised producers as consequences of industrialisation, and as an aspect of the oppression of working people in a capitalist state. Read says: 'The worker has as much latent sensibility as any human being, but that sensibility can only be awakened when meaning is restored to his daily work, and he is allowed to create his own culture'. 'The whole of our capitalist culture' he concludes, 'is one immense veneer'.[3] If such vivid sentiments now seem surprising, that is a measure of the extent to which the promises made under the pressure of wartime needs have been revoked.

An alternative cultural style was already in view, to some degree. Quality paperbacks for a large-scale market were a recent innovation; in January 1941 John Lehmann courageously established a literary journal in that form. *Penguin New Writing* had an egalitarian air about it, with limp covers, economy paper and sales of up to 100,000 at 6d. Lehmann found many previously unpublished young authors and encouraged them to write about everyday experience, often in the relatively de-classed context of the armed forces. He believed these were 'revolutionary circumstances' for the development of literature and the arts.[4] However, *Penguin New Writing* was not entirely revolutionary: it maintained the Bloomsbury mode of sensitive individual response. Then as now, it was hard to envisage modes of creativity outside the traditional conception of art.

It was generally assumed that the new society should be organised by the State; its responsibilities had been growing steadily since the mid-nineteenth century, and they took a huge leap with the wartime organisation of the economy. Furthermore, to maintain production the Government was obliged to do something about the dreadful conditions in which very many people lived – conditions which hitherto had been assumed to be problems merely for the individual and his or her family (this notion has reappeared lately in Thatcherism). Now it was demonstrated, for all to see, that the employment, health, diet and housing of the people could be improved by state action – when the State wanted to act. Sir William Beveridge believed it was simply a matter of will: 'all men have value when the State sets up unlimited demand for a compelling purpose. By the spectacular achievement of its planned economy war shows also how great is the waste of unemployment'.[5]

The underlying ideology that informed the post-war reforms was that the good things of life customarily enjoyed by the leisure classes were now to be available to everyone.

All the people were to have a stake in society, an adequate share of its resources as of right – a job, a pension or social security, a roof over your head, healthcare, education. This, quite explicitly, was the pay-off for wartime suffering.

And 'good' culture, which hitherto had been the special prerogative of the leisure classes, was also to be available to everyone. By the end of the war, state support for the arts was firmly on the agenda. The Arts Council was formed in 1945 and the BBC Third Programme in 1946.

A key post-war assumption, significantly challenged only recently by Thatcherism, was instituted at this point in the 1940s: that the condition of culture is in substantial part a responsibility of the State.

The Festival and its Critics

The 1951 Festival of Britain was conceived, by the Labour administration, largely in this new spirit. It was a massive and unprecedented act of state patronage. Fifty architects and a hundred designers were commissioned, most of them under forty-five years of age.[6] The budget was £11 million, all State funded; no explicit sponsorship was sought. The idea was to represent the history and potential of the British people – not just of distinguished individuals.

The artwork on the Festival site did enact a relatively popular conception of good culture. It was not a matter of paintings hanging in designated culture-halls. In collaboration with the architects, murals and mobiles were designed into the structure of the pavilions; often they were not on canvas or in oblong shapes with frames; some were in poster-style, some in the open-air. The whole project seemed to break free of the conventions for appreciating art. The critic G.S. Whittet recalled in 1956: 'For the only occasion in my experience painting and sculpture became even the tiniest bit proletarian'.[7]

The attempt to filter good culture through populist lenses

was evident in the Lion and Unicorn pavilion, which was supposed to house an exposition of 'the British character, with overtones of national traditions and achievements, though warlike achievements were strictly excluded'.[8] There was a good deal about Shakespeare, the King James translation of the Bible, and so on. But lower-class contributions to language were included. 'The British do not simply leave the development of their language to the professionals of literature', it was explained in the official Guide, written by Ian Cox. 'There is no closed shop among practitioners of the English tongue. At times, indeed, the walls and streets of British towns can make most lively reading. The Cockney has added a local vocabulary to the national one; and every British county has contributed a proverb, or a telling phrase'. Craftsmanship was represented not only by old furniture, but also sporting guns, fishing tackle and tailoring.[9]

Many in the cultural establishment were unhappy with such a project, for 'good' culture seemed linked ineluctably to the leisured classes, and incompatible with both the State and the people. Lady Violet Bonham-Carter defended State intervention, but felt obliged to observe that historically 'the leisure and money of the "privileged" have guarded and preserved for the few much that was rare, precious and lovely.' Whether or not the essential qualities of these values can survive intact', she pondered, 'when they are shared by the many, still remains to be seen'.[10] The threat from the egalitarian ethos of the time was a persistent theme in *Horizon*, which had been started by Cyril Connolly in 1940 with the aim of keeping aesthetic standards alive in wartime. 'Look at the way Shostakovich has been ruined by the dogmatism of the Soviet regime', Edward Sackville-West (cousin of Vita) wrote.[11] State involvement threatened the entire ideology of art as the personal expression of individual genius. The initial co-editor of *Horizon* was Stephen Spender: in *The God that Failed* he explained his repudiation of Communism largely in terms of his commitment to literature.

185

Spender could not identify with the working classes, he found, though he sympathised with their oppression, because the sensibility of 'the creative artist ... which is decided for him in his childhood, is bourgeois'.[12]

An egalitarian conception of art was almost, it seemed, a contradiction in terms. It was understood in this way on the left as well. Aneurin Bevan in his book *In Place of Fear* (1952) acknowledged that the individual might be uncomfortable in the current climate of social change. 'Personal relations have given way to impersonal ones', he said, so it was understandable that 'those whose habits and possessions are bound up with the vanishing social order are filled with pessimism'. But this was necessary in 'a change from one type of society to another'.[13] In other words, if leisured-class aesthetes were uneasy, it was because they had been over-privileged before. However, in Bevan's view this did not mean the end of art but its reorientation, as the possession of everyone, under the benign guardianship of municipalities and the State – he compared it to the erstwhile commissioning of popes and monarchs. In the new society Bevan expected the 'emancipation' of artists, 'restored to their proper relationship with civic life'. This was precisely what Connolly feared.

Within this context, the slant of Coward's song may be understood.

> We know we're caught
> And must support
> This patriotic prank
> And though we'd rather have shot ourselves
> We've got ourselves
> To thank.

Why? Because 'we' voted in the Government that is sponsoring the Festival. But that is an interesting 'we'. Coward, of course, did not vote Labour; he is putting his own distrust of the Festival into the mouths of the majority who had allowed it to occur. In fact, most people *liked* the

Festival, and they even carried on voting Labour (when Labour lost office in 1951 they still got the largest share of the vote). The majority did not altogether feel their 'shoulders sag beneath a heavy yoke'; that was how conservatives like Coward felt. He knows this: his song has to acknowledge that 'We all get terribly heated' if the Festival is 'treated / As a joke'. This 'we' is not Coward, but people who may resent his jocular song. His cartoon version of us, with mauve noses and hair plastered down in the rain, is placed alongside his vision of 'ordinary folk' with 'sturdy hearts of oak'. He cannot decide whether to represent us as pathetic dupes or sterling stuff.

Coward was by no means the only sceptic. Sir Thomas Beecham called the Festival 'a monumental piece of imbecility and iniquity'. An advertisement for a travel agency in the *Listener* suggested as 'the best idea for the Festival year – a trip to South Africa'.[14] It seemed the ultimate impertinence of the Labour Government. Conservative newspapers were against it, especially the Beaverbrook *Express* stable. 'Those who most loudly attacked Socialist austerity equally deplored Socialist festivity', remarked the *Picture Post*.[15] In 1961 Evelyn Waugh published *Unconditional Surrender*, about the war period, and the last chapter concludes with the Festival:

> Monstrous constructions appeared on the south bank of the Thames ... but there was little popular exuberance among the straitened people and dollar-bearing tourists curtailed their visits and sped to the countries of the continent where, however precarious their condition, they ordered things better.

Meanwhile, in what remained of good society, 'Some of the young men wore hired evening-dress; others impudently presented themselves in dinner-jackets and soft shirts'.[16]

Such attitudes flourished despite the co-option of establishment figures onto the Festival Council. Coward himself was for a time a member; so were Sir Kenneth Clark, John Gielgud, Sir William Haley, Sir Malcolm Sargent and

T.S. Eliot. But most of these worthies 'came under considerable pressure from their friends' and 'some of them were privately of the opinion that the whole thing ought to be called off'. Eliot opposed the 1944 extension of secondary education; he held that quality culture had to be founded upon a strong upper class.[17] That class, however, and its ability to support traditional culture, were perceived as in decline. In September 1946 *Horizon* had asked writers what they thought they should live on while writing. Connolly agreed with nearly half his respondents: the State must 'step in'. It must give young writers scholarships and older writers sabbatical years: it must, with its official blessing, 'thrust leisure as well as money on them'.[18] State intervention was acceptable when it fitted in with the established idea of the artist and good culture.

The crucial uncertainty – as to whether a new kind of funding would mean a new kind of culture – arose again when the BBC opened the self-consciously highbrow Third Programme in September 1946. It was presented by the BBC as potentially for everyone. The new Director-General, William Haley, described his three programmes as 'a broadly based cultural pyramid, slowly aspiring upwards'. His ambition, he said, 'was to lead listeners from the Light Programme to the Home and from the Home to the Third until eventually the Home and Light should wither away leaving the Third over all'.[19] But of course the Third Programme did not transcend the traditional organisation of the arts, and Connolly and his friends found they could welcome it without reserve. 'The State is ourselves', he wrote, '*l'état c'est toi*'. The Third's share of listeners fell to 1 per cent in 1949 and then to fewer than 36,000.[20]

The Arts Council, at its inception, was also supposed to have broad popular appeal. However, under the chairmanship of John Maynard Keynes – the Bloomsbury apostle of the mixed economy – the largest slice of the money was committed immediately to turning Covent Garden, which had been a *palais de danse* run by Mecca with a two-month opera season, into an international opera and ballet house. Even so, Keynes hoped that Covent Garden would justify its subsidy in popular terms by performing 'at least a month of Gilbert and Sullivan every year'. These aspirations were largely abandoned by 1951.[21] The Arts Council organized an exhibition of paintings alongside the Festival, *Sixty Paintings for '51.* 'If the Festival of Britain is to achieve its avowed aim of showing the British way of life in all its various facets', the writer of the Foreword to the exhibition Catalogue remarked, 'it is clearly appropriate that a number of our distinguished painters and sculptors should have been given an opportunity to make their contribution.' In its view, the Festival's aim is only 'avowed' until the Arts Council gives 'opportunity' to painters and sculptors. Actually, many such people *had* contributed – within the ethos of the South Bank site – Henry Moore, Barbara Hepworth, Keith Vaughan, Victor Pasmore, Ben Nicholson, John Minton, John Piper, Feliks Topolski, Jacob Epstein, Frank Dobson, Graham Sutherland, Reg Butler.[22] But there was no art exhibition in the conventional sense – with oil paintings on canvas for hanging on walls, on subjects chosen individually by artists. The emphasis of the Festival, the Catalogue implies, is temporary, almost frivolous, whereas *Sixty Paintings* had 'the hope of handing down to posterity from our present age something tangible and of permanent value'.

This drag back towards a traditional idea of culture shows how, even when there is a wide constituency for radical change, you cannot simply jump out of the prevailing conceptual structures. For who was to arrange the new cultural future if not the experts? – And they, for the most part, were products of the old system. State intervention in culture (as in other areas) took its tasks, its personnel and much of its tone from the current establishment. The Labour Party manifesto of 1945 assumed, virtually, that posh culture could simply be offered to everybody: 'By the provision of concert halls, modern libraries, theatres and suitable civic centres, we desire to assure to our people full access to the great heritage of culture in this nation'.[23] In this, as in other aspects of the post-war settlement, it was an opportunity missed. Raymond Williams recalls:

> I thought that the Labour government [of 1945] had a choice: either for reconstruction of the cultural field in capitalist terms, or for funding institutions of popular education and popular culture that could have withstood the political campaigns in the bourgeois press that were already gathering momentum. In fact, there was a rapid option for conventional capitalist priorities – the refusal to finance the documentary film movement was an example.[24]

This falling away from wartime promises occurred partly because the Labour leadership was implicated in the old assumptions and barely able to respond to the radical mood of 1945 (they had expected to lose the election).[25] In fact most of them were brought up in the old posh manner. Clement Attlee 'suffered acutely if the port was circulated the wrong way at his dinner table'.[26] The exception was Herbert Morrison, the Festival enthusiast in the Cabinet.

The State, the People and the Market

'I want to see the people happy', Morrison said, and he thought he knew how that was to be done. The worrying aspect of the Festival ethos, to my mind, is not that the State paid, but that the people had rather little to do with it. Certainly the notion of what would make them happy was very educational – 'a national display illustrating the British contribution to civilisation, past, present and future, in arts, in science and technology, and in industrial design'.[27] The Director-General of the Festival was Gerald Barry, editor of the liberal *News Chronicle*, and his collaborators were mainly professionals, senior civil servants and technocrats. Michael Frayn, in a justly celebrated essay, calls them 'herbivores' (as opposed to the carnivores who make capitalism work) – 'the radical middle-classes – the do-gooders; readers of the *Guardian* newspaper.'[28] The herbivores were prepared to compromise the posh idea of art in the interests of equality and social justice. Frayn sees the Festival as the last fling of middle-class radicalism before the onset of the carnivorous 1950s (one of the first actions of the incoming Conservative administration of 1951 was to smash almost everything on the South Bank site).

The organisers' top-down conviction that they knew what people want is in part the ground for Coward's grumpy song:

> Although as servants of the state
> We may have been coerced,
> As we've been told to celebrate
> We'll celebrate or burst.

'We envisage this as the people's show', said Barry, 'not organised arbitrarily for them to enjoy, but put on largely by them, by us all, as an expression of a way of life in which we believe'.[29] What is so striking about such pronouncements is the speakers' inability to hear the patronising tone that is so blatant to us. The official guide said of the events organised in two thousand cities, towns and villages that they were 'spontaneous expressions of citizenship'; the herbivores could not conceive of any mechanism through which a will more popular than that of the town council might express itself.[30] There is a nice instance in the official guidebook, when visitors are informed that there is a correct route to follow round the displays. But suppose we prefer not to take it? 'This is a free country', the guidebook declares, 'and any visitors who, from habit or inclination, feel impelled to start with the last chapter of the whole narrative and then zig-zag their way backwards to the first chapter, will be as welcome as anyone else'. But there is a penalty: 'such visitors may find that some of the chapters will appear mystifying and inconsequent'.[31]

The point about patronisation is easy to make. Yet was the Festival ethos altogether misconceived? The 1960s idea of managing without authority altogether surely contributed to the dissipating of the ideals which we associate with that decade. You can't organise a Festival, or anything, without expertise. And people did respond. Despite poor weather, eight and a half million visited the main site. When their opinion was asked, many said there was too much written detail for anyone to take in, but they remembered one or two items and the general effect.[32] In a poll conducted by Gallup, 58 per cent of people said their impression of the South Bank was favourable, while 15 per cent found it unfavourable. Most significantly, 'the police were struck by the absence of hooliganism and other crime'.[33] This I take as a key indicator of the extent to which people, after all is said, respected the South Bank as somehow *their space*. Though it was set up for rather than by them, many appreciated the thought.

The aspiration of the post-war reforms was not ignoble: it was to run society by and large on the basis of general consent. We were supposed to feel that the State was organised not just for the leisured classes, or for business, or for the meritorious, or the fortunate. It was organised, to a degree rarely attempted in history, on an ideology of sharing and reconciliation, in a hitherto divided Britain. The guidebook refers repeatedly to the overcoming of earlier divisions – between town and country, workers and experts, workers and machines, conquerors or immigrants and indigenous peoples, women and men, servants and masters. The Festival was offered as 'one united act of national reassessment, and one corporate reaffirmation of faith in the nation's future'.[34]

The over-insistent tone is matched by a complacency about what has been achieved:

> The Tolpuddle farm-hands broke down the last fence of resistance to the freedom of labour. In the early years of the present century, Mrs. Pankhurst's suffragettes forced the break-through which at last brought British women fully into public life.

Far, far more substantial changes would have been needed to make even an approximate actuality of the ethos of sharing, and these were rarely contemplated. The Festival represented, in the manner of the post-war settlement generally, only a partial and gestural amelioration of the injustices of the twentieth-century world economic system. And even that amelioration, as we have seen, is subject to easy reversal, besides depending on continuing and structural injustice in much of the rest of the world.

I have said that there was no sponsorship for the Festival, but the official guide did contain advertisements. They are collected at the front and back so as not to contaminate the cultural effect; they are in bright colours while the text is mainly in austere black and white – the market is banished to the margins of the Festival; it is waiting there, we might say, to resume centre-stage in the bright, glossy consumer world of the 1950s. Already, though, the separation between culture and the market is somewhat forced. As William Feaver has observed, despite the educational impetus, the artistic and design effects on the South Bank site strongly resemble those that were appearing in contemporary advertising. They 'reflected the marketing devices of Daks, Kia-Ora, BOAC, Mr Cube and Mr Therm. The World as advertised'.[35] To Feaver this indicates that the Festival was wrapped up in a world of fantasy. This is too austere: with the benefit of nostalgia at least, the adverts seem rather jolly. But the distinction between people's culture and commercial culture breaks down.

That convergence of design values corresponds to a conceptual awkwardness. Ian Cox wrote; 'the South Bank Exhibition is neither a museum of British culture nor a trade show of British wares; it tells the story of British contributions to world civilisation in the arts of peace'.[36] In fact, beneath the egalitarian manner I have been discussing, the Festival *was* what is repudiated in that formulation: an uneasy amalgam of museum and trade fair. 'Export or Die' was a key Labour government slogan, and the Festival was conceived partly as a way of beefing-up economic performance. The demonstration of achievements in science, technology and design was both 'a tonic to the nation' and an advertisement for foreign visitors.[37] It is the vulgarity of this economic appeal that provokes some of Coward's animus:

> We've never been
> Exactly keen
> On showing off or swank
> But as they say
> That gay display
> Means money in the bank.

So the Festival was not a pure people's space, shielded by Socialism from the market. The market was in there all the time, humanised with a veneer of culture. And that is the story, generally, of art and the post-war settlement. The 1945 Labour government and most middle-class radicals could not see very far past the prevailing structures of capitalism and the art establishment, and we have not got much further today. The key factor in the current conception of art is still, despite Thatcherite insistence on a role for the market, the aura inherited from the pre-war leisured class. Whether there might be a concept of good culture corresponding to an ideology of sharing we may still ponder. The Festival manifests the post-war pattern whereby democratic culture gets squeezed between art and commerce.

Notes

[1] Noel Coward, *The Lyrics*, Methuen, London 1983, p343-4. I am grateful to Isobel Johnstone and Hilary Lane, of the South Bank Centre, for prompting much of this paper, and to Paul Hendon for his help. See further Sinfield, *Literature, Politics and Culture in Postwar Britain*, Blackwell, Oxford 1989, ch3.
[2] Robert J. Scrutton, *A People's Runnymede*, Andrew Dakers, London 1941, pp154-5.
[3] Herbert Read, *To Hell with Culture*, Kegan Paul, Trench, Trubuer, London 1941, pp43-9.

[4] John Lehmann, *I Am My Brother*, Longman, London 1960, p92.
[5] William Beveridge, *Full Employment in a Free Society*, Allen and Unwin, London 1944, p29.
[6] Robert Hewison, *In Anger*, Weidenfeld, London 1981, p49.
[7] Quoted in Mary Banham and Bevis Hillier (eds), *A Tonic to the Nation*, Thames and Hudson, London 1976, p182.
[8] *Ibid*, p96.
[9] Ian Cox, *South Bank Exhibition: Festival of Britain: Guide*, 1951, p68.
[10] *Other People's Lives*, Contact Publications, London 1948, p89.
[11] Quoted in Cyril Connolly, *Ideas and Places*, Weidenfeld, London 1953, p113.
[12] *The God that Failed*, Right Book Club, London n.d., p237.
[13] Aneurin Bevan, *In Place of Fear*, Heinemann, London 1952, pp36, 93 and 50-51.
[14] John Montgomery, *The Fifties*, Allen and Unwin, London 1965, p28.
[15] *Picture Post*, 5 May 1951, quoted by Paul Hendon, 'The Festival of Britain and After ... Political Theatre on a Grand Scale', unpub. diss, Sussex University 1987, p6.
[16] Evelyn Waugh, *Unconditional Surrender*, Penguin, Harmondsworth 1964, p238.
[17] Michael Frayn, 'Festival', in Michael Sissons and Philip French, (eds), *Age of Austerity 1945-1951*, Penguin, Harmondsworth 1964, pp334, 340-1; T.S. Eliot, *Notes Towards the Definition of Culture*, Faber, London 1948, pp47, 42.
[18] Connolly, *op cit*, p124.
[19] Harry Hopkins, *The New Look*, Secker and Warburg, London 1963, p227; Francis Williams, *Nothing So Strange*, Cassell, London 1970, pp271-2.
[20] Connolly, *op cit*, p135; Hopkins, *op cit*, p235.
[21] Robert Hutchison, *The Politics of the Arts Council*, Sinclair Browne, London 1982, pp48-9, 97-9, 90, 117-8.
[22] Other high-cultural events in London associated with the Festival included three hundred concerts, Wagner at Covent Garden, thirty public exhibitions (eleven of them arranged by the Arts Council) and seven plays in repertory at the Old Vic. Britten's *Billy Budd* was commissioned, and new ballets, choral and orchestral works. Hewison observes that it all confirmed the role of the Arts Council, giving it confidence in its infant stage: Hewison, *op cit*, pp51-6.
[23] Frances Borzello, *Civilising Caliban*, Routledge, London 1987, p129.
[24] Raymond Williams, *Politics and Letters*, New Left Books, London 1979, p73.
[25] Ralph Miliband, *The State in Capitalist Society*, Weidenfeld, London 1969, pp106-13; Ralph Miliband, *Parliamentary Socialism*, 2nd edn, Merlin, London 1972, ch9; Douglas E. Ashford, *The Emergence of the Welfare States*, Blackwell, Oxford 1986, pp264-81.
[26] Francis Williams, *op cit*, p222.

[27] Banham and Hillier, *op cit*, p27.
[28] Frayn, *op cit*, p331.
[29] *Ibid*, p336.
[30] Hewison, *op cit*, p49; Banham and Hillier, *op cit*, p36.
[31] Cox, *op cit*, p8.
[32] Montgomery, *op cit*, p31
[33] Frayn, *op cit*, pp347, 351.
[34] Cox, *op cit*, p6 and pp17, 19, 27, 63, 71. See Hendon, *op cit*, pp7-12.
[35] Banham and Hillier, *op cit*, p53.
[36] Cox, *op cit*, p8.
[37] Hewison, *op cit*, p49.

Betrayed Spring: The Labour Government and British Literary Culture

Andy Croft

I've been listening of course to the election results all day with mounting excitement, and now know that Labour have got a clear majority and a strong one, and still 50 seats to go. It's much more than I thought possible, and at this stage fills me with exultation and apprehension. Oh if only this time they can prove strong enough! ... O the whole world is soaring and spinning now in wild hopes of health. Here there is everywhere a jolly atmosphere of gaiety and celebration; everyone pretending it means the beginning of the revolution, giving the clenched fist salute and breaking into the Red Flag or the Internationale ...

Randall Swingler to Geraldine Swingler,
Gradisca, 26 July 1945

Corporal Randall Swingler had certainly earned the right to share in the election celebrations. He had fought with the Eighth Army through North Africa and then for two years up through the mud of Italy, where he was twice awarded the Military Medal. But for Swingler the military victory in Europe, like the election result, also marked the end of a decade-long political struggle against Fascism and its Tory appeasers, to which he had given his services as a writer before becoming a soldier. Few had been so energetic or so effective in mobilising writers and readers against Fascism in the emergent 'People's Front' of the late 1930s; editor of *Left Review*, literary editor of the *Daily Worker*, active in the Left Book Club, the Workers' Music Association and Unity Theatre.[1]

After four years in the Army, Swingler was impatient to claim his place in the progressive cultural movement he had done so much to encourage. He was also eager to see the political and social changes which he was convinced the War had made in Britain, as in Italy and Yugoslavia. When the Japanese surrendered, it seemed that the defeats of the 1930s – especially Spain – were avenged at last:

> I feel more than ever now that a whole lifetime of the world is over, the work of one life achieved, and somehow we're all getting a second life, 'a second chance'. Everything's open and clear as after the flood, immense chaos, but new, primeaval chaos, a young world, all barriers down, a chance, a real chance to make socialism, to build, to create, to live ... The whole struggle lies ahead, the whole great shining magnificent exhilarating struggle of life ... my heart is full of hope, no, more than hope, conviction in the future.[2]

But how quickly those hopes were disappointed and the conviction broken. For though the Labour victory in 1945 owed much to the imaginative culture of the People's Front and its reflorescence in the 'cultural upsurge' of the People's War, the Attlee Administration presided over its dramatic collapse. As a result the Government quickly found itself intellectually isolated and unable to address its natural constituencies except in rhetorical terms, or by political confrontation.

The Best for the Most

The principal organisations behind the 'cultural upsurge' of the War were the Council for the Encouragement of Music and the Arts (CEMA), the Entertainments National Service Association (ENSA), the Army Bureau of Current Affairs (ABCA), Penguin Books (whose Pelicans were frequently published in collaboration with the Forces Book Club), *Penguin New Writing* and the Communist magazine *Our Time*.[3]

CEMA emerged at the end of 1939 as a Pilgrim Trust venture to continue the work of the British Institute of Adult Education (BIAE). The Government took over the funding of the Council, recognising the need to maintain civilian morale in war-time. But CEMA was always more radical and ambitious than this, seeking to provide 'The Best for the Most'. Under the leadership of Vaughan Williams, Mary Glasgow, Tom Jones and the popular broadcaster Walford Davies, CEMA was especially committed to the amateur and the regional, encouraging 'music-making and play-acting by the people themselves'. Early in the War it established a team of drama advisers in the regions to work with amateur drama groups, at the same time working closely with national organisations such as the British Drama League (BDL) and the YWCA (where CEMA funded a National Drama Adviser) to bring professionals and amateurs closer together. In 1942 CEMA formed its own theatrical circuit with fourteen touring companies. Meanwhile a team of 'music travellers' worked with local professionals and amateur groups and the Rural Music Schools Council to organise a nationwide series of concerts. Nine CEMA travelling companies were launched to take plays to Royal Ordinance Factory hostels.

The results were spectacular, a people's culture for a people's war. CEMA organised parties of musicians to play in underground shelters during the blitz of 1940; by October there were sixty such parties, each playing two to three concerts a night in the areas most affected by enemy action.

The 'Art for the People' exhibitions were seen by over 300,000 people in eighty towns that year. In 1942 the travelling companies played over a thousand shows in nearly 300 war-hostels (an estimated 98 per cent of these audiences had never seen a play before), as well as one night shows in 160 towns that had no theatre. To celebrate the 400th anniversary of the birth of the composer William Byrd in 1943, CEMA helped to organise fifteen Byrd festivals; that year it organised 4,500 factory concerts to audiences of up to 7,000. By 1944 it was giving an estimated seventy factory concerts a week, and another thirty in churches and village halls. By 1945 CEMA's travelling players had played to an audience of over half a million.[4]

> At one vast factory-concert the final item was *My Heart Ever Faithful* by Bach. 'It roused tremendous enthusiasm,' says Rita Sharpe, one of the performers. 'Who said that Bach was dull? They wanted more and yet more; but we had to finish punctually at one o'clock so that we did not interfere with the night's output ... In a Bristol factory: Jean Pougnet played *Meditation*, From *Thais*, and one worker stood poised, a cup of tea growing cold in his hand ...'[5]

At the same time the Blitz forced a general cultural diaspora from the metropolis. Sybil Thorndike and Lewis Casson took a tour of the Old Vic to the pit villages of South Wales and County Durham, before finding a permanent home in Burnley. Joan Cross led an opera company tour of Lancashire, South Wales, Lancashire and Durham, playing in Miners' Welfares and staying with miners and their families. Sir Thomas Beecham's London Philharmonic Orchestra began a tour of provincial theatres supported by CEMA (as a result several new provincial municipal orchestras were formed). When Virginia Woolf remarked, in a lecture to the Workers' Educational Association (WEA), that the ivory tower was beginning to lean a little, the South Wales miner and writer B.L. Coombes replied that it was already too late, that the old, pre-war ivory tower was already falling.[6]

On the whole, metropolitan cultural life was clearly invigorated and democratised by the experience (the London Philharmonic Orchestra (LPO) turned itself into a co-operative, 'Musical Culture Ltd')[7]. But more importantly, ordinary people began to participate in reconstructing a provincial artistic life where before the war the only culture had been imported, expensive and alien. In Middlesbrough for example, the Teesside Guild of Arts was launched in July 1943 in collaboration with CEMA. There were drama, theatre, writing, gramaphone, film and photography groups – so much activity that the Guild was soon publishing a monthly newsletter. In 1943 the Guild organised a regular series of lunch-hour madrigal concerts, soon followed by a well-subscribed series of evening concerts. The Adelphi Players visited Middlesbrough, so too did the Pilgrim Players with productions of *Candida* and *The Whole Armour of God* (An ABCA play about the resistance of the Churches in Occupied Europe). Together with the British Drama League and CEMA, the Guild organised an annual drama festival in Middlesbrough; CEMA brought its touring art exhibitions to Teesside and the Guild organised three local exhibitions of painting and photography.

Towns which had no professional theatres before the war suddenly had flourishing amateur theatres; by 1943-4 the BDL claimed a record membership of over 5,000 affiliated amateur dramatic groups. When the commercial theatre in Coventry was destroyed by enemy action, the Coventry People's Theatre was formed; their success led to a campaign for a municipal playhouse in the city. To help meet the demand for performance spaces, the Co-op formed a People's Entertainment Society (PEPS) with the expressed aim of bringing the theatre into common ownership. While PEPS began buying regional theatres, the Society's own company toured a production of *Men of Rochdale*. By the time Glasgow Unity brought a triumphant production of *The Lower Depths* to London for the General Election, it was evident that the relationship between London and the provinces, between professional and amateur, mainstream and radical, had changed fundamentally.

One of the moving spirits in the formation of CEMA was W.E. Williams, Secretary of the BIAE, a director of Penguin Books and editor of the popular Penguin Special series, one of which, Harold Laski's *Where Do We Go From Here?*, sold more than 80,000 copies. When Penguin launched *Penguin New Writing* in 1941 the intention was simply to reprint work from the earlier *New Writing*. But soon John Lehmann was publishing much livelier work by a new generation of writers, such as Alun Lewis, Sid Chaplin, Roy Fuller and Stuart Hood. *Penguin New Writing* was soon selling up to 100,000 copies an issue. Despite paper rationing, total expenditure on books rose dramatically during the War from £9m in 1939 to £23m by 1945.

Williams was also appointed Director of the ABCA when it was formed in 1941. The Bureau organised a programme of weekly discussions in the Forces at platoon level on issues like 'Do We Deserve Our Empire?', 'What's Wrong with Democracy?' and 'What Are We Fighting For?' Despite opposition from Churchill, ABCA material developed an increasingly radical strain, evident in the *Why We Fight* series. The 1943 ABCA handbook, for example, looked to an educated citizen's army like the Parliamentary armies of the 1640s, where every soldier 'knows what he fights for and loves what he knows'. In 1943 the ABCA established a play unit under Michael MacOwan which produced lively propaganda plays such as *Where Do We Go From Here?* for British troops all over the world. Many of the unit's writers were Communists who had written for Unity Theatre before the war – Ted Willis, Andre van Gysegham, Jack Lindsay, Mulk Raj Anand and Miles Tomalin. J.B. Priestley (who was a member of Unity's General Council) gave his militant 1943 play *Desert Highway* to the ABCA as 'a gift to the Army'. In its first six months, the ABCA play unit performed fifty-eight different shows to an audience of more than 20,000.

We have given the troops verse at two o'clock in the afternoon and heard them applaud it to the echo; we have made them leap in their seats with realistic dive-bombing and listen, hushed, to a Japanese cradle song. We are still learning, and, we hope, still shaking them.[8]

Less high-minded though no less propagandist, was Priestley's 1944 ENSA comedy *How Are They At Home?* ENSA organised several million concerts, lectures, performances and exhibitions to men and women in the forces (in 1943 alone 2.5 million performances). Although at first much of its work was based on pre-war assumptions about 'popular' culture, it soon found itself responding to new and surprising demands. Basil Dean reported after a visit to Italy that the troops there wanted more opportunities to see opera. In 1943 Louis MacNeice's 'Salute to the Red Army' was performed at an ENSA pageant at the Albert Hall to music by Alan Rawsthorne. That year an ENSA 'Forces Centre' was established at Salisbury, where each week nearly two thousand men and women attended adult education courses, celebrity concerts, brains trusts, gramaphone recitals, talks, play-reading and play production groups, and discussion groups. At an ENSA festival in 1943, the LPO players were struck by the reaction of the audience, mostly hearing a symphony orchestra for the first time:

The concentration of attention was almost unbearable to watch, and there was no relaxation of stress in the pause after the first movement or after the second. Even after the final chord had been hammered out there was a moment's silence. Then came a volley of applause that nearly lifted the great galvanised-iron roof ... Standing by me was a tough ordinary seaman with a scarred face and gnarled hands. His eyes were wet with tears ... he had never heard an orchestra until the festival began, and now he couldn't keep away from it. 'It's worse than the drink or women, the way it gets you,' he said.[9]

Several Tory newspapers, principally the *Daily Express*, led an unremitting campaign against CEMA; 'The government gives £50,000 to help wartime culture. What madness is this? There is no such thing as culture in wartime!' Questions were asked in Parliament about J.B. Priestley's popular Sunday evening talks on the Home Service, and he was taken off the air. Churchill personally tried to dissolve the ABCA in 1942. In 1943 a summary of the Beveridge Report prepared by the ABCA was suddenly withdrawn on the grounds of 'lack of balance'.[10] As late as 1944 Tory MPs were protesting against the funding of CEMA because of the 'poor quality and debasing effect' of its work, especially its popular art exhibitions.

For *Our Time*, this was the cultural 'Third Front', against the 'Diehard Division and Country House Brigade who have fought progress from every Tory ditch since the Reform Bill'. In the climate of the People's War, *Our Time* and its sister magazine *Seven* expanded rapidly articulating the demands of this cultural upsurge, publishing the work of men and women in uniform, and a new generation of radical artists and critics, such as E.P. Thompson, Elizabeth Shaw, Eric Hobsbawm, Hamish Henderson, Felix Topolski and Paul Hogarth.[11]

A Time to Live

It is easy to over-state the range and radicalism of this wartime 'cultural upsurge' and the extent to which it contributed to the election result in 1945. But *something* remarkable happened during the war in British cultural life which made the arts more accessible and more enjoyable for many more people than before. And that widened enjoyment helped to construct a wartime climate of feeling, informed a public sense of the immediate past, shaped a popular apprehension about the future, which – if nothing else – encouraged high hopes for cultural opportunities under the new Labour government. And among those whose vision of

Britain was defeated in 1945, the responsibility of the People's War culture for the Labour government was clear:

> It is the legitimate fruit of much earnest endeavour. Classes, discussion groups, summer schools, brains trusts, BBC talks, instruction in world and other citizenships, chairs of international relations, book clubs, and bureaux of current affairs, have brought it into being. A vast wash of words, both written and spoken, has prepared the way for its coming, and now it has come. It may be seen there – earnest faces, slight tendency to premature baldness; company suggestive of concert or art gallery or British Museum reading room ... They are bores.[12]

For a brief period, the developing momentum of wartime culture seemed to gather pace in the more relaxed conditions of peacetime. In 1945 the Ballet Rambert organised a three week ballet festival for the Forces at Salisbury, with performances, lectures, exhibitions and a special library. Sadlers Wells held their fourth annual CEMA ballet in the LCC open-air theatre in Finsbury Park. ENSA organised a touring exhibition of paintings by Duncan Grant, Vanessa Bell and Christopher Wood. The British Drama League hosted its first national conference since 1919 in response to a call by Michael Redgrave (blacklisted by West End management before the war) for new relationships between amateur and professional theatres. The Old Vic made a triumphant return to South Wales. The ABCA Play Unit was playing at the Arts Theatre. Theatre Workshop was re-formed, based first in Kendal and then the following May at Ormesby Hall outside Middlesbrough. There was even talk of cinemas being rebuilt as theatres. George Harrap announced a competition for new manuscripts from writers serving in uniform. The BBC Third Programme began broadcasting in September 1946. The National Book Council became the National Book League, organising the first Children's Book Week. Several of the pre-war provincial arts festivals began a tentative revival (Stratford and York); the first Cheltenham Music Festival took place that summer. And in June 1945 Maynard Keynes, chair of CEMA, announced that the work of CEMA was not only to be maintained in peacetime but extended in the form of an Arts Council. There was every good reason why the Artists' International Association (AIA) called their 1945 exhibition 'This Extraordinary Year!'

In that extraordinary year the Amalgamated Engineering Union (AEU) marked its silver jubilee with an ambitious programme of arts commissions. The launch of a history of the union was accompanied by a film, *We Who Make the Tools*, an exhibition, 'The Engineer in British Life' prepared by the AIA and opened by Ernest Bevin at the Whitechapel Gallery, and a play about the history of the union by Montagu Slater, *Century for George*.[13] The play was performed in the newly re-opened Scala Theatre as part of a season of trade union sponsored plays by Theatre '46 under Bernard Miles. Other plays included a Home Guard comedy by Miles, a new version of *Faust*, a dramatisation of *Pilgrim's Progress*, and a documentary play by Jack Lindsay and B.L. Coombes, *The Face of Coal*, drawing on the techniques of the ABCA play unit and Unity Theatre.

Unity Theatre was one of the few London theatres to stay open during the war (it also played in the underground shelters). In the wartime cultural and political climate Unity expanded rapidly.[14] By 1945 there were strong Unity Theatres (many with their own premises) in Glasgow, Leeds, Aberdeen, Cardiff, Bristol, Edinburgh, Reigate and Redhill, Mid-Rhondda, Birmingham, Manchester and Merseyside, and in 1946 London Unity felt confident enough to launch a professional company. When the coal industry was nationalised in January 1947, the Ministry of Fuel funded a production by the Unity company of a documentary play, *Coal*. The first-night audience included Government Ministers and leaders of the Coal Board and the National Union of Mine Workers (NUM). At the height of the fuel crisis of 1947 the play went on to tour in the north, the

Midlands and Scotland, while the NCB sponsored a touring exhibition, 'The Miner Comes to Town' which ran for six months at the Marble Arch Gallery. That year too, Harold Heslop's novel about the history of the Durham miners, *The Earth Beneath* was published in Britain and the USA, to great critical acclaim.[15]

It certainly looked as if Virginia Woolf's tower had finally collapsed under the rubble of war. This seemed the beginning of the popular and radical peacetime culture that many expected the Labour government to encourage, constructed upon new relationships between the State, the Labour Movement, the arts, and the new audiences created by the war. The high point was undoubtedly the re-opening in 1945 of Sadler's Wells theatre with the 'people's opera' *Peter Grimes*, written by Benjamin Britten and Montagu Slater.[16] Hailed as the first British opera since Purcell and Handel, *Peter Grimes* was the clearest example of the way radical artists had moved from the edges of British cultural life to its very centre.[17] Slater was also head of film scripts at the Ministry of Information; Ted Willis was now director of Unity Theatre's professional company; Unity's Ann Davies was working full-time as national organiser for the British Drama League; Alan Rawsthorne was writing music for the Old Vic and for Ministry of Information films; Alan Bush was commissioned by Nottingham City Council to write a symphony to mark the city's quincentenary; Geraldine Swingler, having spent much of the war playing concerts for the Ballet Rambert, CEMA and ENSA, was about to embark on a European tour. Such was the optimism in this 'Springtime of Nations' that British Communist poets felt confident enough in 1945 to publish a collection of poetry written during the War under the title *New Lyrical Ballads*, an affirmation of what they saw as a new, direct and active relation between poetry and life brought about by the war:

> If you should be tempted to despair, remember,
> Remember at once, and be humbled and quickened,

That already the lands live, where men
Spread forth their life like an ordered and opening flower.[18]

For cultural contacts were now reopening with the liberated countries of Europe. In 1945 the British Council sent a collection of modern British painting from the Tate to exhibit in European capitals. That year the French Resistance writer Louis Aragon visited Britain. The British Council organised an exchange visit between the French Comedie Française (the theatre of the Resistance) and the Old Vic; there were exhibitions of work by Dutch Resistance artists, and – to the horror of the Tory press – by Picasso and Matisse. In 1947 there were successful exhibitions of paintings by Van Gogh in London, Birmingham, Manchester and Glasgow, and of 'Fifty Years of British Painting' at the Tate.

As PEN (the association of writers) centres began reopening in liberated Europe, the first post-war International PEN Conference was held in June 1946 in Stockholm. The cultural policies of Franco's Spain were denounced, and an attempt by some anti-communist exiles to establish émigré PEN clubs was overwhelmingly rejected. Ominously, the conference was dominated by an American attempt to block a Dutch proposal to publish the names of writers who had collaborated with the Nazis. More ominously, there were no delegates from the Soviet Union (though the conference expressed its regret at their absence).

But the Soviet Union was still the ally which had defeated the Nazis at the cost of twenty million dead, and cultural exchanges were still encouraged by both sides. Early in 1945 the Society for Cultural Relations (with the Soviet Union) established a Writers' Group, with J.B. Priestley in the chair. John Gielgud and Beatrix Lehmann made recordings of Shakespeare especially for use in the Soviet Union. Two Soviet exhibitions came to Britain, 'The Friendship of the Peoples of the USSR' and an exhibition on the Soviet theatre accompanied by a programme of recitals and lectures on Soviet cultural life. The following year Priestley went to the

Soviet Union for the première of *An Inspector Calls* in Moscow and published an enthusiastic account of the trip, *Russian Journey*, on his return.

Meanwhile, the long-awaited combatants' poetry of the war began at last to appear, most notably Hamish Henderson's *Elegies for the Dead in Cyrenaica* (which won the Somerset Maugham Prize), Swingler's *The Years of Anger* and collections by Keith Douglas, John Jarmain, Sidney Keyes, Roy Fuller and Alun Lewis. There was a new generation of novelists too, Alexander Barron, Howard Clewes, Sid Chaplin and Dan Billany, writing about their experiences in the war. Meanwhile the older generation of *Our Time* novelists continued to press the claims of the People's War in peacetime fiction, notably Patrick Hamilton, John Sommerfield and Jack Lindsay. At the end of Lindsay's *Time to Live* the inhabitants of Holly Street want to turn the local drill hall into a community theatre:

> We're not going to let all this blossoming fade out. No areas are more culturally starved than the big cities, the great deserts of the suburbs ... How far have we got to go from Holly Street before we can listen to good music, see a decent painting, see a play of any kind? ... We're going to change all this. And the first thing we can do is to make a centre for our own activities ...[19]

The Arts Under Socialism

A Time to Live was inspired by one of the Arts Councils's first initiatives, *Plans for an Arts Centre*, a booklet and touring exhibition which outlined ambitious plans for new arts centres where professionals and amateurs could work together. The plans were, however, dimissed by Keynes as 'rubbish' and no arts centres were built. For it was soon evident that the Arts Council was going to be a very different organisation from CEMA. Keynes's aim was to increase the *audience* for the arts, to improve 'standards', encourage training, and advise local authorities on matters of cultural policy. He had always disliked CEMA's involvement with amateurs, especially the 'music travellers' scheme, and the Arts Council was from the first more interested in working with professional institutions in London than in the regions. Covent Garden was to be a 'special case'. In 1948 it received £68,000 out of a total grant of £428,000 to the Arts Council. On the other hand, the council consistently refused to give any support to Theatre Workshop, and in 1947 it withdrew funding to Glasgow Unity Theatre in order to subsidise West End theatre. There was no financial support for literature, except tiny sums to the Apollo Society and the 1947 Festival of Spoken Poetry. Keynes had always been opposed to the educational emphasis of the 'Art for the People' travelling exhibitions with their guides and illustrated talks, and when in 1949 the Arts Council took over the exhibitions, they were rapidly moved out of factory canteens and shops and into art galleries. Many small arts centres had developed in the regions as a result of the work of CEMA; however the Arts Council never spent more than 1 per cent of its total budget in support of their work, and in 1952 it withdrew funding from all arts centres since it 'wished to reserve its formal association for a select number of professional undertakings'.[20]

What was achieved in the war now proved too radical in peacetime. The People's War was over; the leaning tower had survived the Blitz. Within a few years the cultural forces unlocked by CEMA had been frustrated and the high hopes present at the formation of the Arts Council severely disappointed. This was partly because the social basis of the wartime culture had ended with the war, but it was a process exacerbated by the policies of the Arts Council which seemed as remote from the needs and concerns of professionals as it was from those of amateurs. When Keynes died in 1946, his successor as Arts Council Chair was Ernest Pooley, a career civil servant who continued the movement away from the legacy of CEMA. In particular, Pooley contrived to get rid of

Mary Glasgow, Secretary of first CEMA and then the Arts Council in 1951. In its report that year, the Council was explicit about the changing emphasis of its work, away from 'spreading' cultural opportunity to 'raising' artistic standards. Having come this far in six years, it was only a short step to the élitist policy announced in the 1950s of 'few but roses'.

The Labour Party did not have a history of interest or involvement in cultural issues. It lacked the cultural traditions of other parts of the Labour Movement such as the ILP, the Communist Party, the Co-operative Movement and trade unions such as the Miners. It had no publishing house, newspaper, cultural magazine or theoretical journal. Suspicion of both the avant-garde and the People's Front had isolated it from the most exciting cultural developments of the previous decade. Consequently, the Attlee government was unable to recognise one of the sources of its own hegemony, or to mobilise the culture that had done so much to bring together, focus and express the aspirations of its own supporters. Important centenaries – the Rochdale Pioneers, the Chartists' third Petition, the 1649 Commonwealth, and the publication of the *Communist Manifesto* – were left for others to celebrate, and without any support or encouragement from either the Government or the party in government, the celebrations were muted, off-stage.

Of course, the Government had other priorities, and might be forgiven more than most for neglecting the arts. But this is the best that can be said, that the Labour government neglected the arts. Its most important initiative in this field – granting a Royal Charter to the Arts Council in 1946 – was inherited from the coalition wartime Government; the Arts Council owed more to R.A. Butler than to any Labour Minister. And though the Labour government inherited a fundamentally flawed Arts Council, it did nothing to address the problems. The Arts Council was not funded by the Ministry of Education but by the Treasury, which meant that it was vulnerable to the Treasury's capital expenditure cuts in 1947. With no ministerial lobby for the arts, there was no pressure on Cripps to honour his promise to increase funding. The Attlee government's only important legislation affecting the arts was Clause 131 of the 1948 Local Government Bill, inserted at the last minute to enable local authorities to fund cultural activities on a 6d rate.[21] It was an important opening for the peacetime regeneration of provincial cultural life, led by democratically elected local authorities. But it owed nothing to Cripps or to government policy, rather to the efforts of the Health Minister, Nye Bevan.

Even then, not all local authorities imposed the additional rate, and the general prohibition on new building meant that municipal provision in the arts expanded only very slowly. In fact, after the opening-up of forms of ownership in the last years of the War, under the Attlee Government there was a rapid narrowing of control in the theatre. By 1948 three-quarters of all theatre seats in London and the provinces were owned by A.S. Cruickshank and Prince Littler (who also had controlling interests in important production companies like Tennent's). Meanwhile, in the absence of a financial commitment from the Government, talk of a National Theatre remained just that.

British theatre seemed to be in constant crisis in the late 1940s, though the Government did not seem to notice or care. As Basil Dean observed, the theatre was the only industry to emerge from the war without re-organisation. The wartime working relationships between professional and amateur were soon broken, accelerated by the Arts Council's preference for funding only the former. When the Entertainment Tax on the theatre was halved in 1948, this helped only commercial theatre (since amateur theatre companies were exempt from the tax). The crisis was addressed by J.B. Priestley in a 1947 Fabian pamphlet, *The Arts Under Socialism* in which he advocated the transfer of the theatre to State control. There was no other way, he argued, of guaranteeing either artistic achievement or popular participation:

What is the use of spending hundreds of thousands of pounds every year teaching children that Shakespeare is a great dramatist, if every playhouse accessible to those children and their parents is completely controlled by men who are determined to present nothing but leg shows and stupid farces? ... this is not simply because of the transition from a wartime to a peacetime economy and production in a half-ruined world, for this we can all understand; but it is also because there are too many people in authority here who fail to appreciate the importance of art to a society like ours.[22]

Priestley's call for a national conference to deal with the crisis was widely supported in the theatre world and in February 1948 he chaired a three day National Theatre Conference in a belated attempt to reconstruct the alliances that had brought theatre alive to so many people during the war. The conference called on the Government to address the number of major towns that did not possess either a civic or a commercial theatre. Cripps attended and promised more funds for the Arts Council, but the Government did nothing.

On the other hand, the independence of the Arts Council from the Government disappointed those who had hoped for direct State involvement in the arts. Cyril Connolly, for example, used the pages of *Horizon* from 1946 onwards to express his disappointment at the failure of the Government to replace the role of the private patron. Post-war writing was in crisis, he argued, as standards declined in proportion to its rewards, and while writers might still be honoured their work was usually neglected. In particular, only government intervention could rescue the publishing industry:

The fact remains that a Socialist Government besides doing practically nothing to help artists and writers has also quite failed to stir up either intellect or imagination; the English renaissance, whose false dawn we have so enthusiastically greeted, is further away than ever ... [23]

213

For publishing too was in crisis. Paper rationing was still 65 per cent of pre-war usage at the end of 1945, and yet London publishers required ever longer print runs even to meet their costs. This meant that new books were expensive to buy, and that publishers were cautious of new works and new authors. The increasing importance of book club deals hardly encouraged publishers to take risks, or writers to risk innovation. They were not helped by a severe cut in the supply of paper in 1947, when no magazines were published for a fortnight. Writers and publishers tried in vain to persuade the Government to help the industry. A group of publishers, booksellers, educationalists, writers and literary agents issued *The Battle of the Books*, a collection of essays pleading with the Government to support the industry. 'The Government,' they argued, 'is helping to precipitate a crisis in British publishing which will not easily be remedied. The present policy would seem logically to end in the supremacy of the dross and the desperation of every decent publisher.'[24]

By 1947 the honeymoon between art and politics was clearly over, and the support of the metropolitan intelligentsia for the Government was now provisional. By the time the Government announced capital expenditure cuts of £180 million for 1948, *Our Time* had lost patience with the evident lack of a coherent cultural strategy:

> To rouse the enthusiasm of the people, to harness their instincts ... for the work of reconstruction, to enrich their leisure, to add to their skills; in these ways British art, writing, music, and science have great contributions to make ... We cannot afford the capital cuts unless we are prepared to acquiesce in economic and social suicide.[25]

Or as *Horizon*'s 'military spokesman' put it:

> The offensive against Art is developing according to plan. It is too early to prophecy total victory ... There exists, as you

know a fifth column in this country. There are artists, writers, poets, crypto-artists and crypto-writers, survivors from the bad old days ...[26]

Horizon and *Our Time* were survivors of the intellectual culture that had moved from the People's Front through the People's War to the enormous hopes invested in '1945' and their subsequent disappointment. But by the end of the 1940s this disappointment was all they shared, as British cultural life began to splinter under the pressures of the Cold War and the peculiarly British form of McCarthyism described in the next chapter. And the survivors 'from the bad old days' were dwindling. Within a few years all the most lively literary magazines *Writing Today, New English Review, Life & Letters Today, John O'London's Weekly, Penguin New Writing, Horizon* and *Our Time* had folded.

Persecution Mania

London literary life was vulnerable to Cold War pressures, since it was still dominated by survivors from pre-war metropolitan culture, for whom 1945 represented the end of an interruption rather than a new beginning. Some, like Eliot and Waugh, were never part of the anti-Fascist literary movement; others like Spender, Lehmann, Connolly and Toynbee, had spent the war in London, largely unchanged by the experience. Anyway, a defensive literary culture which had been inspired by anti-Fascism clearly required new inspiration to hold it together. Sentiments which had been mobilised against Fascism were now clearly harnessed by those who sought to defend 'Intellectual Liberty' against Communism. 'Fifteen years ago,' argued Orwell, 'when one defended the freedom of the intellect, one had to defend it ... against Fascists. Today one has to defend it against Communists and "fellow-travellers" '. Eric Ambler, whose People's Front thrillers had re-invigorated the British political novel, invented the Cold War spy-novel with *Judgement on Deltchev*. Storm Jameson, whose pre-war novel *In the Second Year* depicted life in a Fascist Britain, now dramatised the consequences of a Soviet invasion of Britain in *The Moment of Truth*. Disguised as heterodoxy (Koestler, Orwell, Spender, Crossman's *The God that Failed*) anti-communism quickly assumed the authority of orthodoxy. During the autumn of 1946 the Tory press discovered a sudden interest in literary freedom when the Leningrad Communist Party Secretary Zhdanov attacked the writer Zoschenko for his short story, *The Adventures of a Monkey*. Connolly's eagerness to accept State patronage was rather tempered by the affair, in which he saw Evelyn Waugh as Zoschenko and Nye Bevan or John Strachey as Zhdanov. But *Horizon* was not *Leningrad* and the Government did not want to censor Connolly any more than it wanted to sponsor him. Randall Swingler could be forgiven for wondering what Connolly and Orwell were so worried about.[27]

Meanwhile, Communist writers who had come in from the cold during the war soon found themselves quickly again excluded. Hamish Henderson spent his Somerset Maugham Award visiting Italy in order to translate Gramsci's prison writings; while he was there he addressed Communist Party meetings about popular song and the American threat to European folk cultures until, under American pressure, the Italian authorities expelled him. When he returned to Britain he could not find a publisher for his book. Even Jack Lindsay could not find a publisher for his translation of French Resistance poets, since they were 'brigands'. Randall Swingler found himself effectively blacklisted at the BBC. By the end of the 1940s he was publishing what proved to be his last collection of poems, watching *Our Time* fail, seeing the Communist Party and its cultural energies marginalised and then turned inwards in the disputes that would see him leave it in 1956.[28]

To be fair, there was not much any government could have done to relieve the pressure of the Cold War on British intellectual life, given Britain's relationship to the USA. The British government could do nothing, for example, to prevent the Americans blocking Julian Huxley's appointment as first General Secretary of UNESCO. Anti-communism was a dangerous tiger to ride: even a death-bed statement by Orwell could not prevent readers and reviewers from seeing *Nineteen Eighty-Four* as a satirical attack on the Attlee government. But the Labour government intensified the pressure, publicly purging Communists in the Civil Service, the BBC, and (less publicly) in adult education; Swingler, who taught at Goldsmith's, was not the only tutor to have his courses investigated.[29] Priestley tried unsuccessfully to calm the hysteria:

> We are deafened and bedevilled now by people who believe in enormous elaborate plots. Like most public men, I have had from time to time letters from unhappy victims of persecution mania, giving me in bewildering detail their accounts of fantastic conspiracies ... I find the same hysterical tone, the same nightmare atmosphere, in much writing and talking, these days.[30]

But Priestley's voice had already lost its wartime authority. When his wartime utopia *They Came to a City* was filmed, Rank refused to handle it.[31] The 'Group' (West End managements) succeeded in damaging Priestley's 1948 National Theatre Conference (thereby embarrassing Cripps) by running a campaign in the Tory press attacking the conference as a Communist front because Ted Willis was one of the organisers. One of the few journals to report the conference, *Theatre Today*, was not surprised to discover that it lost all its West End advertising.

In this cold climate John Lehmann used *Penguin New Writing* to warn young writers against 'the dust-storms of false and foolish theories that are apt suddenly to blow about their paths, particularly in these highly political days.' He urged them not to write about the war, the problems of returning to civilian life, and the political possibilities of

Labour Britain. 'May every author who stands now at the beginnng of his career sweep such pernicious nonsense from his mind.'[32] Not surprisingly, a new kind of writing about the war began to appear by the end of the decade, by writers such as Eric Williams, Elizabeth Bowen and Nicholas Monsaratt, reconstructing a rather different kind of war from that of People's War fiction. Randall Swingler was struck by the way anthologies of poetry from the war were dominated increasingly by poets who had not seen any action.

The Wroclaw Peace Congress of 1948 may be seen as an attempt to recreate the geography of the People's War. But it was too late. It was condemned as a Communist front even before the British delegates had left for Poland (though they included A.J.P. Taylor, Richard Hughes, Louis Golding and Olaf Stapledon).

When the Second World Peace Congress was called two years later in Sheffield, Attlee declared it 'bogus'. Two-thirds of the foreign delegates were prevented from entering Britain, including Robeson, Aragon, Neruda, Seghers, Zweig and Shostakovich. With so many leading figures absent, the Congress was abandoned and transfered to Poland.[33] Four days later the United Nations General Assembly rejected a Soviet proposal to ban the atom bomb.

Paradise Postponed

Relationships among editors and writers dating from the Spanish Civil War broke under the pressure of the Cold War. Provincial writers such as Harold Heslop, B.L. Coombes, Jack Hilton and Walter Brierley found themselves out in the cold again, and the old relationships of patronage and privilege, London and the provinces, restored.[34] Regional writers only survived by turning picturesque, as did Walter Greenwood, Herbert Hodge, Jack Jones and James Barke. It was the lasting achievement of the Labour government to re-establish authority within the well-kept gardens of cultural privilege. This was Bloomsbury's finest moment.

The chief surviving spokesman for Bloomsbury-Modernism was T.S. Eliot. While Ezra Pound paid the price of anti-semitism in a mental institution, Eliot was quickly rehabilitated, awarded the Nobel Prize for Literature and the Order of Merit. He repaid the Government with an attack on its educational reforms in *Notes Towards a Definition of Culture*. Disputing whether education made people happier, he rejected any extension of educational opportunity, specifically the 'Mute Inglorious Milton Dogma' (for Eliot, of course, one Republican Milton was enough), the fallacy that education might open cultural opportunity:

> there is no doubt that in the headlong rush to educate everybody, we are lowering our standards ... destroying our ancient edifices to make ready the ground upon which the barbarian nomads of the future will camp in their mechanised caravans ...[35]

By the time of the 1951 Festival of Britain, it was all over. Although the Festival was the kind of state patronage towards the arts for which many had long given up hoping, there was not much room for the barbarians. The only literary commission was given to Cecil Day Lewis – for a translation of the *Aeneid* for the Third Programme. The Festival poetry competition attracted over 2,000 entries, but the judges (Sir Kenneth Clark, Sir Maurice Bowra, Lord David Cecil, Professor Basil Willey, George Rylands and John Hayward) were not impressed. Their contempt for the entries and for the popular sources of poetry was a fair measure of the development of British literary culture under five years of Labour government. As Eliot's friend Hayward explained:

> What was striking in by far the largest number of poems submitted was the lack of what may be called any literary ancestry, of any evidence, explicit or implicit, that their authors had any knowledge of the English poetic tradition. Many of them, so it seemed, could rarely have read any poetry

worth the name, or if they had, were entirely unaffected by it
... To all appearances the extent of their knowledge was
confined to popular anthology pieces, to hymn-books, and to
dimly recollected set-passages from school primers ... There is
... no point in encouraging such writers ...[36]

And so the Arts Council's poetry committee was born, and
poetry was taken back by those whose education and
sensibility had at least taught them how to police literature.
The cultural limits were established for the next decade and
the values of the Arts Council for the next thirty years; a
high-walled garden in whose grounds the ivory tower was
fully restored, where *New Lines* and the Movement poets
could flower and Philip Larkin's poetry be mistaken for a
spring. The paradise briefly glimpsed in 1945 by Randall
Swingler was, as his friend John Mortimer would later write,
indefinitely postponed. The chance had been missed.

Notes

I wish to record my thanks to Arnold Rattenbury and Ken Worpole for
their comments on earlier drafts of this essay, to Judy Williams for
permission to quote from her father's letters, and to Jim Fyrth for his
patience with a MS that was originally twice the length he wanted.
[1] With Alan Bush he edited the *Left Song Book* for the Left Book Club; he
wrote songs for the Workers' Music Association, plays for Unity Theatre
and a widely performed mass declamation, 'Spain'. He launched *Our Time*.
[2] Randall Swingler to Geraldine Swingler, 15 August 1945.
[3] For this period, see Robert Hewison, *Under Siege*, Weidenfeld &
Nicholson, London 1977; Andrew Davies, *Where Did the Forties Go?*
Pluto Press, London 1984; Alan Ross, *The Forties*, Weidenfeld &
Nicholson, London 1950, and Jack Lindsay, *After the Thirties*, Lawrence &
Wishart, London 1954.
[4] For CEMA see B. Ifor Evans and Mary Glasgow, *The Arts in England*,
Falcoln Press, London 1949.
[5] Jack Lindsay, *British Achievement in Art and Music*, Pilot Press, London
1945, p10; in a BIPO survey of musical taste commissioned by the
Musician's Union in 1947, 31 per cent of those questioned said that as a
result of the work of CEMA and ENSA, they were more interested in
attending concerts than before the war, while 24 per cent preferred

symphony music to any other kind of music.
[6] Virginia Woolf in 'The Leaning Tower', *Folios of New Writing*, Hogarth Press, London, Autumn 1940; Coombes reply 'Below the Tower' appeared in *Folios of New Writing*, Spring 1941.
[7] Thomas Russell, *Philharmonic Decade*, Hutchinson, London 1945.
[8] Quoted in Andrew Davies, 'A Theatre for a People's Army? the Story of the ABCA Play Unit', *Red Letters*, Spring 1982.
[9] Jack Lindsay, *British Achievement, op cit*, p12.
[10]Perhaps this was the ABCA pamphlet which Edward Thompson received a few weeks before the battle of Cassino:

> The squadron leader came out of his tent with it in his hand, spotted me, and said: 'Oh, Thompson! HQ insists that we get all the men together and run discussions on this. Do you mind taking it on? I'd do it myself, but it's rather difficult to argue *against* a thing when you don't know anything about it.'

E.P. Thompson, *Writing by Candlelight*, Merlin, London 1980, p82.
[11] *Our Time* estimated that the total cost of CEMA activities for the whole of 1944 was less than the cost of a small destroyer; for *Our Time* see Charles Hobday, *Edgell Rickword: a Poet at War*, Carcanet, Manchester 1989.
[12] *New English Review*, 1946 May; R.A. Butler in *The Art of the Possible*, Hamish Hamilton, London 1971, blamed the ABCA for the election result; the character of the sinister Dr Beamish in Evelyn Waugh's *Love Among the Ruins*, Chapman and Hall, London 1953, connected the nightmare of post-war England with the culture of the Popular Front.
[13] Francis Klingender wrote *Art and the Industrial Revolution*, 1947, as a result of his involvement in the AEU exhibition.
[14] See Colin Chambers, *The Story of Unity Theatre*, Lawrence & Wishart, London 1989.
[15] See Harold Heslop, *Out of the Old Earth* edited by Andy Croft and Graeme Rigby, Bloodaxe Books, Newcastle-upon-Tyne 1994.
[16] For the collaboration between Britten and Slater see Philip Brett, *Peter Grimes*, Cambridge University Press, Cambridge 1983.
[17] For the Communist Party Writers group in the 1940s see Andy Croft, 'Writers, the Communist Party and the Battle of Ideas 1945-50', *Socialist History*, Number 5 1994.
[18] Randall Swingler, 'The Possible', *New Lyrical Ballads*, edited by Honor Arundel, Maurice Carpenter and Jack Lindsay, Poetry London/Nicholson and Watson, London 1945.
[19] Jack Lindsay, *A Time to Live*, Andrew Dakers, London 1946, p266, 267; for the fiction of the People's War, see Alan Munton, *English Fiction of the Second World War*, Faber and Faber, London 1989, and Ken Worpole, *Dockers and Detectives*, Verso, London 1983.
[20] See the interview with Mary Glasgow, *Our Time*, January-February 1948; Robert Hewison, *In Anger*, Weidenfeld & Nicholson, London 1981;

Robert Hutchinson, *The Politics of the Arts Council*, Sinclair Brown, London 1982; Janet Minihan, *The Nationalisation of Culture*, Hamilton, London 1977, and Geoff Mulgan and Ken Worpole, *Saturday Night or Sunday Morning?*, Comedia, London 1986; Raymond Williams later recalled that

> the Labour government had a choice: either for reconstruction of the cultural field in capitalist terms, or for funding institutions of popular education and popular culture that could have withstood the campaigns in the bourgeois press that were already gathering momentum ... the failure to fund the working-class movement culturally when the channels of popular education and popular culture were there in the forties became a key factor in the very quick disintegration of Labour's position.

Politics and Letters, Verso, London 1979, p73.

[21] The theatre owners' lobby had defeated the proposal of the 1924 Labour government to allow local authorities to spend a penny rate on culture and entertainment.

[22] J.B. Priestley, *The Arts Under Socialism*, Fabian Society, London 1947; see also Peter Ustinov, *Listener*, 30 January 1947, and Ann Lindsay, *Theatre*, Bodley Head, London 1948.

[23] *Horizon*, July 1947; when in September 1946 *Horizon* ran a questionnaire on 'The Cost of Letters', half of the contributors (including Elizabeth Bowen, Cecil Day Lewis, Laurie Lee, Henry Reed, William Sansom and Dylan Thomas) said they thought the State should support writing by supporting writers.

[24] G. Hopkins (ed), *The Battle of the Books*, Alan Wingate, London 1947; see also Dennis Kilham-Roberts, Secretary of the Society of Authors, on the crisis of the publishing industry in the *Observer*, 10 March 1946, and Arthur Calder-Marshall *The Book Front*, Bodley Head, London 1947; the Society of Authors campaigned unsuccessfully in 1947 against the low levels of contributors' fees at the BBC, and in 1949 to persuade the Chancellor to re-adjust income tax on authors' royalties.

[25] *Our Time*, December 1947.

[26] *Horizon*, November 1947; compare the hopeful spirit of Priestley's *Three Men in New Suits*, Heinemann, London 1945 and *Letter to a Returning Serviceman*, Home and Canthill, London 1945, with the disappointment of his *Bright Day*, Heinemann, London 1946, Priestley's article in the *New Statesman*, 2 July 1949; other novels about the disappointed hopes of these years were Jack Lindsay, *Betrayed Spring*, Lane, London 1953, John Sommerfield, *The Inheritance*, Heinemann, London 1956, and Margot Heinemann, *The Adventurers*, Lawrence and Wishart, London 1960.

[27] Although the 'documents' relating to the controversy were published in both *Horizon* and *Modern Quarterly*, Zoschenko's *The Adventures of a Monkey* was not; see also the discussion of Soviet literature in *New*

Writing, Autumn 1946 and *New Statesman*, 6 September 1947; the exchange between Orwell and Swingler is in *Polemic*, Sept-Oct 1946.

[28] For the fortunes of British Communist writers in the Cold War see Andy Croft, 'Authors take sides: Writers and the Communist Party, 1920-1956', in Kevin Morgan, Nina Fishman and Geoff Andrews (eds), *Opening the Books, New Perspectives in the History of British Communism*, Pluto Press, London 1995.

[29] For the witch-hunt in adult education, see Roger Fieldhouse, *Adult Education and the Cold War*, University of Leeds, Dept of Continuing & Adult Education, Leeds 1985.

[30] *New Statesman*, 2 October 1948.

[31] Rosselini's film *Open City* was shown in British cinemas in 1947 only after references to the Italian Communist partisans had been cut.

[32] *Penguin New Writing*, July 1946, no. 28.

[33] Bill Moore, *Cold War in Sheffield*, Sheffield Trades Council 1990; Picasso, who *was* allowed to reach the Congress, protested at the Government's treatment of the other delegates by refusing to attend an exhibition of his work in London; the Stockholm Peace Appeal is discussed in Angus Wilson, *Hemlock and After*, Secker & Warburg, London 1952.

[34] When Walter Brierley (whose best-selling *Means-Test Man* was one of the most influential novels of the 1930s), sent the BBC some new scripts after the war, someone wrote across the BBC's internal copy of their rejection letter, 'Do Midland know him? What is his stuff like?'.

[35] T.S. Eliot, *Notes Towards a Definition of Culture*, Faber and Faber, London 1949, p111.

[36] *Poems, 1951*, Penguin, Harmondsworth 1951; one of the poems rejected by the competition judges was 'The Place Called Choice' by Edward Thompson, whose evident lack of 'poetic knowledge' was exposed when the poem was published in *The Heavy Dancers*, Merlin, London 1985.

British 'McCarthyism' and the Intellectuals

Steve Parsons

There are ninety and six ways ... of enabling Communists to earn a livelihood, but I do not think that teaching and broadcasting should be among them. That is too great a risk, seeing the times in which we live.

Lord Vansittart, House of Lords, Parliamentary Debates (Hansard), 1950

The Cold War brought a fundamental shift in the British political climate. Attlee, who in 1944 thought that Britain would facilitate good relations between the USA and the USSR, had concluded at the Potsdam Conference in 1944 'that there was no possibility of real Anglo-Soviet co-operation'.[1] Some of Britain's Cold War policies are well known – among them the suppression of the Communist-led resistance movement in Greece,[2] and the 1947 decision to allow hundreds of war criminals from the Baltic States to settle in Britain.[3] Others, such as the part of the Labour leaders in galvanising anti-Communism within the Scandinavian Social Democratic parties,[4] and Britain's role in establishing underground anti-Communist guerrilla armies in waiting in western Europe, are not well known or still obscure.[5] Here I shall concentrate on the impact of the Cold War on British 'intellectuals' – members of the professions and those involved in education and the arts.

Britain is often compared with the USA, where thousands lost their jobs because of their political allegiance or views, in order to disparage the idea that there was any 'British McCarthyism'. Here, comparatively few people were dismissed and none went to prison on political grounds. (Nor were any killed as in the Soviet Union). In fact, a number of Americans sought refuge in Britain, and some even established themselves as 'names' in their professions (Sam Wanamaker and Clancy Sigal spring to mind). Douglas Hyde, who visited the USA in 1948, after breaking with the British Communist Party, said that, in comparison with the American one,

> the British witch-hunt seemed pretty 'civilised'. That does not mean that it may not have been as effective – even more effective from the Government's point of view, but clearly the policy was, so far as I could see … 'we' [that is to say the Government] set out not to make martyrs whereas McCarthy made them left right and centre.[6]

The British government proceded in its own way and considered that US inspired anti-Communist propaganda was not appropriate to Britain – a viewpoint in time accepted by American Intelligence, which saw social democracy as one of the most effective forces in neutralising Communisn in Europe.[7]

British Communists were never forced into semi-illegality, as in America. Communists still held academic, professional and trade union posts and were never completely isolated from their colleagues. Nevertheless a series of official, and privately inspired, measures were taken which undermined certain civil liberties, which led to a rise in open, and not so open, political discrimination, and which created an atmosphere of cultural caution, in which all intellectuals who were left of centre had to work. These measures were part of a process which the historian Edward Thompson later observed, 'led the nation into a wasteland of spirit …

destroyed any socialist vision, dragooned people into flocks of Atlanticist sheep or pro-Soviet goats, and blocked off any "third way".[8]

From War to Peace

Throughout the war MI5 and Military Intelligence monitored the activities of the British Communist Party (CPGB), but official policies towards Communists working in the State and Armed Forces were highly idiosyncratic. Some Communists were turned down from fairly innocuous posts, while others were involved in important secret work. The sheer scale of the need to mobilise resources, coupled with the desire for good relations with 'our Soviet ally', accounted for some of the vagaries.[9]

A change took place early in 1944, following the conviction of Dave Springhall, National Organiser of the CPGB, for passing information on munitions to the Soviet government. Churchill ordered the removal of all Communist Party members from the Secret Service, and the Government agreed that all known Communists engaged in confidential work in the Civil Service should be transferred to 'safe' areas. Churchill, however, opposed demands that MI5 be responsible for informing Government departments of any Communists on their staffs and resisted calls for a public statement on 'Communists and Espionage'. And although in future Communists were to be prevented from joining the Army Education Corps, the twenty individuals, identified by MI5 as Communists, already working for the Corps were to be removed only if their own overt acts warranted it.[10]

Early signs of divergence between East and West were seen in the scientific field (the withholding from the USSR of the 'secrets' of the A-bomb and radar and the rise of Soviet-inspired espionage). In the closing days of the war, in a clumsy move criticised by the bulk of the press, the Government banned eight senior scientists from among a

226

party of twenty-eight from going to Moscow to celebrate the 220th anniversary of the Russian Academy of Sciences.[11] But it was at the beginning of 1946 when Alan Nunn May, a British scientist who had worked on the atom bomb project, was charged with spying for the Russians, that matters took on a momentum. Public coverage of the matter was fairly restrained, compared with the way the issue of 'nuclear spies' was dealt with just a few years later. Nunn May's sentence of ten years aroused some opposition, but that soon petered out. The trial seems to have led to security measures against a number of politically 'suspect' civil servants, causing the Secretary of Staff Side of the National Whitley Council to say in March 1947 that; 'Certain of our constituent bodies have reported cases to us of alleged victimization of civil servants merely on the grounds that they are members of the Communist Party'.[12] When three scientists in government employment had their promotion countermanded as a result, it was claimed, of MI5 intervention, the press was interested and there were questions in Parliament.

The most significant consequence of the Nunn May case was the establishment in May 1947 of a Special Cabinet Committee on Subversive Activities, chaired by Attlee. The files of this Committee remain closed, but it set the groundwork for the new arrangements for the political vetting of civil servants which were announced by Attlee in the following year. Until 1948 government measures concerning 'security' and combatting Communism remained behind the scenes. When Herbert Morrison rejected a call by a Conservative MP for the establishment of a Select Committee on Un-British Activities, and expressed his confidence that the Communist Party could be easily dealt with by 'the other political parties', the Committee on Subversive Activities had already been in existence for nearly six months.

In an equal degree of secrecy, and on the initiative of Christopher Mayhew, a self-acknowledged 'hardened cold warrior', an anti-Communist propaganda unit was set up early in 1948. This body, known as the IRD (Information and Research Department), was staffed with some forty officials and financed from the 'Secret Service Vote'. Its existence remained unknown to Parliament and the general public. Its job was to fight the propaganda war against the Soviet Union abroad and its sympathisers at home, and to this end it produced a mass of reports, with no identification of origin, which were sent to journalists, trade union leaders, MPs and political officials. Although a former official of the Department claims that their material was to provide background information for those who wished to speak on Communism, one writer feels, 'A more accurate description of recipients, judging by the reports, would be "anyone wishing to denigrate Communism".'[13] In a memorandum to the Cabinet, detailing the formation of the IRD ('a small Section of the Foreign Office'), Ernest Bevin pointed out that his paper, 'The First Aim of British Foreign Policy', had shown:

> that the Russian and Communist Allies are threatening the whole fabric of western civilisation, and I have drawn attention to the need to mobilise spiritual forces, as well as material and political, for its defence. It is for us, as Europeans and as a Social Democratic Government, and not the Americans, to give the lead in spiritual, moral and political spheres to all the democratic elements in Western Europe which are anti-Communist ... we must now take this more definitely anti-Communist line in our publicity.[14]

Attlee, Bevin and Morrison were among Labour leaders who were explicit in their attacks on the British Communist Party from an early stage, though careful at first to refrain from undue criticism of the Soviet Union. When the CPGB applied for affiliation to the Labour Party in 1946, an 'official Labour' response was published in the shape of a pamphlet by Harold Laski entitled *The Secret Battalion*, which characterised Communists in Britain as 'organised as a conspiracy'. This was echoed by Morrison at the Labour

Party Conference that year when he also described the Communist Party as more a conspiracy than a normal political party. The Labour establishment became increasingly hostile to those Labour members whom they considered to be pro-Soviet, commonly termed 'fellow travellers'. The list of proscribed organisations which had been instituted by the Labour Party before the war was revised to include new bodies such as the British Soviet Society. Labour's Organisation Sub-committee also prohibited Labour Party members from attending particular 'suspect' events, and from associating with Communists. Extensive information was collated on 'wayward' Labour members, and the indications are that British Intelligence helped with its collection.[15]

1948 – 'The Turning Point'

Eric Hobsbawm has described the year 1948 as 'the turning point' as far as the Cold War atmosphere went in Britain;

> Anybody that got a job in the university or Birkbeck before then, as I did, was extremely unlikely to be sacked. However, from I would say 1948, that is the Berlin crisis period, things tightened up substantially.
>
> My evidence for this is that in 1947 I and some other progressives were still hired by the Foreign Office to go to Germany and help in the 're-education of the Germans in democracy'. We were reinvited for the next year but the invitation was cancelled in May 1948.[16]

International developments, in particular the Prague Coup, heightened the Cold War atmosphere, and on 15 March 1948 the Prime Minister announced that members of the Communist Party and those 'associated with it' would be excluded from any work 'vital to the security of the State'. As a cosmetic exercise Attlee added 'Fascists' to those who would be covered by the ban.[17] Yet in procedural terms the announcement was merely an extension of the security arrangements that had already been set in motion in June 1946. However, the public impact was significantly greater, and while the Labour *Daily Herald* thought that the ban was reasonable, and that it was for Parliament to ensure that it was not implemented in a mood of panic, and that Communists were distinguished from leftwingers, other quarters emphasised that 'fellow travellers' would be vetted as thoroughly as CP members.[18] Officially, in the period 1948 to 1954, 124 civil servants were removed from their posts, the majority being transferred, with only some thirty outright dismissals.[19] Undoubtedly many more resigned of their own volition and others found their career advancement sidetracked.[20]

Another area immediately affected by Attlee's announcement was the BBC. A clear change took place there in a period of a few weeks, as is shown in the records of meetings held between senior government, Opposition and BBC figures. At a February meeting Churchill complained about undue prominence given to the Communist viewpoint on the radio. The Director-General of the BBC replied that the matter would be investigated, but that he did not believe there were many Communists employed by the Corporation, and anyway no one should be 'penalised for their political convictions'.[21] At the end of March, in a memorandum on 'Communists in the BBC', produced for Morrison by one of his officials, the Director-General was assuring the Government that the BBC was well aware of the dangers of Communist infiltration and realised 'that the BBC is just the sort of stronghold that the Communists would like to capture'.[22] Reference was also made to the fact that MI5 had been vetting *all* new recruits to the corporation for the past ten years. However, even at this stage, the Director-General expressed the position of the BBC Governors, that no proceedings be taken against any employee except on the grounds of 'specific dereliction of duty'. The following month he told the Broadcasting Committee, which included

Morrison and Churchill, 'that the Corporation attached such importance to complete impartiality that if it became apparent that an employee's political views would urge him to prejudice this standard, suitable action would be taken, even though no actual offence had been committed'.[23] On 10 April the Communist actor, Alex McCrindle, who had gained fame as 'Jock' in the radio series 'Dick Barton Special Agent', was dismissed by the BBC. From this time a comprehensive monthly list was made of any Communist speaker, or any reference to Communism on the radio, to ensure that both 'be kept in proper perspective'.[24]

Guarding the Schools

The possibility of Communist ideas being spread in schools attracted attention from the early Cold War years. Already in the 1920s and 1930s worries had been expressed by establishment figures about left wing subversion in schools, and in 1948 a Conservative and Unionist Teachers' Association was formed with the aim of fighting Communists and Socialists in the profession.[25] At the Association's first annual conference, R.A. Butler told the three hundred delegates that:

> there is in the teaching profession a definite Communistic element and I think it is important to remind you of events in Czechoslovakia; if the country did not believe it before, we now see Communists – not as a real political party in this country, but as actually part of the army of the enemy itself, and the more clearly we can express those views, and the more we can thrust out the Communists in our midst the happier we shall be.[26]

Complementing this activity, the Tory peer Lord Vansittart drew attention to the fact that many publicly active Communists were school teachers, as much as 1 per cent of the profession (Communist teachers were said to number two thousand at this time).[27] It was inevitable, Vansittart claimed, that these teachers would attempt to inculcate their pupils with Communism. Such attitudes were not restricted to Conservatives. At one of the Cabinet Committee meetings, chaired by Attlee, held to co-ordinate action against Communism, the minutes record that, 'Ministers were disturbed at the extent of Communist infiltration in this country, especially in the trade unions and in the teaching profession'.[28]

In the National Union of Teachers (NUT) a determined scare was launched against Communists from 1948. Various fraudulent 'letters' were sent to London schools from a bogus 'Young Communist Action group', in order to discredit Communists standing for election to the leadership of the London Teachers' Association. The magazine *Teachers' World*, which had a large circulation among primary school teachers, carried a series of items directed against Communists in the profession.[29] By 1949 these efforts had borne fruit; all but one of the five Communists on the NUT Executive failed to secure re-election and Communist teachers were removed from the executive of the London Teachers' Association. In the schools developments were less dramatic, and although there were some local calls for the removal of individual teachers, they retained their jobs unless they worked outside the state sector.

George Rudé, later to be recognised as an eminent historian, was dismissed from St Paul's, the London public school, was subsequently unable to obtain an academic post in Britain and was refused a BBC post because of his political commitments.[30] Attempts were made to institute bans on the appointment of Communists to teaching posts in State schools by the London County Council and by Surrey and Essex Councils, but only in Middlesex were moves in this direction enacted. The 'Middlesex ban' was brought in by the County Council in 1950, after a Communist Party member was appointed to the headship of one of their schools; his appointment was revoked and a resolution approved which laid down that, 'members of Communist (or Fascist) parties' or persons 'associated with either in such a way as to arouse doubts about their reliability be debarred from appointment' as 'principals of technical institutes ... heads of county primary ... secondary ... and special schools and (to) the staffs of training colleges'.[31]

Watching For Subversive Lecturers

Eric Hobsbawm's observation that 1948 represented a cut-off point for known Communists being appointed to academic posts seems to have been generally true. The Cambridge economist Maurice Dobb wrote in 1950 that he was one of three who were considered for an appointment at the University of London in 1946 all of whom, he was led to believe, were turned down on political grounds, but that was at a time 'when such cases had not become so common'.[32] By 1948-9 it was the general procedure for attention to be drawn to Communists' politics if they were candidates for university appointments. The matter was often approached surreptitious-ly, as an article in the *New Statesman* reported, 'It is already becoming a habit in some academic circles to append to a testimonial (often eulogistic in terms of the candidate's capacities) the statement that he is a member of the Communist Party'.[33] The interview of a highly recommended scholar, who happened to be a member of the Communist Party, for a professorship is probably fairly typical:

> After RHT had been interviewed and left the room, Professor C. of Manchester said that he was clearly out of the question. Local education authority representatives asked why since he seemed to be a good candidate. C. turned in an obvious fashion to R. Pascal, a well known Communist and Professor of German at Birmingham since 1939, who is RHT's professor and was on the board, and asked to what political party RHT belonged. RP said this was an improper question, and C. withdrew it – but by this time the cat was out of the bag.[34]

In 1949 Brian Simon applied for a job at Bristol University, was interviewed and assumed he had been appointed, yet to his surprise the post went to someone else. Only later did he learn from one of his referees that the reason was that they had found out that he was a member of the Communist Party; in fact the referee was reprimanded for not telling them that he was. Yet it was by chance that Simon had his suspicions confirmed; he was never officially informed that he had been turned down because of his politics.[35] The unofficial nature of these political tests and the confidential nature of the proceedings of appointing bodies ensured that much evidence on this matter was hearsay and unattributable.

The issue gained a degree of publicity in 1950 when the School of Slavonic Studies at London University dismissed Andrew Rothstein, the only Communist among the school's lecturers, for 'inadequate scholarship'. Rothstein, although he had significant support within the school, failed to get the backing of the Association of University Teachers. That Rothstein had been teaching at the school for four years suggests that political considerations played a part in his dismissal and his forthright advocacy of official Soviet politics (in his 1950 Pelican *A History of the USSR* he defended the 1930s show trials uncritically) undoubtedly contributed.[36]

The Security Services kept a close eye on Communists (and those classified as 'fellow travellers') in the academic world, and Lord Vansittart, who specifically targeted Birmingham University as an area of 'Communist infiltration' in a major speech in the House of Lords (29 March 1950) on 'Communists in the Public Service', appears to have been supplied with comprehensive information from MI5 and the Special Branch.[37] But it was in the field of adult education, which received a significant influx of Communist lecturers at the end of the war, that official restrictions were openly taken against Communists and those 'suspected of having been Communists'. The outstanding case arose from the concern of the Workers' Educational Association and the Oxford University Extra-Mural Delegacy that Communist and 'fellow travelling' tutors working in North Staffordshire constituted a Marxist threat. Steps to remove the 'threat' culminated in refusal, in 1949, to renew the contract of the Warden of the Wedgewood Memorial College at Barlaston Hall, where many trade union courses took place, and the dispersal of other tutors who had worked with him. The aftermath as described by Roger Fieldhouse

> was a reduction in the number of Marxist tutors (employed by the Extra-Mural Delegacy), a muzzling of Marxist ideology and a concerted effort to inhibit the remaining left-wing tutors and prevent any more from being appointed.[38]

Where extra-mural and adult education departments provided tutors for the Armed Services they proscribed individual lecturers because of their 'Communism', and on occasion directly intervened in the teaching process to object to anti-government or pro-Soviet bias. Outside of adult education, the Admiralty told Pangbourne Nautical College, at the time of the Chinese bombardment of the British warship *Amethyst* in July 1949, to get rid of a Communist member of staff.[39]

Protecting the Young Mind

'Communist infiltration' of education was seen as a deliberate attempt to influence 'the susceptible minds of the young'. The State therefore monitored the activities of the World Federation of Democratic Youth (WFDY) from its inception in wartime Britain among refugees (when it was called the International – later World – Youth Council), and the prominent part played in its activities by named Communists was noted.[40] A request by the World Youth Council for facilities for visiting delegates to a conference in London was turned down by the Foreign Office but was reversed by Cabinet decision in August 1945. The conference went ahead in November 1945, and the World Federation of Democratic

Youth was officially formed. Communists were considered to have manipulated the event (the Soviet delegation numbered sixty with an average age of forty) and the six member executive of the British section of WFDY was said to include two Communists. A year later the attempt by WFDY to achieve recognition as a consultative non-governmental organisation by the United Nations was rebuffed, the British government resolutely opposing the application. A few years later Herbert Morrison characterised WFDY as a Fifth Column body; and in August 1951 the Government attempted to prevent students and others from attending a WFDY/International Union of Students Festival of Youth in Berlin. Many were refused visas for the journey and some eighty were held at Saalfelden under guard for a night by American soldiers, who refused to let them travel on to the Festival.[41]

A few months before the Festival of Youth, Herbert Morrison had attempted to get the Government to enforce a ban on the import of a propaganda film that had been made of a similar event the year before, a Free (East) German Youth mass rally. Although Morrison agreed that the Government could be accused of interfering with the liberty of the subject, if they did not act they might be,

> criticised for allowing a foreign publication of such a dangerous propaganda nature to enter the country and be shown to immature persons who have not the political wisdom to see through it. I do not see why we should allow this film to be imported any more than we would have allowed Nazi anti-semitic films.

After a private showing of the film for Ministers the Cabinet decided that it was not practicable to take any action.[42]

Protecting Western Culture

There is little evidence that established academics who were Communists could not get their work published for that reason, even during the worst years of the Cold War.[43] But at the end of 1949 the Government decided that an informal approach be made to Surrey Dane, joint managing director of Odhams Press, to persuade him to encourage more anti-Communist material in the press's publications.[44] Writers such as Rebecca West in the *Sunday Times*, became increasingly strident in their anti-Communism. Even the more serious mainstream journals could, on occasion, print such intemperate attacks as did an unsigned review in the *Times Literary Supplement* of Jack Lindsay's *Byzantium into Europe*. The reviewer not only questioned Lindsay's scholarly honesty, and linked his book to a Soviet re-writing of history, but alleged that Marxist historical materialism as an ideology was irreconcilable with western scholarship and scientific method:

> It raises the question, which will have seriously to be faced, sooner rather than later, by those concerned with academic appointments, whether, in fairness to his pupils, any individual that adheres to the Communist doctrine can be allowed responsibility for the teaching of history. [45]

Later the *TLS* refused to review Lindsay's political trilogy on post-war life, *The British Way*, but attacked it in a leading article. Lindsay, as a well known Communist writer outside academia, continued to get his books into print, according to himself, only because his publisher, Nicholson of the Bodley Head, 'was a genuine liberal who refused to be dictated to by Cold War pressures'.[46]

However, the change in the cultural climate had less to do with McCarthy-type witch-hunting and more to do with the dissipation of anti-Fascist optimism and with an operation of commercial criteria. And as *Our Time*, a periodical of the more independently minded cultural figures in the Communist Party, ruefully commented, the Government showed no concern for cultivating British literature, film and music while the Arts Council had been allowed to decline, and:

> when the censorship is not directly reactionary, it can operate by means of profit expediency – English 'anti-Red' writers have already had large American sales, and it might well become as difficult here as in America for a Left-wing writer to find a publisher.[47]

Local authority funding could, nevertheless, be used to effect political changes, as when the London County Council withdrew financial support from the London Philharmonic Orchestra in 1949, after the orchestra's secretary, the Communist Thomas Russell, had taken a well publicised trip to Moscow.[48]

Communists Under Siege

British Communists experienced increasing unpopularity and public hostility in the period 1949-51 following the Chinese shelling of the British warship, *Amethyst*. These were the years of the British military campaign against the Communist insurgents in Malaya and the outbreak of the Korean War. Party-organised meetings were broken up; councils refused to hire out their buildings to Communists and the police began interpreting the offence of 'obstruction' in such a manner as to clamp down on the selling of the *Daily Worker*, street meetings, poster parades and leafleting.[49] An National Council for Civil Liberties (NCCL) memorandum recorded ten separate police interferences with Communist activities, including four arrests for 'obstruction' – selling papers and speaking in public – between the 10 June and the 5 July 1950.[50]

In 1950 the Government considered its most far-reaching measures against 'Communist activity', when an explosion at

Portsmouth dockyard caused panic and fear of sabotage in official circles.[51] Chuter Ede, the Home Secretary, sent a memorandum to the Cabinet suggesting the need for new legislation. Although British troops were fighting in Korea as part of the United Nations forces, Britain was not technically in a state of war, which meant that, although incitement to sabotage would be criminal conspiracy, incitement to obstruct or hinder the movement of troops or supplies would not be illegal. The initial response from the Prime Minister's Office was reasoned:

> Unless the Home Secretary can say that the Portsmouth explosion was an act of sabotage, the Government will not be able to say in support of such legislation that there had yet occurred any incident of the kind at which legislation would be aimed or to adduce any evidence that any such incident was likely to occur ... is it better to show that the Government are preparing for all possibilities, or is it better to avoid putting ideas into people's heads?[52]

However, what were seemingly Attlee's reservations did not end the matter and various drafts of a bill entitled 'Overseas Operations (Security of Forces) Bill' were presented to Cabinet. One provision made it an offence 'systematically' to publish '... orally or in writing, statements or matter likely to prejudice the carrying out of operations outside the United Kingdom by His Majesty's forces or any associated forces or to assist persons opposing such operations by force ...'.[53] Conviction could mean up to fourteen years' imprisonment, although the prosecution had to prove 'intent' – that those in question had knowingly used untrue statements that were against the public interest. A later revision of this clause allowed for a defence only on the basis that the facts published were true; a *belief* that they were true was no longer adequate. In discussions over the proposed Bill the difficulties and drawbacks of implementation became apparent. A possible court case that revolved around the truth or otherwise of something printed in, for example, the *Daily*

Worker, could result in a propaganda victory against the Government. It was also felt that the Government would be open to criticism if it introduced such legislation 'while doing nothing to counter a general Communist conspiracy against essential services in this country'.[54] A decision was taken in late November 1950 not to introduce the Bill 'in present circumstances'. By this time Labour had less than a year in power left. A general legislative assault against Communists was rejected as likely to be counter-productive, drive Communists underground and reduce the flow of intelligence concerning their activities. In the discussions surrounding the proposed legislation Morrison and Chuter Ede argued that banning the Communist Party, as in Australia and South Africa, was not practicable because 'public opinion' would not accept such a move.[55]

Consequences

Anti-Communism in Britain never reached the pathological heights that it did in the USA; no one was imprisoned because of their Party membership; fear and hatred of Communism were never used to measure one's patriotism and national identity. Yet a series of significant developments took place in post-war Britain – a domestic impact of the Cold War that has generally been passed over in silence. According to one American scholar, it 'seems clear, on both the local and national level ... that actions against the Left during the Cold War were carried out more as a war of attrition than the outright battles that took place in the United States'.[56] How individual Communists experienced and responded to that 'war of attrition' varied. In March 1951 the London County Council imposed a ban on the employment of Communists, and as a result a number of party members, including several architects and planners, were allowed to 'drop their party card' while others became secret members. A decision was taken by the party leadership, as a matter of expediency, to disband the LCC Communist Party branch for a period. As a consequence many of those who had 'gone underground' simply dropped out of political activity and never returned to open party membership. Communist architects in private practice found that, for commercial necessity, displays of political radicalism or progressiveness had to be dispensed with. For this reason the leftwing Architects' 'Co-operative Partnership' was renamed ACP.[57]

In contrast, some who were Communists at this time do not, in retrospect, consider that they were isolated. Michael Barratt Brown was in close touch with not only Party members in the academic world but also fellow economists such as Joan Robinson and Dorothy Wedderburn (then Cole) at Cambridge. He was also able to talk to 'Roy Harrod in Oxford and James Meade in Cambridge, who were liberal Keynesians. Douglas Cole was a family friend, as were many of the left in the Labour Party – Stafford Cripps, Konni Zilliacus, Dick Crossman, Ian Mikardo, Michael Foot ...' among them.[58] Although some organisations which included Communists, Labour Party members and others, such as the Socialist Medical Association and the Haldane Society of Socialist Lawyers, experienced splits and dissention, links were maintained – the Communist Party was never the completely isolated pariah organisation that it was in America.

British 'McCarthyism' actually helped slow down the political erosion of the party. The writer and journalist Mervyn Jones was, in the confines of his diary, increasingly critical of the British Party and of Soviet policies, but did not seriously consider leaving the Party until three or four years later. In his words:

> The Party was held together by the ferocity of the Cold War, the pressures of enemies on every side, the incesssant onslaughts on the Soviet Union and Communism in the press and in the speeches of both Tory and Labour politicians – onslaughts which contained some home truths, but also a

torrent of distortions and slanders. It seemed cowardly, and even indecent, to withdraw from the battle.[59]

Eric Hobsbawm has expressed a similar view:

> ... people said this isn't the time, you know whatever doubts and hesitations we have, this isn't the time ... The case against anti-Communism was so obvious at the time.[60]

It was an attitude that accepted the dictates of party discipline, which meant that the leadership's word 'was final'. Critical voices within the Party were marginalised and on occasions expelled. From 1949-50 there was a 'purging' of 'factionalist and Titoist elements'.[61] The easing of the Cold War atmosphere and the international events of 1956 finally resulted in an explosion of protest within the Party, the loss of a sizeable segment of its membership and the end of its monopoly of the non-Labour left.

Notes

[1] Kenneth Harris, *Attlee*, Weidenfeld and Nicholson, London 1983, p267.

[2] P. Papastratis, *British Policy Towards Greece During The Second World War 1941-44*, Cambridge University Press, Cambridge 1984; Heinz Richter, *British Intervention in Greece*, Merlin Press, London 1986.

[3] Ed Harriman, 'A Cupboard Full of Nazis', *New Statesman*, 5 August 1988; David Cesarani, *Justice Delayed*, Heinemann, London 1992.

[4] See Vibeke Sorensen, *Social Democratic Government in Denmark Under the Marshall Plan, 1947-1950*, PhD thesis, European University Institute, Florence 1987.

[5] These secret armed groups, established in 1949, were based on anti-Communist and right-wing nationalist elements in the wartime resistance movements. A Belgian parliamentary investigation established that 'Gladio' was initiated and co-ordinated by a secret committee with representatives from Britain, France, Holland, Belgium and Luxemburg (Henrick Lisberg, 'Danmark i hemmelig haer i 30 ar', *Politiken*, 3 September 1991). By the 1950s the CIA was increasingly involved in Gladio.

[6] Douglas Hyde, letter, 21 September 1990.

[7] Alan Ryan; article marking the passing of the CIA funded magazine *Encounter*, 'Killed by its own success', *Times*, 2 February 1991.

[8] E.P. Thompson, 'Mr Attlee and the Gadarene Swine', Guardian, 3 March 1984.

[9] See R. Kisch, *The Days of the Good Soldiers – Communists in the Armed Forces of World War Two*, Journeyman Press, London 1985; Bill Moore and George Barnsby (eds), *The Anti-Fascist People's Front in the Armed Forces – The Communist Contribution 1939-46*, Our History Pamphlet, Number 81, 1990.

[10] See F.H. Hinsley and C.A.G. Simpkins, *British Intelligence in the Second World War – Volume 4, Security and Counter Intelligence*, HMSO, London 1990.

[11] Dora Russell, *The Tamarisk Tree* – Volume 3, Challenge to the Cold War, Virago, London 1985.

[12] 'Alleged Victimization of Civil Servants – Cases Being Considered', *The Times*, 28 March 1947.

[13] William Crofts, *Coercion or Persuasion? Propaganda in Britain After 1945*, Routledge, London 1989, p246; Christopher Mayhew, *Time to Explain*, Hutchinson, London 1987, Chapter 11, 'The Cultural Cold War'.

[14] Ernest Bevin, 'Future Foreign Publicity Policy', Memo from the Secretary of State for Foreign Affairs, 4 January 1948, PRO CAB 129/Volume 23.

[15] See Joan Mahoney, *Exporting McCarthyism: British Civil Liberties and the Cold War*, PhD thesis, University of Missouri, Kansas City, 1989; Joan Mahoney, 'Civil Liberties in Britain During the Cold War; The Role of Central Government', *The American Journal of Legal History*, Volume XXXIII, 1989.

[16] E.J. Hobsbawm, letter, 11 June 1991.

[17] Peter Hennessy and Gail Brownfield, 'Britain's Cold War Security Purge, the Origins of Positive Vetting', *The Historical Journal*, December 1982, p968; 'The 10,000 "fellow travellers" ... will be vetted as thoroughly as the party members. They are regarded as more likely to divulge secrets than those who are open about their allegiance', *Daily Express*, 17 March 1948. The *Daily Mirror* reported the estimated number of Communists in the Civil Service as about 1000, 13 March 1948; one of the first to be purged was Arthur Prince, a clerical officer in the Ministry of Supply, who had been a Communist for a period but was now ward treasurer of Maldon, Surrey, Labour Party. *Daily Worker*, 10 May 1948.

[19] Mahoney, *op cit*, pp181-2.

[20] There were unofficial ways of getting rid of Communists from the Civil Service. Some Communist civil servants 'seeing the way the wind was blowing' decided on new careers before the 1948 ban. Christopher Hill left the Northern Department of the Foreign Office and returned to academic life as soon as he could after the Labour victory-interview Christopher Hill, 2 July 1991; Stephen Boddington who was refused permanent status, in the wartime Admiralty, 'pioneered the concept of linear planning: one of his first tasks was to route merchant vessels from port to port with the minimum of wasted journeys', *Obituary*, *Guardian*, 1 January 1990.

Sometimes 'polite' action was taken, for example '... my mother was politely asked to resign from an MOD establishment, where she had been selling the *Worker*', letter, R. Abraham, 6 December 1990.

[21] 'Political Broadcasting', Minutes of meeting, Lord President's room, House of Commons, 25 February 1948, PRO CAB 197/5.

[22] Letter from David Stephens (Office of the Lord President) to Lord President, report of meeting with William Haley, Director-General of the BBC regarding 'Communists in the BBC', 30 March 1948, PRO CAB 197/5.

[23] 'Political Broadcasting', Minutes 22 April 1948, PRO CAB 124/31.

[24] Letter from William Haley, Director General of the BBC, to Winston Churchill, 5 March 1950, PRO CAB 124/31, detailing measures taken by the BBC re Communists. Communists in the BBC first became an issue in 1948 after Churchill complained about the prominence given to two British Communist leaders in two news bulletins. Morrison demanded action and was assured by the Director-General (via a meeting with David Stephens, see Note 22) that the matter had been dealt with.

[25] See Martin Lawn, *Organised Teachers and the Labour Movement 1900-1930*, PhD thesis, Open University, 1982, Chapter 11, 'Purge of the Left'.

[26] R.A. Butler, MP, *The Right Angle*, (Journal of the Conservative and Unionists' Teachers Association), Volume 1, Number 1, June 1948.

[27] Lord Vansittart, 'Communism Among School Teachers', *Parliamentary Debates* (Hansard), House of Lords, 7th Volume of Session 1948-49, 7 December 1949, 1261. There were more like 1000 members of the Communist Party Teachers Group, Max Morris, taped interview, 7 November 1991.

[28] 'Anti-Communist Propaganda: Policy and March', GEN.231/3rd Meeting 1, Confidential Annex, 19 December 1949, PRO CAB 130/37.

[29] According to Max Morris (interview cit.) the anti-Communist Campaign in the *Teachers' World* was inspired by the former NUT General Secretary, Fred Mander.

[30] Doreen Rudé, letter, 3 March 1989; according to Eric Hobsbawm, Rudé's PhD supervisor (1951) Professor George Cobban, effectively 'did him down', presumably by mentioning his politics in references, Hobsbawm, taped interview 19 June 1991.

[31] Quoted in *Educational Bulletin*, Volume 3, Number 1, October 1951.

[32] Maurice Dobb letter to Miss Allen, 4 November 1950, NCCL Files, Brynmor Jones Library, University of Hull, DCL/2/8.

[33] 'Academic Liberty', *New Statesman and Nation*, 24 June 1950.

[34] Rodney (Hilton) letter to Christopher (Hill), 31 October 1950, NCCL Files *cit.*

[35] Brian Simon, taped interview, 2 July 1985.

[36] A letter of protest against the operation of 'unofficial political tests' in the making of appointments to university teaching posts, written by five academics (Dobb, Beryl Smalley, Joan Robinson, H.S. Davies and J.C.H.

Whitehead) to the *New Statesman*, 13 May 1950, caused something of a stir, and the NCCL, on Rothstein's suggestion, attempted without success to launch a commission of enquiry into the matter.

[37] John Costello, *Mask of Treachery*, Collins, London 1988, p699, 'Notes and sources' number 55.

[38] See Roger Fieldhouse, *Adult Education and the Cold War: Liberal Values Under Siege 1946-51*, Leeds Studies in Adult and Continuing Education, Leeds 1985.

[39] Peter Cadogan, taped interview, February 1983.

[40] Cabinet Memo, 'World Federation of Democratic Youth' by the Minister of State, Volume 11, 28 June-30 July, PRO CAB 129.

[41] *The Journey to Berlin – Report of a Commission of Inquiry into Certain Events at Brussels, the Channel Ports, Innsbruck and Saalfelden in August 1951*, National Council of Civil Liberties, London n.d.

[42] Cabinet Memo, 'Propaganda Film of the Berlin Youth Rally' by Secretary of State for Foreign Affairs, 19 March 1951, PRO PREM 8/1411.

[43] There is 'no evidence *at all* that the Cold War prevented or restricted publication. Some may have thought it not worth trying, but that is a guess ...', Christopher Hill, letter 21 July 1991. Two eminent Communist academics, Arnold Kettle and Edward Arthur Thompson were among those who had influential works published at this time, the former on literature, the latter on ancient history. There were problems in fields where the material was considered to be too overtly political; Hutchinson's University Library turned down Hobsbawm's first book, which they had 'more-or-less commissioned', on the basis that it was 'too biased' – Eric Hobsbawm, taped interview, 19 June 1991.

[44] William Surrey Dane, 1939 Director at the Ministry of Information; 1941-45 Director at the Ministry of Supply; 1947-57 Joint Managing Director of Odhams Press Ltd; 1949 (October)-1960 Chairman of the *Daily Herald*.

[45] Unsigned leading article, *Times Educational Supplement*, 21 July 1950.

[46] Jack Lindsay, *Life Rarely Tells*, Penguin, Harmondsworth 1982, p805.

[47] 'We Want to be Un-American', *Our Time*, Volume 7, Number 3, November 1947.

[48] For further details on Thomas Russell, the LPO and the LCC see my Ph.D thesis *Communism in the Professions: the Organisation of the British Communist Party Among Professional Workers*, University of Warwick 1990, p280-281 (footnote 63).

[49] Pollitt was assaulted at a public meeting in Plymouth a few days after the '*Amethyst* affair'. Wembley Council tried to ban a CP meeting in the town hall, but were prevented by a legal injunction. The Labour Party in Stepney, where there were twelve Communist Councillors, 'used the *Amethyst* incident in an incredibly vicious campaign to get the Communists off the council'. Bert Ward, *I'll See Socialism in My Time*; Teesside Communist Party, Middlesbrough n.d., p18.

[50] 'Memorandum on Interference with Communist Party meetings and

other activities', July 1950, NCCL Files, Brynmor Jones Library, University of Hull DCL/21/3. Olive Gibbs's husband, who headed a small Oxford firm of accountants was advised by a CID detective sometime in 1949-50, to sack one of his staff who was a Communist. See *Our Olive – The Autobiography of Olive Gibbs*, Robert Dugdale, Oxford 1989, p133.

[51] A young woman party member was transferred from her job at Hampshire County Council town planning department at Fareham during the panic following the explosion; see my PhD thesis, *Communism in the Professions, op cit*, pp272-3.

[52] Letter from the Prime Minister, signed Brook, 19 July 1950, PRO PREM 8/1525.

[53] 'Overseas Operations (Security of Forces) – Defeat of a Bill', 1950, PRO PREM 8/1525.

[54] Memorandum from the Prime Minister 'Overseas Operations (Security of Forces) Bill', 15 November 1950, PRO PREM 8/1525/

[55] See Peter Wilby, 'Conspiracy Obsessed the Attlee Cabinet', *The Sunday Times*, 4 January 1981; also Joan Mahoney's PhD, *op cit*, pp113-115. Attlee reported to the Ministry of Fuel & Power that Citrine, Chairman of C.E.B. feared Communist sabotage of power stations, PRO PREM 8/1275.

[56] Joan Mahoney, *op cit*, p203.

[57] More details are given about architects/planners in the LCC and elsewhere in my PhD, *op cit*. The Head of the Architectural Association school, Robert Jordan, resigned in 1950 following criticism of his toleration of Communists on the teaching staff, see *The Builder*, 24 November 1950, which carries a prominently placed 'witch-hunting' article, 'Architecture and Politics', on the matter.

[58] Michael Barratt Brown, letter, 26 February 1992.

[59] Mervyn Jones, *Chances – An Autobiography*, Verso, London 1987, p117.

[60] Eric Hobsbawm, taped interview, 19 June 1991. The composer Rutland Boughton, who was a party member from an early period, was critical of the Party 'line' on Yugoslavia. He remained a member throughout the Cold War, a time when 'he became so alarmed that MI5/Special Branch might destroy his music that he got a Czech comrade to photograph his scores for safe-keeping', Richard Abraham (grandson), letter, 6 December 1990.

[61] See Eric Heffer's autobiography *Never a Yes Man: The Life and Politics of an Adopted Liverpudlian*, Verso, London 1992, for his expulsion from the CP. For CP crackdown on Titoist and factionalist elements, grouped together with police and MI5 spies, see resolution of Political Committee, 25 May 1950, published in *World News and Views*, Volume 30, Number 22, 3 June 1950.

The Days of the New Look: Consumer Culture and Working-Class Affluence

Angela Partington

[Class conscious has to be understood as] a proper envy of those who possess what one has been denied. And by allowing this entry into political understanding, the proper struggles of people in a state of dispossession to gain their proper inheritance might be seen not as a sordid and mindless greed for things of the marketplace, but attempts to alter a world which has produced in them states of unfulfilled desire.

Carolyn Steedman, *Landscape for a Good Woman*, 1986[1]

From the point of view of working-class women, the Second World War could be said to have 'ended' in 1947, the year of the 'New Look' in fashion, which symbolised a shift from austerity to affluence. More accurately, it signified the burgeoning of consumer capitalism, since the New Look was one of the first examples of 'mass consumption' in that it referred to a range of high fashion commodities marketed specifically for working-class women as well as for the middle-class fashion consumer. The years which followed saw the gradual end of rationing and the appearance of more and more goods targeted at working-class consumers who had not previously been considered a market for them, but whose purchasing power was now becoming essential to capitalism's survival.

The post-war working class was a relocated and fragmented one which depended increasingly on shared leisure and consumption practices for a sense of shared identity, rather than on traditional forms of 'community' which had developed in the early urban, industrialised centres of working-class life. Working-classness was to be increasingly articulated through the exercise of choices in relation to goods and services, practices which were located in the private, domestic sphere and for which women were better equipped than men. Working-class culture was to be found in the home as well as in the pubs and streets, and represented through design and media products as well as through sing-songs and football matches.

There is a commonly held view that in the 1950s, consumerism eroded the distinction between working-class and middle-class culture to produce a 'national consensus culture',[2] that affluence dismantled working class resistance and totally subordinated women.[3] A more optimistic view suggests that the changes in those years created a 'democracy of style', or the beginnings of the collapse of the cultural hierarchy which had treated middle-class taste as superior. Both interpretations assume that class differences were either eradicated, absorbed or rendered meaningless. I shall challenge these interpretations and argue that consumerism provided new opportunities for the expression and celebration of class and gender differences, and of oppositional values and beliefs.

Consumer Culture

In the mid-1950s Labour based its electoral appeal on the contrast between the poverty and unemployment of the 1930s and the welfare state of the 1940s; whereas the Conservatives more successfully compared 1940s austerity with 1950s affluence. Labour failed to see that the assertion of class and gender struggles could be made by consuming goods in different ways; ' "needs", "rights" and "demands" were OK, but desire, pleasure and personal fulfillment (were) grounds for suspicion'.[4]

The Left has tended to see the tastes which affluence made possible as merely manufactured by the marketing industries in a way that reinforced working-class subordination or, worse, prevented people from knowing their subordination. Some feminists have likewise tended to see the pleasures which consumerism offers women as helping to keep them in their subordinate position and blind them to this reality.

Working-class women did not become bourgeoisified leisured housewives during the post-war period, however. The modernisation of working-class homes and the expansion of the service industries meant that the number of women in paid employment remained at wartime levels during the 1950s.[5] It was hardly necessary to stimulate women's desire to consume following a lengthy period of shortages and sacrifices, and this meant that they were even more likely to work outside the home as well as in it, in order to be able to afford new goods. By the end of the 1950s four out of five families were hire-purchasers of goods worth a total of £1000 million.[6]

Culture is not simply the expression of anterior economic conditions or social positions. It is created from the shared knowledges, competencies and skills specific to a social group. The use of this 'cultural capital' through consumption gives commodities meanings, and produces pleasures that are not available to other social groups.[7] In this way post-war consumerism produced new ways of being working-class as well as new forms of class conflict.

During the 1950s both the housewife and the teenager were identified as target markets. It has generally been assumed that while the housewife was a passive consumer of commodities offered her, the teenager had the capacity for subversion and appropriation, innovating styles which then became adopted by other age groups within the same class;

for example the changing width of trouser legs, from bags to drainpipes to flares to tapered legs. But it was women who innovated and influenced the overwhelming majority of changes in style within class groups and who acquired the necessary consumer skills to do so. And when new styles originated among young males it was generally women who disseminated them among older men. In this way women ensured the reproduction of class differences, and a single code of dress was replaced by a whole range of codes.

Contradictions in Consumerism

Consumerism is necessary to capitalism, yet it has intensified the contradictions inherent in the system. As needs are expanded, the pressure for higher wages increases and the rate of profit is reduced. Affluence is witness to capitalism's instability and a condition of continuing struggle between classes and ways of life.

The extension of consumption, while uniting manufacturing and cultural industries in their pursuit of new markets, also brought them into conflict. One strategy of the marketing industries was to load goods with meanings, and encourage emotional investment in them (the 'libidinisation' of consumption). But at the same time there were attempts to educate the consumer, train affluence and regulate consumption being made by the social services, promoters of home management, elements of the cultural leadership such as the design profession, and by some sections of the media. This tendency towards regulation derived from a desire both to rationalise the economy and to legislate certain (middle-class) tastes against the vulgarities of 'conspicuous consumption'. But the regulation of consumption is in conflict with its libidinisation, because it attempts to strip meanings from goods, discourage emotional identification, and promote rational and disinterested relationships with them instead. Yet the emerging mass market system, of which this process of regulation was a part, relied precisely on the conspicuousness of consumption and the articulation of different tastes among the consumers. This contradiction, between a strategy to channel desires into stable and predictable demands and a strategy to develop diverse preferences and choices, provided a terrain for the development of new forms of class difference and class struggle, for example over the meaning of the 'New Look'.

Attempts both to regulate consumption and to libidinise it were made within each industry, and post-war reconstruction provided even advertisers with an atmosphere of working towards a 'planned', peaceful, prosperous society. These groups envisaged themselves as among '... "the ranks of the planners" and the "directors of the good society", and ... (as) play(ing) their part in the psychological guidance of the masses. ... advertising had become honourable, shifting its motivation from private profit to public welfare'.[8]

The New Look

This is rarely acknowledged; for example, fashion is often dismissed as built-in-obsolescence, a mechanism for stimulating consumption; mass-produced or popular fashion in particular tends to be seen as part of the post-war proliferation of 'false needs'. But late 1940s and 1950s fashion was the focus for attempts to regulate consumption as well as to libidinise it. For example, although fashion historians argue that the industry loved the New Look because it was a way of seducing the consumer into buying much more fabric, the British fashion establishment opposed the style; a delegation representing 300 clothing companies went to the Board of Trade in March 1948 asking for a ban on long hemlines.[9] The new style actually meant less product for their investment of materials and labour. Utility styles continued to be promoted by designers and manufacturers, as they had been in the Britain Can Make It Exhibition of 1946, while the New Look

251

was regarded at best as only a frivolous and impractical bit of fun, at worst as unpatriotic and regressive.

In trying to impose certain tastes on consumers, the design profession and the marketing industries were attempting to create 'good' i.e. predictable consumers, but they succeeded only in creating the opportunity for the rules of 'good consumption' to be broken, inadvertently allowing consumers to produce unexpected meanings around goods, none more so than fashion commodities. The rules and regulations of good taste – restraint – and of modern design – functionalism – were promoted in media products aimed at working-class women (for example, Hardy Amies's weekly column in *Woman*). 'Glamorous' styles were acceptable only as a complement to sensible and practical ones, and appropriate only on certain occasions. But British women consumed the New Look 'improperly' by adapting it as an everyday style.

There was nothing intrinsically submissive about the New Look,[10] even though it restricted movement and emphasised the curves of the body. Its strong colours, severe shapes, and theatrical styling could equally well be read as 'stroppy' and defiant compared to the twee floral prints and sensible cuts of utility styles. The way it was adapted and worn by working-class women transformed it into a hybrid style, 'unfaithful' to the designer's vision, and they appropriated it for working and for relaxing in, as well as for 'dressing up' occasions. The 'functional' of Utility clothing and the 'decorative' of the New Look were copied, sampled, and re-mixed by working-class women to produce hybrid styles. This suggests that knowledge of the contrast between Utility and the New Look was being used not to uphold the distinction between practical and glamorous, or between efficient and frivolous, but to undermine it. By refusing to keep the functional and the decorative separate, consumers were not only breaking the rules of good design and taste, but using goods to satisfy desires other than those assumed by the marketing industries.

252

Consumerism did not take popular culture away from the working class. The very system through which goods were made available enabled the rearticulation of class differences through style in new and more complex ways.

Mass Markets – New Skills

A mass market system develops consumer skills to create markets for goods – thereby encouraging a multiplicity of cultural codes, different ways of relating to objects, different meanings and values around objects. Although the marketing industries aspire to control the meanings of goods, the consequence of their activities is actually to preserve and expand the consumer's capacity for her own symbolic investments in them.

It was during the 1950s that terms such as 'lifestyle' were coined, a new language which replaced the old ways of describing class distinctions, yet which suggested that differences remained. 'Market segmentation', or the division of people into smaller and smaller groups with distinct preferences, made it possible to design, package and merchandise otherwise similar prodcucts for more and more consumers. The best example of market segmentation in response to the demands of industry in the 1950s was the creation of the 'teen-ager'; but working-class women became the target for massive quantities of advertising, editorial, and other forms of promotion such as design exhibitions.

Mass-market systems are often understood as ones which enable new styles to be 'diffused' from a middle to a working-class market. On the assumption that subordinate groups emulate dominant ones, popular fashions are understood as those which 'trickle down' from élite groups to 'the masses'. This has been invoked in support of the notion that differences have been eroded, absorbed, or concealed, as an affluent working class has aspired to the tastes and preferences of the middle class.

In fact there is virtually no 'trickle down' within a mass market fashion system. On the one hand the re-invented fashion 'season' enables the co-ordination of manufacturing and merchandising strategies which allow simultaneous adoption of new styles across socio-economic groups. On the other hand the development of a repertoire of styles in the same fashion season allows for different choices and tastes. Innovators within more and more market segments are targeted, not just those in privileged groups. Fashion marketing is based increasingly on media forms which have specific audiences or readerships, disseminating information within, rather than across, class groups.[11] So differences exist in the *ways* in which fashions are adopted, and in the selections and discriminations made between styles; for example, privileged groups can ignore new fashions and wear variarions on 'classics', while women on a very limited clothes budget may be very keen to adopt the latest fashions but customise them to make them more adaptable. Exclusivity is enjoyed by all consumers, since they can shop at retail outlets intended specifically for them. Simultaneous adoption does not mean identical adoption therefore. Although the fashion industry may determine the range of styles from which choices have to be made, certain styles or 'looks' become much more popular amongst some consumer groups than others, and certain styles completely fail to be adopted by some, or even all groups.

The pursuit of working-class markets has established a fashion system in which there is very little 'vertical flow' (down or up) in the ways in which styles are innovated or adopted by specific class groups. Post-war culture is not one in which distinctions and hierarchies collapse, but a 'horizontalized' one in which differences multiply.[12] The too little recognised power of the working-class consumer is not a consequence of mere accessibility to goods, but of the accumulation of cultural capital stimulated by a mass market system. For example, Dior's licensing system (developed from the late 1940s and acknowledged as a crucial part of the modernisation of the fashion industry) spelled the end for couture as the cutting edge of 'Fashion', by limiting it to craft-based dressmaking with a shrinking market whose main value to the industry was a form of publicity, precisely because it encouraged the production of popular knowledges and competences in relation to fashion. Multiple chain stores heralded the emergence of popular fashion, where styles could diversify and multiply not just be cheaper and/or 'watered down' versions of couture. These developments were consequences of economic strategies deployed by manufacturing, marketing and leisure industries in the pursuit of profit, nothing to do with a 'democracy of style'. Consumerism did not create the illusion of a classless society, neither did it reinforce already established class relations; it altered the conditions, means and processes through which class differences were to be articulated and the resources for which class struggles were to be conducted.

Problems of Mass Markets

Both manufacturing and cultural industries depend on specific modes of production and distribution for the successful merchandising of a product within a mass market system. The divisions of labour, forms of management and 'quality control' that were developed (initially in the USA) to ensure efficient and regularized production in manufacturing became equally important in the development of cultural and leisure products for working-class markets in Britain.

In the case of Hollywood films, for example, the industry, which already had a strong foothold in the British market in the wake of the Second World War, a 'studio system' had long ensured a 'house style' which enabled the consumer to identify and choose the product in terms of their already established tastes and preferences. Also, the 'vertical integration' of film production and exhibition in the same corporate framework enabled greater accuracy in the identification of markets for films. By the 1950s the system had developed to ensure that the Hollywood product was differentiated and 'customized' according to even finer distinctions. There was now control over the way in which a film was styled in terms of its 'stars', 'images' and its 'look'. As the creation of designers as well as directors, the film was now packaged, merchandised and exhibited through cinema 'chains', allowing the investment of more capital in fewer films and reducing product uncertainty. A greater proportion of the budget was spent on its appearance-in-the-market-place. In other words the industry was now able to target its consumers as well as control the quality of its products.

The 'big' picture of the 1950s transformed the women's film into the full-blown melodrama, which found an audience with working-class women, despite the film industry's growing competition from television and other leisure industries. Although they were spending more on other consumer goods and other forms of entertainment, working-class women continued going to the cinema, but as a special 'treat' rather than a weekly habit.

But mass market systems have created as many problems for industries as they have solved. For instance, in the fashion industry, the turnover of styles and the diversity of markets has prevented the total mechanization of production, making long-term planning and investment impossible.[13]

Within every industry, there are competing groups of professionals who come into conflict over the problem of how to find markets for goods; whether to 'libidinise' consumption or to 'regulate' it. A classic example concerns the role of design in manufacturing, in which the conflict is between the notion of design as a marketing tool, and that of design as solving 'real' problems and 'improving the quality of life'. In the 1950s, for example, the disparity 'between the pieces illustrated in the Council of Industrial Design's publications and those displayed in the shop windows of high street furniture retailers' highlighted a widening gap between their different definitions of mass taste.[14] Even when contemporary designs became more widely available, retailers simply 'added' them to the ranges of traditional furniture which they already carried, as another 'look' which certain consumers might prefer. At different points, and with different products, either quality, function, price, or 'the look' can become the most promoted aspect, depending on which group (manufacturers, designers, advertisers, retailers) manages to gain control in that instance. For example, designers gained control over the production of textiles in the 1950s but not over that of television sets.

The consequences of such conflicts have influenced the development of mass market systems. Department stores differentiated themselves from multiples by concentrating on supplying particular groups of consumers; for example, by buying couture models and having copies made up for exclusive sale in the store. The deployment of design in merchandising and retailing accelerated the production of visual languages for expressing class differences – not only did the consumer discriminate between commodities, but between the ways they were packaged, advertised, and displayed.

These developments provided new conditions for forms of contestation and struggle between groups. Contemporary 'styles' in furniture, for example, were associated in the 1950s with particular kinds of specialist 'up-market' retailers and therefore with middle-class consumers. They became 'popular' only when 'translated' or 'customized' through 'copies', and through advertisements, magazines, and shops which could address the specific preferences of working-class women. This was not emulation but a refusal to consume that which did not address already established preferences, even if those preferences were changed as a result. The 'translation' of a design changed the product from the 'original' in such a way that the design establishment no longer approved of it, and was therefore a kind of appropriation. Variations in 'make', label, retail 'brand', fabric, style, quality or price, as well as forms of publicity and styles of packaging, guaranteed that the simultaneous adoption of new styles was not identical adoption, but that fashions were adopted in class-specific ways.

Consumer Power

A mass market system has to accommodate a massive rejection of goods on the part of consumers. It has been estimated that as much as 90 per cent of new products fail to find a market.[15] Shopping is about selecting and discriminating; the rejection of goods affects marketing and industrial realities, often forcing changes in business strategy and even causing entrepreneurial failure. The consumer's rejection of commodities is as effective in challenging capitalism as is industrial action.

The size of the proportion of rejected goods is an indication of the extent to which goods are consumed 'improperly' – in ways not anticipated by industry. Of the 10 per cent which do find a market, how many are consumed by the targeted consumers in the way that was expected? From clever fashion followers who mix designer originals with high street bargains, to working housewives who hang Austrian blinds in their bathrooms, consumers not only choose, they appropriate and customize. 'Improper' consumption is standard behaviour, and it depends on the consumer's ability to produce her own meanings around goods.

The only way to understand how goods acquire meanings for working-class women is to consider how they make commodities refer to each other by using knowledges which are specific to them. During the late 1940s and the 1950s, working-class women found themselves in a position to accumulate and develop knowledges and competences which allowed them to do this. Knowledge about fashion could be used to decode films, familiarity with films to interpret interiors; reworkings of the symbolic and functional in a domestic context could inform the way the New Look was worn. Class and gender-specific knowledges were used to make goods refer to each other in specific ways, and so to acquire meanings not intended or assumed by the producers. Just as the New Look was adapted as an 'everyday' fashion, and so consumed 'improperly', so was domestic design.[16]

A double burden of paid and domestic labour was now common for women. So their knowledge of modern design was acquired not simply as 'housewives', but as waged workers whose homes needed to provide the pleasures of a feminine and familial domain, not of a 'machine for living in'. Therefore the 'functional' could not be kept separate from the 'homely' any more than it could be from the 'glamorous'. For instance, although the architects of new houses did away with 'the front parlour' on the grounds that it was mostly 'unused', the women who furnished and decorated it managed to restore its equivalent.[17] And although 'new ideas in design' were well represented in women's magazines, very often the application of these ideas gave them meanings which were incompatible, or even in direct conflict with, the ideals and principles of modernist design. Weekly magazines of the period suggest that, despite designers' emphasis on domestic efficiency, commodities were being put to all kinds of different uses which were entirely dependent on social and cultural contingencies, rather than on a rationalised functionalism. For example, the need to combine old and new furniture, while giving the room a 'designed' look, could result in blatant camouflaging and faking, by decorating or re-covering old pieces to make them 'go' with the new ones.[18]

While the design profession approved of electric fires 'which did not pretend to be anything else' working-class women continued to set them into fireplaces used for the display of trinkets, ornaments, pictures, documents of family events and souvenirs.[19] Adding to, removing, or rearranging such objects on the mantelpiece or hearth, remained one of the ways in which women maximized the symbolic and ritual uses of the fireplace. Features such as brass fenders, iron grates, wooden mantelpieces, and ceramic tiles, were often 'unnecessarily' retained or reintroduced. These remained important as articulations of emotions – from pride and pleasure, to anger and frustration – even if the reason for their 'practical' use (solid fuel) had disappeared. The fireplace continued to be used as the central decorative focus of the room, and as a family gathering place, suggesting the preservation of its symbolic connotations despite the disappearance of its practical necessity.

Through their consumption of new goods, working-class women asserted a need to *display* both their possessions and their domestic skills, often using the storage units, which designers assumed would reduce clutter, in ways which brought them into direct conflict with the design profession's attempt to isolate function. The 'no clutter' dogma often resulted in an outrageous formality in the arrangements of ornaments or pictures, which became excessive or paradoxically decorative, beyond the bounds of 'good taste'. Certain items of furniture, which had no practical function in the working-class home, such as display and cocktail cabinets and sideboards, became very popular. The traditional practice of cleaning in order to achieve a spectacular shine and brilliance, rather than to be efficient or hygienic, remained very important. This was completely different from the practice of leisured or middle-class housewives, in that it denied the home the status of 'haven' from the world of work. It made work visible, while the marketing industries were trying to make it invisible by promoting the myth of 'labour saving' goods.

Reading the Images

Women were able to use exclusive skills acquired through the whole range of media products targeted at them, to consume fashion and design goods improperly. For instance, working-class women's familiarity with fashion and style was due as much to their consumption of feature films as it was to their readings of advertisements and magazines. Conversely, their readings of films depended on knowledges about designed commodities, so that the appearance of women wearing denim jeans in Hollywood melodramas, for instance, could suggest meanings for working-class women which contradicted the ideological message of the films, since the audience was already familiar with such images from the fashion media. The early scenes of the 1952 film *Ruby Gentry* showed the central character in denim jeans, while she wore Parisian-style couture later in the film. It was possible to read the clothes symbolically, representing her humble origins which contrasted with her married status as a rich woman. But for the audience, the jeans would have connoted sexuality and youthful glamour rather than poverty, since they appeared fashionable rather than scruffy. Ruby's fashionable-ness would have had particular poignancy and resonance for a working-class audience, since it is despite her poverty that she manages to achieve it. While middle-class women would have read the clothes as expressions of character, working-class women may have used them as means of exercising new consumer skills while at the same time celebrating working-classness.

The pleasures of watching films in order to see clothes, hairdos, make-up, cars, houses and interiors are distinct from the pleasures of following a narrative or identifying with fictional characters, and are only available to viewers who can produce specific intertextual readings, because they have the necessary consumer skills. The images in *All That Heaven Allows* (1955), for example, were compared to the pages of a glossy women's magazine by critics in women's weekly publications in such a way that this was assumed to have resonance and meaning for the audience. It can be argued that this resemblance enabled the production of meanings which countered the ideological message of the film's narrative, or the values which the director had attempted to address through it.[20]

* * *

Consumerism did not destroy or marginalise 'authentic' working-class culture. The expansion of capitalism necessitated the dissemination of consumer skills, providing new conditions for the production of class and gender-specific meanings and realities, and reproducing class and gender differences. Working-class women were able to use knowledges, acquired as a result of being targeted by marketing industries, to produce intertextual meanings to which neither male nor middle-class consumers had access. Consumerism provided the conditions for a distinct culture for this subordinate group. There was no consensus culture or hegemonic domination of middle-class values.

In post-war culture, class consciousness and class struggle not only survived despite consumption, they became impossible without it. Working-class affluence and consumer culture allowed the development of needs and provided the means by which working-class women in particular could struggle 'to alter a world which (had) produced in them states of unfulfilled desire'.

Notes

[1] Carolyn Steedman, *Landscape for a Good Woman*, Virago, London 1986, p3.
[2] Laura Mulvey, 'Melodrama in and out of the Home', in Colin MacCabe (ed), *High Theory, Low Culture*, Manchester University Press, 1986, p2.
[3] Jon Clarke *et al*, 'Subcultures, Cultures and Class', in T. Bennett *et al* (eds), *Culture Ideology and Social Progress*, Open University/Batsford, London 1981, p60.
[4] Frank Mort and Nick Green, 'You've Never Had It So Good, Again!', in *Marxism Today*, May 1988, p33.
[5] Ann Oakley, *Housewife*, Penguin, Harmondsworth 1974, p59.
[6] Janice Winship, 'Femininity and Women's Magazines', Unit 6, *The Changing Experience of Women*, Open University, Milton Keynes 1983.
[7] Pierre Bourdieu, 'The Aristocracy of Culture', in *Media Culture and Society*, Volume 2, Number 3, 1980.
[8] Ernest Mandel, *Late Capitalism*, Verso, London 1972, pp197-210.

[9] Kathy Myers, *Understains: the Sense and Seduction of Advertising*, Comedia, London 1986, pp17-19.

[10] The New Look derived from Christian Dior's 'Corolle' line of 1947, and ironically referred to a nineteenth century silhouette which emphasised the curves of the body and depended on the draping and folding of fabric and on the use of padding and corsetry, to create full, swinging skirts, a 'nipped in' waist, and rounded shoulders. The design establishment's distaste for the style remains in evidence, for example, in Colin McDowell's recent claim that Dior was only a 'stylist' not a proper designer.

[11] Charles King, 'A Rebuttal of the "Trickle Down" Theory', in G. Wills and D. Midgeley (eds), *Fashion Marketing*, Allen and Unwin, London 1973.

[12] Rudi Laermans. 'The Relative Rightness of Pierre Bourdieu: Some Sociological Comments on the Legitimacy of Post-Modern Art, Literature and Culture', in *Cultural Studies*, Volume 6, Number 2, 1992, p256.

[13] Ellen Leopold, 'The Manufacture of the Fashion System', in J. Ash and E. Wilson (eds), *Chic Thrills*, Pandora, London 1992, p111.

[14] Penny Sparke, *An Introduction to Design and Culture*, Bell and Hyman, 1986, p128.

[15] John Fiske, *Reading the Popular*, Unwin Hyman, London 1989, p5; also Mica Nava, 'Consumerism Reconsidered' in *Cultural Studies*, Volume 5, Number 2, 1991, p161.

[16] Angela Partington, 'Popular Fashion and Working-Class Affluence', in Ash and Wilson, *op cit*.

[17] Judy Atfield, 'Inside Pram Town', in J. Atfield and P. Kirkham (eds), *A View From the Interior: Feminism, Women and Design*, Women's Press, London 1989.

[18] Angela Partington, 'The Designer Housewife in the 1950s', in Atfield and Kirkham, *op cit*.

[19] Adrian Forty, *Unit 20: British Design*, 1975, p60.

[20] Angela Partington, 'Melodrama's Gendered Audience', in S. Franklin *et al* (eds), *Off-Centre; Feminism and Cultural Studies*, Unwin Hyman, London 1991.

Adults Learning – for Leisure, Recreation and Democracy

Roger Fieldhouse

> ... given understanding, the human spirit can rise to the challenge of events ... therefore the aim of any programme of adult education must be to provide men and women with opportunities for developing a maturity of outlook and judgement, for increasing their sense of responsibility and awareness, for helping them to evolve a philosophy of life, and to develop interests which will enrich their leisure.
>
> *Further Education*, Ministry of Education pamphlet, 1947[1]

A New Role For Local Government

During the Second World War there was an immense spread of adult education, both in the forces through informal groups as well as the Army Bureau of Current Affairs (ABCA), and among civilians anxious to understand the war and the world which might follow it.

The 1944 Education Act responded to this interest by, for the first time, requiring local education authorities (LEAs) to secure adequate facilities for organised cultural training and recreative activities for anyone over compulsory school leaving age who was able and willing to profit by them. The Ministry of Education's 1947 pamphlet *Further Education* called this 'learning for leisure'.[2] Local authorities were expected to extend educational and social resources greatly so

264

as to enable people, 'to deal competently and democratically with the complex political questions of our time, or to develop those interests and activities which go to the making of a full and satisfying life', thereby 'making for individual happiness and ... a civilised community'.[3] This exemplary liberal perspective envisaged further education as 'a synthesis between the utilitarian and the cultural – so that a wide choice of educational activities may be brought within the range of the imagination of all'.[4] In a written reply to a parliamentary question in February 1946, Ellen Wilkinson, the Minister of Education, made it clear that the Government regarded the LEAs' responsibility for adult education as no less important than their other further education functions.[5]

The evening institutes were the focal point of much of this 'learning for leisure'. As a result of the encouragement given to this area of adult education, they became 'less junior vocational institutes and much more adult non-vocational centres'. The number of institutes more than doubled between 1947-1950, from just over 5,000 to almost 11,000 and the number of students increased from about 825,000 to nearly one-and-a-quarter million. Local community centres, whether provided by LEAs or other bodies, also increased considerably, and some progress was made in several counties with village or community colleges based on the ideas and practice of Henry Morris in Cambridgeshire.[6]

This 'learning for leisure' provision was expected to fall into three categories – theoretical studies, foreign languages and practical activities. The first would develop an appreciation and understanding of cultural traditions and achievements. Although the number of people interested in this category would be small compared with those engaged in the practical activities (which were 'far the most popular form of adult education'), nevertheless the importance of the group far outweighed its size 'for from its ranks come many of the leaders of those groups and associations which are such an important part of democratic society'. 'Women's specialized interests' which would enable 'young women contemplating marriage, as well as those already married, to increase their skill in housecraft' were also to be encouraged, as was the use of exhibitions, films, public libraries, and broadcasting.[7] But in this broad, if somewhat traditional, programme of formal and informal adult education, there was no mention of literacy or what would now be called adult basic education, which is surprising considering the Armed Services' extensive experience of illiteracy during the war.

The response of local authorities to the 1944 Act and the 1947 blueprint varied considerably, but overall, during the late 1940s, the Ministry found it difficult to persuade the Treasury to increase the resources for further education because of the LEAs' failure to use all the resources available. In 1947/48 they took up only £4 million of the £6 million available for further education priorities.[8]

When there was an expansion of further education, it was largely through direct LEA provision, but most LEAs expected their educational partners to undertake much of the cultural and academic liberal adult education envisaged in the Ministry's 1947 pamphlet. Circular 133 had reminded them that the Act required them to consult with the universities, educational associations and other bodies when preparing their schemes for further education.[9] Further education was a community effort in which the authority must play a leading part, but 'the first need is co-operative action by authorities, universities, and voluntary organisations of every kind'.[10] In particular LEAs should subsidise other bodies to make provision which they were unable or unwilling to make themselves.[11] To a very considerable degree, this was a continuation, or extension of the support which LEAs had long given to the 'Responsible Bodies' – the universities and the Workers Educational Association (WEA), but it also involved them in collaboration with others such as women's institutes, the YMCA, young farmers' clubs, youth organisations, drama and music societies.[12]

The Workers Educational Association

It is perhaps not surprising that the Labour government was favourably disposed towards the 'Responsible Bodies', especially the WEA: as many as fourteen members of the Government in 1945, including the Chancellor of the Exchequer, (as well as a very large number of MPs) were either former tutors or students, or members of the WEA Executive.[13]

The revised further education regulations, issued in August 1945, increased the scope and responsibilities of the universities and voluntary associations in the field of liberal studies and laid down specific machinery for consultation and joint planning between them and the LEAs. They sustained the practice of allowing grant aid of 75 per cent towards the Responsible Bodies' teaching costs to be given by the Ministry directly, in addition to any financial support which the LEAs gave for local organisations. The Ministry clearly saw liberal adult education as having 'a special value and significance' and expected it to increase substantially. It deflected the Treasury's concern about the financial implications on the grounds that its grant towards the teaching costs represented in practice only about 50 per cent of the total costs to the Responsible Bodies.[14]

Thus the WEA entered the post-war era in a mood of confidence. It had every expectation of Government support and believed that it had an important role to play in preparing people for the greater democratic participation in the affairs of the nation, widely expected under the new administration. In terms of branches, membership and student numbers, the WEA was already experiencing a boom by the end of the war. But this proved to be only temporary. Membership began to decline after 1947, and even an apparent 13 per cent increase in the number of students between 1945/6 and 1954/5 was somewhat illusory because so many of them were attending shorter courses.[15]

The WEA was failing to live up to two of its fundamental

principles: to be the agency for high level (university standard) liberal adult education; and to concentrate on the educational needs of the working class. Both failures have their origins in the pre-war period but they were now becoming all too apparent.[16] The first, exemplified by the drift away from three year tutorial classes to short courses, was summed up by R.H. Tawney in 1948:

> the valid – and very serious – criticism is ... that, in its eagerness to increase the number of classes and students (the WEA) has steadily relaxed the demands which it makes upon them ... Short classes have not been a preparation, or supplement to, tutorial classes, but a substitute for them ... a soft option.[17]

Similarly the WEA was 'gradually losing its claim to be a specifically working class organisation' as more and more of its students were drawn from the middle class and it became 'a more universal provider'.[18] One possible reason which it saw for its failure to attract working-class students after the war was the social reform programme of the Labour government. This was hailed as the realization of the social emancipation for which adult education had been preparing the working class for half a century. There was a widespread belief – shared and encouraged by the Government – that (apart from a few temporary post-war reconstruction problems), what they had been striving for had now been achieved. And as the WEA had cast its appeal to the working class partly as the educational instrument for achieving this social emancipation, its apparent arrival with the welfare state somewhat reduced this appeal. It was slow in re-defining its social purpose in the post-war world.[19]

The evolution of the WEA into a universal provider and the encouragement to the LEAs after 1944 to both expand and to spread their adult education wings put these intended partners on a collision course. It is true that the LEAs were still tarred with the 'night-school' brush and expected to concentrate on the less glamorous, bread-and-butter techno-logical, commercial and practical further education, while the WEA and the universities claimed the more prestigious liberal adult education.[20] But the differences were being narrowed to the extent that a few years later the Ashby Committee recognised that the LEAs had 'a lively interest in liberal adult education' and received evidence from the local authority Association of Education Committees calling for the abolition of the direct grant to the WEA, and its reduction to the status of an LEA agency. The suggestion that the LEAs could and should take over the functions of the WEA had been made from time to time ever since the passing of the 1944 Act. The consultation processes and joint planning required by the Act were insufficient to avoid occasional eruptions of mutual distrust.[21]

The Universities and Adult Education

Meanwhile, the universities were expanding their extramural staff and programmes. By 1947 all but one university (Reading) had established departments for this purpose, and in 1948 the new Universities Council for Adult Education announced that its members could no longer be bound to work through the WEA. Non-WEA university extramural provision began to expand very rapidly. Moreover, the universities took full advantage of the flexibility of the new regulations to enter fields hitherto regarded as the preserve of the WEA. In particular, they embarked on a massive expansion of one-year and shorter courses indistinguishable from the WEA's programme.[22]

Although the university extramural departments, like the WEA, were part-funded by the Ministry of Education as Responsible Bodies, the Government's influence over them was insubstantial in practice. His Majesty's Inspectors (HMI) were expected to ensure that they complied with the further education regulations, but apart from the requirements that the Responsible Bodies should confine themselves to liberal adult education (which they were quite willing to do), these were very unrestrictive. However, there was some concern within the Ministry of Education about the tendency throughout the country for the Responsible Bodies to change the pre-war balance between part-time tutors and full-time staff (who represented a much greater financial commitment). This came to a head in 1946 when the Oxford Extramural Delegacy appointed seven new full-time tutors, mostly to the north Staffordshire area, without prior consultation with the Ministry. HMI Dann was despatched to Oxford to warn the delegacy that this proportion of full-time tutors would require special justification as a long-term policy, and to ensure that in future the Ministry should be informed beforehand about appointments. An Oxford memorandum of a meeting between Dann and delegacy officials records the Ministry's concern about the post-war expansion of Oxford's full-time staff.[23]

Political Concerns – Cold War

The same memorandum (probably dating from early 1947) also notes that the Ministry felt some concern about the possible political bias of the staff.[24] This was not a new phenomenon: the old Board of Education had exercised a discreet surveillance over the Responsible Bodies for many years.[25] In 1944 the HMI's adult education committee had expressed concern that with the growth of informal adult education during the war, there had been a downgrading of the premium on tutors' qualifications, with a resultant decline in educational conduct and objectivity. Some of this was a genuine concern about pedagogical quality but it also apertained to what was seen as political bias, intemperance and injudiciousness.[26] This HMI suspicion about political reliability was carried over into the post-war world. The election of a Labour government did nothing to change it.

In some respect this is surprising because much of adult education was non-political and many of those engaged in it reflected the moderate Labourist ideology. The deflation of the WEA's social purpose – its sense of education for social, political and economic emancipation, 'knowledge for power' – had become muted, and its specific commitment to the working class had grown increasingly less visible.[27] The universities' refusal in 1948 to restrict themselves to workers' education, instead offering their services to any groups or bodies capable of providing suitable students, signalled a similar withdrawal from overt political commitment.[28]

However, there were tendencies in the other direction. The increase in full-time staff after the war drew a number of politically progressive and committed people into adult education which they saw as part of the process of changing British society fundamentally for the better. 'Many of those who sought social change after the second world war turned hopefully to the adult education movement, and expected its liberal structures to provide opportunities for attaining their objectives'.[29] In the 'battle of ideas' that grew in intensity as political polarisation sharpened after 1947, they saw it as legitimate and desirable to question and confront the dominant bourgeois ideological orthodoxies. In particular, through the Responsible Bodies' links with the trade unions, they saw their role as educating the trade union activists and combating the bourgeois tendency in the Labour Movement.[30] Therefore the considerable expansion of trade union work undertaken by both the WEA and some universities was seen as politically sensitive, especially as the left-wing politics of some of the tutors were anathema to many of the Labour Party's leading trade union supporters.[31]

There was little overt government influence exerted on the Responsible Bodies because in most cases they could be relied upon to take action themselves to contain any overstepping of the acceptable political limits.[32] They had learned the lessons of previous decades.[33] But occasional episodes do reveal that the Government maintained a surprisingly close surveillance

271

of the more politically sensitive activities of the Responsible Bodies. One occurred when a political debate involving three MPs (Labour, Independent Labour and Conservative) and a Liberal peer, was organised by the Newbury WEA branch and the Oxford Delegacy one Saturday in March 1948. The following Monday morning, the Labour MP was buttonholed by the Home Secretary, Chuter Ede, and asked to explain why he had been involved in a Communist meeting at Newbury. The incident reveals a significantly Cold War use of the term 'Communist' and a somewhat disconcerting degree of attention by the security services and their political master.[34]

A similarly close watch was kept by the Colonial Office on Oxford's extramural activities in West Africa during 1946-49. Initially Arthur Creech-Jones, the Secretary of State for the Colonies (and a former member of the Oxford Tutorial Classes Committee) supported this work. But when the suspicions grew that it was aiding and abetting the independence movements in Nigeria and the Gold Coast, Creech-Jones and his civil servants curtailed Oxford's activities and encouraged the British Council and other, politically more reliable, universities to take over from Oxford.[35] Likewise David Wiseman, a much respected former secretary of the British Institute of Adult Education, was prevented in 1950 from taking up an adult education post in the Gold Coast because of his previous membership of the Communist Party.[36]

In this rather indirect way did the Labour government maintain a degree of control over the Responsible Body liberal adult education it had encouraged to expand after the war.

Meanwhile, it took a very tentative first step towards opening up a new route of mature entry into higher education for a few adult students. In July 1947 George Tomlinson activated a section of the 1944 Education Act to provide for the award of twenty state scholarships 'for students of mature age'. These scholarships were 'to provide opportunities for

University Education to men and women over 25 years of age who were unable to undertake a University course at the normal age but whose aptitudes and qualifications subsequently appear likely to enable them to derive full benefit from a University course of study'.[37] This very cautious arrangement was continued and slightly expanded during the later years of the Labour government.[38]

The Limits of Achievement

After 1944 the LEAs were encouraged to adopt a broadly liberal and co-operative approach to non-vocational further education in collaboration with their 'Responsible Body' partners. However, there is little evidence that this stemmed directly from government policy rather than the inclinations of senior Ministry officials. The result was a considerable, if uneven, expansion of non-vocational further education provision. There was also an initial expansion of WEA provision, smiled upon by a friendly government, but this was not sustained, partly because the WEA's once protected territory was increasingly encroached upon by both the LEAs and the universities, and partly because the WEA was slow to formulate a new approach to adult education to suit the post-war welfare society. The universities were also allowed to take advantage of a lax state funding mechanism and the equally non-restrictive new further education regulations to expand and broaden their adult education activities.

However, when this generally liberal and expansionist *laissez-faire* approach was somewhat undermined by the Government's concerns about possible political bias or political activism in adult education after the outbreak of the Cold War, the WEA and the universities experienced a greater degree of restraint.

By 1951 adults were offered greater opportunities for education than at any time in the past, and many more of them than before the war were using those opportunities to

273

enrich their leisure. But the post-war vision of large numbers of adults learning 'to deal competently and democratically with the complex political questions of our time' in a participatory democracy had faded.

Notes

[1] Ministry of Education, Pamphlet Number 8, *Further Education*, HMSO 1947, paragraphs 74-5 and 102.

[2] *Ibid*, pp32-70.

[3] *Ibid*, paragraphs 74-5.

[4] *Ibid*, paragraph 196.

[5] PRO ED 34/35.

[6] Ministry of Education, *Further Education*, paragraphs 128-30; N.A. Jepson, 'The Local Authorities and Adult Education', in S.G. Raybould (ed), *Trends in English Adult Education*, Heinemann, London 1959, pp83-119 (pp102, 105-8); PRO ED 135/10 and 136/730.

[7] Ministry of Education, *Further Education*, paragraphs 103-19, 123-4.

[8] P. Gosden, *The Education System Since 1944*, Martin Robertson, 1983, p165.

[9] Ministry of Education, Circular 133, *Schemes of Further Education*, 1947 paragraph 5.

[10] Ministry of Education, *Further Education*, paragraphs 76-7.

[11] *Ibid*, paragraph 95.

[12] N.A. Jepson, *op cit*, pp104-5.

[13] E.J. King, 'The Relationship Between Adult Education and Social Attitudes in English Industrial Society', unpublished PhD. thesis, University of London 1955, p265; M. Stocks, *The Workers Educational Association*, George Allen and Unwin, London 1953; p143; B. Jennings, *Knowledge is Power: A Short History of the WEA 1903-78*, Hull University 1979, p50. Mary Stocks put the number of WEA MPs as 56, but Margaret Cole counted over 100 (paper presented by F.V. Pickstock to the International Graduate Summer School, Oxford, 109 August 1978).

[14] Ministry of Education, *Further Education*, paragraphs 94-5; PRO ED 34/35 and 46/448.

[15] R. Fieldhouse, *The WEA: Aims and Achievements 1903-1977*, Syracuse University 1977, pp 15, 19, 34, 40 and 46.

[16] *Ibid*, pp15-34.

[17] Letter from R.H. Tawney to S.G. Raybould, 29 September 1948, quoted in Fieldhouse, *The WEA, op cit*, pp26-7.

[18] *Ibid*, pp30 and 24. The WEA had long faced rivalry in the field of workers' education from the National Council of Labour Colleges (NCLC), which was financed by trade unions, and adopted an

uncompromisingly socialist approach. In the post-war period the NCLC mainly ran correspondence courses, but the WEA faced new rivalry from educational schemes run by trade unions themselves, independent of both the NCLC and the WEA's Trade Union Committee (WETUC).

[19] J.F.C. Harrison, *Learning and Living*, Routledge and Kegan Paul, London 1961, pp344-5, 350 and 359. One of the WEA's claims to consideration was its voluntary, democratic character. Most of its work was carried by voluntary workers, a feature which it pointed out made for cheap provision, as well as an example of how democratically run voluntary bodies could co-operate with the State to provide services without bureaucracy.

[20] *Ibid*, pp314 and 325.

[21] Ministry of Education, *The Organisation and Finance of Adult Education in England and Wales* (The Ashby Report), HMSO 1954, pp28-31 and 40-41; N.A. Jepson, *op cit*, p117; Fieldhouse, *The WEA, op cit*, pp31 and 36-7.

[22] *Ibid*, pp34-5.

[23] Oxford Extramural Delegacy archives (now in the Bodleian Library), staff tutors' files, undated memorandum and Tutorial Classes Committee Minutes, 22 November 1947; PRO ED 80/29, note on discussion concerning full-time tutors, 10 December 1946; R. Fieldhouse, *Adult Education and the Cold War*, Leeds University 1985, p29.

[24] *Ibid*.

[25] See R. Fieldhouse, 'Bouts of Suspicion: Political Controversies in Adult Education, 1925-1944' in B. Simon (ed), *The Search for Enlightenment*, Lawrence & Wishart, London 1990, pp153-72.

[26] *Ibid*, pp168-9.

[27] R. Fieldhouse, *The WEA, op cit*, pp43-5 and 49-50.

[28] *Ibid*, p34.

[29] R. Fieldhouse, *Adult Education and the Cold War, op cit*, p1.

[30] *Ibid*, p14.

[31] R. Fieldhouse, *The WEA, op cit*, p37 and *Adult Education and the Cold War, op cit*, pp30-1 and 38-50.

[32] *Ibid*.

[33] R. Fieldhouse, 'Bouts of Suspicion', *op cit*.

[34] R. Fieldhouse, *Adult Education and the Cold War, op cit*, pp23-4.

[35] *Ibid*, pp55-66.

[36] *Ibid*, p67.

[37] PRO, ED 46/472, Ministry of Education Circular Number 185, 1 November 1948.

[38] *Ibid*, minute papers 14 September 1949 and 22 May 1950 and notes of a meeting on 24 October 1949.

Art and Architecture for the People?

Nigel Glendinning

> It is conceivable that we are now entering a period in which the visual arts will once more take their place as the major intellectual interest not only of a few specialists but of the average citizen.
>
> Trystan Edwards, *The Things Which Are Seen, a Philosophy of Beauty*, new and enlarged edition, 1947

The census returns for 1951 listed 16,548 men and women working as painters, sculptors and engravers in England and Wales; 623 more than there had been in 1931. There were 1,089, additionally, in Scotland in the 1950s, but the grand total is only 5,949 more than that of a hundred years earlier, with a very much smaller population. The figures for architects, on the other hand, tell a different story. There were 15,767 in England and Wales, and 1,932 more in Scotland in 1951, as compared with 10,265 in 1931, and 2,971 in 1851, when the master-builder tradition still persisted. The expansion of more than 70 per cent in relation to the 1931 tally reflects the emergence of a new type of architect – the town planner – whose arrival on the scene in increasing numbers was a significant phenomenon in post-war Britain.

Transforming the Home Environment

Town planning was not a new activity; there was already an Institute for it in London by 1910. In the 1920s, George L.

Pepler could define the subject as 'the control of the use of all land, in accordance with a plan having as its definitive object the greatest common good', and planners like Patrick Abercrombie and Thomas Sharp, before and after the Second World War, firmly established the criteria for better cities.[1] The need to relieve the pressure on population centres such as Glasgow and London led, during the war, to the idea for a series of New Towns.[2] No less than fourteen of these were begun between 1947 and 1950, and several leading architects undertook major planning roles: G.A. Jellicoe at Hemel Hempstead; Frederick Gibbert at Harlow; and Bertold Lubetkin at Peterlee – a town named after a famous miners' leader from Durham. Some of the more inventive housing designs were introduced at Peterlee, particularly in the south-western neighbourhood, where two architects from the development corporation, Peter Daniel and Frank Dixon, collaborated with the abstract painter Victor Pasmore.[3]

In major cities, much architectural and planning effort went into the provision of new public housing to replace pre-war slums and bomb-damaged areas. In London, in the wake of the Patrick Abercrombie and George Henry Forshaw plan for the County (1943), well built neighbourhoods, with plenty of open space and appropriate facilities, were the real priority: providing a healthier environment and more pleasant surroundings for the next generation. It was recognised that architecture could be an instrument for social change, with perhaps some input from sociologists. Charles Madge, who was Social Development Officer for the New Town of Stevenage at the time, argued that housing ought to respond to 'the evolving family and ... the nexus of emotion between a man and his wife and children'.[4] Such psycho-social imperatives were just as important for the architect as the internal logic of 'cost, materials, social organisation and economic need'.

Inevitably there were conflicting views about aims and style, but a fresh impulse was given in the modernist direction by technical developments like prefabrication and the on-site casting of concrete slabs. Architects and engineers, some of whom came to England as exiles or refugees in the 1930s, facilitated or encouraged new ways of doing things.[5] Modernist practices were, however, entering a new phase.[6] In 1951 Bertold Lubetkin, for instance, felt that the reaction against the early militant stage of modernist architecture had brought with it 'romantic tendencies, a preoccupation with the particular, with details, with materials as such, and the flight from objectivity'.[7] This was the escape of the petit bourgeois into a world of *gemütlichkeit*, suburban timidity and conformist modesty. Lubetkin and his partners in Tecton struck off in a different direction, and sought to humanize their treatment of abstract forms in public housing, while responding to the normal economic and planning imperatives.

Tecton put these principles into practice in three blocks of flats at Spa Green on Rosebery Avenue, completed for Finsbury Borough Council in 1951, and built on the box-frame principle (for the first time in Britain) on a pleasantly sloping site opposite the Sadlers' Wells Theatre.[8] The group produced a pattern of dark and light on the outside, through windows, balconies and vents on stairwells. Inside, they civilised the living conditions. Double-doored hatches between the living-room and the kitchen minimised invasive cooking smells. The balcony was intended to serve as extra storage and also as play-space for young children, 'accessible from the living-room, and under supervision from the kitchen'. Special attention was paid to sound insulation; a central heating and hot water supply was included, and there was a Garchey system of refuse disposal. Furthermore, in those pre-tumble-dryer days, the roofs were planned as covered drying spaces, with an aerofoil section to induce a flow of air with the slightest wind.

The same concern to transform the home environment of ordinary people can be found in most post-war developments. A typical example is the Pimlico estate, at Churchill Gardens, which benefited from its proximity to the river. There the young architects Philip Powell and Hidalgo Moya created an imaginative combination of high-rise blocks and grassy open spaces, with lower terraces of housing at the perimeter of the site.[9] A particularly striking feature was the heat accumulator: a giant thermos flask to store hot water for the district heating system, preheated by the exhaust steam from alternators at the Battersea Power Station, and piped under the river to an insulated steel tank within a glass-walled tower. Other facilities included a parade of shops, a community centre, day nursery, three nursery schools, four pubs, and an underground car park for 200 cars, with a service station. Construction was started in 1948, and the estate won an award during the Festival of Britain.

Environmental factors were equally important in other types of building project, such as hospitals, factories and schools. Howard V. Lobb's Bourne Secondary Modern at Ruislip and the Field End Primary at Eastholt for the Middlesex County Council, were the first schools planned to meet the new requirements of the 1944 Act.[10] Peter Peri – Hungarian in origin, but naturalised English – made sculptures on nursery rhymes for Field End (1946). But there was more panache in Denis Clarke-Hall's Secondary school for Richmond in Yorkshire, designed though not built before the war, and considered to be 'the first school in England to illustrate the possibilities of the contemporary architectural idiom in planning and design'.[11] Hertfordshire County Council and its architect C.H. Aslin, soon became a by-word for excellent schools and ingenious use of prefabrication, while Alison and Peter Smithson brought an outstanding structural clarity to the school at Hunstanton in Norfolk they completed in 1954.[12] The Hospital for St Albans and Mid-Herts by the Architects' Co-operative Partnership, and the Londonderry Hospital on a thirty-acre site two miles outside the city with spectacular views, by Yorke, Rosenberg and Mardall, were other influential projects of the period.

New technology, good design and enhanced working conditions were combined in the best factories. Concrete shell structures sharpened the interest of the rubber factory at

Brynmawr, built by the Architects' Co-operative Partnership with engineering support from Ove Arup (1949). Rudolf Frankel introduced a barrel-vaulted roof pattern into a clothing factory at Congleton in Cheshire, and achieved spare and elegant lines in a design for a service station at Birmingham.[13] Social innovation was to be found in the welfare centre built for the North Thames Gas Board at Beckton in East Ham, which was 'the first of its kind in this country', providing canteen, games room with bar and billiards, and other facilities. The same organisation commissioned an attractively glazed canteen by Elie Mayorcas, at Bromley-by-Bow.[14]

The Festival of Britain – Art For All

A particular focus for architecture, art and design in the Labour years was created by the Festival of Britain. The original idea came from a Government committee which had been asked to report on the whole question of British participation in fairs and exhibitions.[15] They suggested that a Universal International Exhibition should be held in Central London in 1951 – one hundred years on from the Great Exhibition of Victorian times. This deadline was ultimately met, although very little seems to have been planned before 1946. In that year, Misha Black combined information about the 1851 Exhibition with some suggestions for 1951 in *The Ambassador*, and Hilton Wright illustrated the article with a modernist Crystal Palace on stilts by the riverside, topped off with a pylon and helicopter pad. The major LCC contribution – a new Concert Hall – was formally announced in the autumn of 1948, yet suggestions for the South Bank in general were still being advanced in architectural journals the following year.[16] Robert Matthew and Leslie Martin's Festival Hall proved a striking new venue for music in the capital, and the acoustics were carefully planned. But external additions in the 1960s unfortunately ruined the elegant north façade overlooking the Thames. Temporary, yet highly inventive, Festival structures included Philip Powell and Hidalgo Moya's Skylon, Ralph Tubbs's Dome of Discovery, and the Royal Pavilion by the Architects' Co-operative Partnership: a plywood construction on a heptagonal plan, with laminated timber arches.

Art was vigorous in the immediate post-war period and played a full role in the Festival. There were murals by Graham Sutherland, John Piper, Keith Vaughan and others inside Festival buildings, as well as sculptures by Henry Moore and Barbara Hepworth.[17] The *New Statesman* cast a slightly ironic eye over these displays, and found the general character of the work self-indulgent and retrogressive: back to Victorianism, back to decoration and away from the functional.[18] But, in relation to the artwork, such a view seems wilfully misleading. The murals were certainly more than mere decoration, and represented the commitment of artists to a wider audience. Some were obviously didactic as well as visually powerful, and there was a clear historical lesson about land ownership in Stephen Bone's *Battle for Land* at the Town Planning Pavilion for the Lansbury Neighbourhood. Outside the Festival, Ivon Hitchens's vast painting on the role of dance in human life, for Cecil Sharp House in Regents Park Road, London (1950-54), had an equally evident social dimension.[19]

During this period artists felt the need to communicate more widely, whatever their style. After the First World War, surrealists argued that the shared imagery of the unconscious mind enabled the general public to respond to their paintings instinctively. The fact that surrealist devices filtered into various types of publicity image in the post-war years, seems to prove their point.[20] Abstract painters, for their part, held that the musical or architectural character of their art guaranteed its expressive or imaginative appeal to others. Ben Nicholson associated abstraction with the sense of liberation, and described it as 'a powerful, unlimited and universal language'.[21]

Artists also faced a more responsive public in the decades after the war. Patrick Heron claimed that the 'section of our population which interests itself in modern art has very greatly increased in numbers since 1939'.[22] Julian Trevelyan felt that a fellow-feeling amongst painters of different tendencies during the war, had led to 'the more tolerant and catholic acceptance of various styles that has come about since'.[23] The hatred and fear of conservatives for surrealism and abstraction, furthermore, no longer found such strident and aggressive expression.[24] The Second World War had brought a reappraisal of the role of the creative artist. Cyril Connolly had voiced the opinion that artists, like scientists, mystics, philosophers and saints, helped to extend 'human consciousness', and contributed to 'the domination of the inhuman world'.[25] The artist was parasitic on, yet energized, the non-artists in society. Connolly's *Horizon* included articles on leading contemporaries and on younger artists of promise. John Piper designed the original cover.

Prints made during the period likewise helped artists to command a new public. The establishment of Contemporary Lithographs Ltd in the late 1930s had made original works by leading artists available at relatively inexpensive prices, ranging from 10s 6d (52.5p) to 30s 9p (157.9p).[26] And the Artists' International Association (AIA) had more specifically targeted a mass audience when it launched a scheme called Everyman Prints in 1939, depicting scenes from contemporary life. After the war, the AIA ran a Picture Hiring Library, lending to individuals and organisations at the fairly modest rate of 7s 6d (37.5p) per picture per month.[27] Modern art also appeared in books and magazines. John Lehmann, Frederick Muller and Poetry London were publishers with an excellent eye for interesting artists. For Muller, Walter Neurath commissioned John Craxton, Michael Ayrton, Robert Colquhoun and others, between 1944 and 1946, to illustrate a series of poetic anthologies called 'New Excursions into English Poetry'. Poetry London published Mervyn Peake's brilliantly atmospheric drawings for

282

Coleridge's *Ancient Mariner*,[28] Lucian Freud's sharp outlines for Nicholas Moore's *The Glass Tower* (1944), and Ceri Richards' exuberant accompaniment to Dylan Thomas's poem 'The Force that through the green fuse drives the flower' (1947).[29] Several artists also reached a larger audience through design work. Prints by Eric Ravilious for Wedgwood Pottery, designs by Sutherland and Henry Moore for Ascher Fabrics, and by Sutherland again for Helios, all featured in the *Britain Can Make It* Exhibition in 1946.[30] Edward Bawden, John Minton, Eduardo Paolozzi and Graham Sutherland also produced wallpaper designs; and posters for Ealing Studios' films were produced by Edward Ardizzone, Barnett Freedman, Edward Bawden and John Piper.[31]

New Patrons

In these cases, industry looked to artists, who were not normally thought of as commercial, for quality and fresh inspiration, and the cachet of their names. The artists probably did not need too much persuasion, although they were beginning, at the time, to enjoy new sources of moral and material support through the Arts Council. The provision of living allowances for artists had long been under discussion in progressive circles. Proposals were already being aired in 1910 in Rupert Brooke's essay on *Democracy and the Arts*, and his text was published in 1946 by Geoffrey Keynes to encourage fresh government thinking on this issue. In that same year, the Dartington Hall *Report on the Visual Arts* made a strong case for the continuation and extension of state patronage for living artists. Not everybody approved of this, but Arts Council acquisitions and bursaries certainly helped contemporary work to flourish in Britain during the next two decades.[32]

A further source of moral, if not financial, support from 1946 was the Institute of Contemporary Arts (ICA), which was soon responsible for organising a series of important

283

exhibitions and events.[33] 'Forty Years of Modern Art', an exhibition held at the Academy Cinema, was followed by 'Forty Thousand Years of Modern Art' at the same venue, in February and December 1948. Exhibitions at the ICA's Dover Street premises started in 1950, and the 'Aspects of British Art' show in December that year coincided with the official opening. Mobiles and stabiles by William Turnbull and Eduardo Paolozzi were among the exhibits – Alexander Calder's seminal work in the genre was seen and much discussed in London at the time – and William Gear displayed a suppleness in the abstract idiom that brought support from the Arts Council, and excited the admiration of John Berger when Gear had a show at Gimpel fils in 1951.[34] Berger was critical of the more rigid and geometric manner of some non-figurative artists, and disapproved of the romantic and literary leanings of many British painters, which made their work too private in his opinion.[35] Several of the younger artists shared Berger's views on the contemporary scene, and confronted the harsher realities of British life more readily than their seniors. David Carr was one of these: a collector and admirer of the stark industrial townscapes of L.S. Lowry, and a recorder himself, as an artist, of working people, factory subjects and the interface between man and machine.[36] Prunella Clough shared his concern and also painted industrial subjects at this time; as did Merlyn Evans.[37] Photographers tackled dour environments even more directly, and between 1945 and 1952 Nigel Henderson, living in Bethnal Green, captured the character of the area in a notable series of photographs and collages.[38]

The interest in popular motifs and folk-art in the 1940s and 1950s reflects a similar preoccupation with non-élitist aspects of British culture: it is evident in John Piper's articles on villages, shops, market squares, pub traditions and interiors,[39] and in two books on popular English art, one by Margaret Lambert and Enid Marx, and the other by Noel Carrington and Clarke Hulton (1945).[40] There was also an exhibition of popular art at the Whitechapel Gallery during the Festival in

1951. A scientific or historical concern to capture accurately the quality and character of craft traditions might well conceal a desire to preserve the past. But the general mood was against looking back. The need to rebuild the economy and create better opportunities for all, and a widely held desire for joint endeavour and social progress, was surely reflected in the art and architecture of the period. Amongst architects, the old-style prima donnas made way for teamwork and partnerships, and design objectives put social priorities above the aesthetic. Sometimes, of course, the social results were not what was planned. High-rise blocks, for instance, designed to provide more open space and better living conditions, created as many social problems as they solved. The new form was soon recklessly exploited, furthermore, to cope with the excessive growth of city population. In art, Arts Countil policy and patronage sometimes seemed to impose a rather limited vision on the public. Yet there was less narrow self-absorption among artists. Even the more romantic souls – be they expressionist, surrealist or abstract – turned to social, national or existential themes, opted for less extreme abstraction in non-figurative work, and added more human figures to their landscapes.[41]

Notes

[1] Quoted by P.L. Dickinson in *An Outline History of Architecture of the British Isles*, Cape, London 1926, p300. Important early contributions to the development of the aims and objectives of town planning had been made by William Morris in his lectures on 'Art and Socialism' (1884), by Ebenezer Howard (1898) and Patrick Geddes (1904).

[2] Wartime discussions on suitable locations for New Towns are reflected in an editorial in the *New Statesman*, 'New Towns and War Industries', 20 June 1942.

[3] F.J. Osborne and Arnold Whittick, *The New Towns. The Answer to Megalopolis*, Leonard Hill, London 1963, pp224ff and Plate 34. The south-western neighbourhood of Peterlee was completed in 1961.

[4] Charles Madge, 'Reflections from Aston Park', *Architectural Review (AR)* 104, 1948, p109. Ruth Glass also contributed to the sociological debate, in 'Social Aspects of Town Planning', *AR* 97, 1945, p67. There was

a section largely concerned with social structures in relation to architecture in *Towards a New Britain*, The Architectural Press, London, n.d., pp30ff, and much analysis of social factors in Tom Harrisson's 'Tomorrow: The City', in *The Saturday Book*, Number 4, L. Russell, (ed), Hutchinson, London 1944, pp73ff. For details of the pre-war social objectives and standards in the Quarry Hill development at Leeds, *cf.* John Madge, *The Rehousing of Britain*, Pilot Press, London 1945, p15.

[5] Notable foreign architects who came to England before the war included Serge Chermayeff and Bertold Lubetkin from Russia, Walter Gropius and Eric Mendelsohn from Germany, and Ernô Goldfinger. Engineers included Ove Arup and Felix Samuel. In relation to innovative techniques, Arup published an important article on box-frame construction in *Architect's Journal (AJ)* 101, 1945, pp439-440. There was an interesting exchange of letters on the subject between Samuely and Arup in the same journal: *AJ* 102, 1945, pp149 and 257-258.

[6] The sense of change is reflected in the term 'post-modern' that begins to be used at the period. Cf. Joseph Hudnut, 'The Post-Modern House', *Architectural Record* 97, May 1945, pp70-74.

[7] *AR* 109, 1951, pp135-146.

[8] Lubetkin explained the technical advances which made a freer treatment of the outside of the Spa Green flats possible. Tecton designs evolved from the traditional load-bearing external walls of Highpoint I (1934), through the transversal wall solution in Highpoint II (1937-38), with some supporting columns, to the Danish system of cross-wall construction used for Spa Green after the war. This last system allowed variations to be made in the external surface, and eliminated the necessity for internal beams and stancheons.

[9] *AJ* 102, 1945, p105. Cf also *AR* 109, 1951, pp70ff.

[10] *AR* 104, 1948, p129. For a critical review by Robert Townsend, cf *AR* 106, 1949, pp154ff.

[11] *AR* 106, 1949, p154.

[12] Cf *The Independent Group: Post-war Britain and the Aesthetics of Plenty*, David Robbins, (ed), MIT Press, Cambridge, Mass 1990, pp109-111.

[13] On Brynmawr, cf *AR* 102, 1947, pp63ff. There was an article on four factories by Frankel in *AR* 105, 1949, pp167ff. Frankel's service station in Birmingham was included in a review of good contemporary work by J.M. Richards in 'The Next Step?', *AR* 107, 1950, pp165ff. Frederick Gibberd's steel-rolling mill at Scunthorpe, and Eric Ross's engine test house and aircraft assembly hall at Filton, near Bristol, were other significant designs of the period.

[14] *AR* 110, 1951, pp49ff and 316-317.

[15] Information on the background to Festival planning is from *The Ambassador: The British Export Journal for Textiles and Fashions*, Number 8, 1946, pp20ff. I am grateful to Hilton Wright for drawing this important article by Misha Black to my attention.

[16] Cf articles by Gordon Cullen and Clive Entwistle: 'Bankside Regained', *AR* 105, 1949, and 'An Alternative Plan for the South Bank', *ibid*, pp113ff. The announcement about the new concert hall – not apparently at that stage a replacement for The Queen's Hall, which it was intended to rebuild – is reported in an article by Desmond Shawe-Taylor, *New Statesman (NS)*, 23 October 1948.

[17] Graham Sutherland's painting was entitled 'The Origins of the Land', and Keith Vaughan's 'Discovery'. There were also murals by Edward Bawden, Kenneth Rowntree, Feliks Topolski and others.

[18] *NS*, 5 May 1951.

[19] On Hitchens' mural painting, cf Patrick Heron, *Ivon Hitchens*, Penguin Books, Harmondsworth 1955, p12 and Plates 30 and 31.

[20] Cf. Bevis Hillier, *The Decorative Arts of the Forties and Fifties*, Studio Vista, London 1975, pp44-49.

[21] For theories of abstraction given by contemporaries, cf *A Tribute to Ben Nicholson*, Exhibition Catalogue, Crane Kalman Gallery, 3 July-10 August 1974, and the essay on 'Art in Europe at the end of the Second World War' by Herbert Read, in *The Philosophy of Modern Art*, Faber, London 1952, pp50-52. The Nicholson quotation comes from *Horizon*, IV Number 22, October 1941, p276. The concept of a universal language, applied by Nicholson to abstraction, was commonly related to all painting by seventeenth- and eighteenth-century theorists.

[22] 'The Criticism of Contemporaries', *NS*, 2 October 1948.

[23] *Indigo Days*, Macgibbon and Kee, London 1957, p131.

[24] Aggressive comments on modern art in the 1930s are particularly common in the pages of a periodical entitled *Art and Reason*. A contributor writing in August 1937 believed that England should follow Hitler's example, and hand over 'artists who persist in following the cult of modernism ... to the State for sterilisation as dangerous lunatics' (*Art and Reason*, Volume III, Number 32, 1937, p3).

[25] 'Comment', *Horizon*, Volume 1, Number 4, April 1940, pp229-234.

[26] Prices are taken from the advertisement inside the cover of *Horizon*, Volume 1, Number 7, August 1940.

[27] *Avant-Garde British Printmaking*, F. Carey and A. Griffiths, (eds), Trustees of the British Museum, London 1990, p19. On the AIA Library scheme, cf. *NS*, 17 March 1951.

[28] On the involvement of Neurath in Frederick Muller commissions, cf. *A Paradise Lost: The Neo-Romantic Imagination in Britain 1935-55*, David Mellor (ed), Lund Humphries, London 1987, p45. For Peake's Coleridge illustrations, cf. *Poetry London*, X, 1944, pp197-204.

[29] *Poetry London*, XI, 1947.

[30] Council of Industrial Design, *Design 46*, HMSO, London 1946, pp26, 54-55, 60 and 90. Cf. also *AR* 111, 1952, pp193-194; and *Did Britain Make It? British Design in Context 1946-86*, Penny Sparke, (ed), Design Council, London n.d., p87.

[31] C.C. Oman and J. Hamilton, *Wallpapers: A History and Illustrated*

Catalogue of the Collection in the Victoria and Albert Museum, London, Sotheby Publications, 1982, pp252-255, (Pattern Books Nos. 707, 709, 710 and Edward Bawden, Nos. 756-769). On posters for British films, cf. article by Osbert Lancaster, *AR* 105, 1949, p88.

[32] R.F. Harrod, *The Life of John Maynard Keynes*, Macmillan, London 1951, p522. Opposition to state patronage of the arts came from Herbert Read in 'The Fate of Modern Painting', *Horizon*, Volume XVI, Number 95, 1947, pp242ff; and Bernard Shaw in 'Art Workers and the State', *NS*, 26 April 1947.

[33] Cf. David Robbins (ed), *op cit*, pp13ff.

[34] *NS*, 1951, pp422-423.

[35] Cf. his review of 'British Painting, 1925-1950' at the New Burlington Gallery, *NS*, 1951, p504. Berger was critical of John Piper and also of Francis Bacon, whose 'horrors' were 'not justified by any spirit of tragedy' in his view.

[36] Cf. Bryan Robertson's essay on Carr in *David Carr: The Discovery of an Artist*, Quartet Books, London 1987, pp13ff.

[37] *Ibid*, pp28-30 (on Prunella Clough), and pp21-22 (on Merlyn Evans).

[38] David Robbins (ed), *op cit*, pp76ff.

[39] *AR* 97, 1945, March; 99, 1946, February; 106, 1949, pp265ff.

[40] Noel Carrington, *Popular Art in Britain*, illustrated by Clarke Hulton, Penguin Books, Harmondsworth 1945; and Margaret Lambert and Enid Marx, *English Popular Art*, Batsford, London 1945 and 1951.

[41] In artists discussed by David Mellor in *A Paradise Lost ...*, *op cit*, the change of direction is particularly noticeable in the work of Leslie Hurry, *op cit*, p84. Barbara Hepworth exhibited thirty-one drawings of surgeons at work in operating theatres at the Lefevre Gallery in 1948. And even Ben Nicholson, in titling his pictures around 1945, moved away from total abstractions like *Painting* or *Painted Relief* to the more concrete or suggestive *Still Life* or *Parrot's Eye*.

Myths of Consensus and Fables of Escape: British Cinema 1945–51

Andy Medhurst

> It's because we are English that we're sticking up for our right to be Burgundian.
>
> Mrs. Pemberton in *Passport to Pimlico* (1949)

This chapter is best begun with a series of denials. It is not a history of the British film industry between 1945 and 1951, nor a detailed critical evaluation of 'great films' produced in those years, nor a survey of the crucial place of cinema-going within patterns of post-war leisure. All of those topics deserve attention, but the limitations of space impose a different focus. What I hope to do is to sketch an outline of the broad thematic concerns of popular British cinema in post-war Labour Britain and to offer some necessarily speculative thoughts on the connections between those texts and their social contexts.

The nature of such connections is, of course, a notoriously problematic area. The spectre of 'reflectionism', that wilfully naive belief that fictional texts can be read as factual documents, shadows any attempt to relate cinema to society, but nevertheless it seems incontrovertible to me that the films of an era must bear the traces of the times that produced them. As to whether those traces were consciously placed there by socially-conscious film-makers, have become apparent with the advantages of hindsight, or are the product of critical over-ingenuity – the jury is still out on that.

One fact can be stated with confidence: the end of the Second World War saw British films at a peak of both audience popularity and critical respectability. In the 1930s, mass audiences had, with significant exceptions (most notably music-hall comedies and imperial epics), preferred Hollywood's product, revelling in its gloss and panache, adoring its stars, relishing its pace, appreciating its apparent egalitarianism. Most British films, by contrast, seemed staid, condescending and parochial. The exigencies of war changed that – British films were forced to democratise themselves rapidly and audiences responded accordingly. The cinema became a prime site of national cohesion, and whether it was Noel Coward going down with his ship or George Formby unearthing Nazi spies, the underlying ideological project was the same.

This is not to say that all wartime films concerned themselves specifically with topical narratives and hegemonic calls for national togetherness. Gainsborough Studios carved out an exceptionally lucrative niche for themselves by producing a series of full-bloodedly escapist historical melodramas (memorably inaugurated by *The Man in Grey*, 1943) which allowed wartime women a welcome breathing-space of rapturous forgetfulness that momentarily banished the horrors and privations that awaited them outside the Odeon.

The critical establishment, however, was sternly, snobbishly disapproving towards Gainsborough's success. For them, such films sullied the acclaimed new maturity of British cinema, which rested primarily on its absorption of documentary influences into feature film-making techniques. A critical palate schooled on the worthy platitudes of Griersonian documentary could hardly be expected to appreciate the saturnine, Heathcliffian sadism of James Mason, or Margaret Lockwood's limited but irresistible repertoire of schemes and palpitations. Richard Winnington, the most astute critic of the day, was so enraged by Gainsborough's *The Wicked Lady* that he quite forgot the progressive liberalism he usually displayed in his columns for the *News Chronicle* and blimpishly damned it as 'an ugly hodge-podge of servant-girls' lore.'[1]

That remark comes from the first, 1946 edition of the *Penguin Film Review*, where Winnington was able to outline his preferred version of British cinema's recent achievements and post-war prospects. Gainsborough-phobia apart, it's a critical text of great richness, precisely summarising the tremulous optimism surrounding national cinema at that moment:

> It is in *Brief Encounter, Journey Together, I Know Where I'm Going, The Way to the Stars, Dead of Night* that you sense the magic possibilities of the British cinema, fragile encompassed, hardly daring to breathe. And when I meet a director or writer who says to me with passion and certainty, 'I'm going to make a film that will shake the daylights out of you even if it isn't box-office', I shall feel we might have started.[2]

The aesthetic advocated here is one which would value films made as personal expression rather than as commercial property, a very European aesthetic, one which Winnington must surely have known stood very little chance of surviving in the context of the British industry. His list of emblematic titles contains some very successful films, but none of them caught the public mood in quite the same way as *The Wicked Lady*, the most successful British film, in terms of the tainted box office, of 1946. It is for this reason that this chapter will not detain itself with accounts of many of the most critically revered and prestigious films of the period – I have no wish to deny the qualities of *A Matter of Life and Death, The Fallen Idol, Odd Man Out, Kind Hearts and Coronets, Black Narcissus, Hamlet,* and *The Third Man,* but their impact as social barometers was, at best, limited.

The artistic merits of *The Wicked Lady*, then, are not the

concern of this chapter, but what is crucial is how that film's narrative relates very closely to the social history of its moment of production. All dolled up in the usual elaborate Gainsborough trappings (the sumptuous excess of that studio's costumes were a strong selling point in an era of clothes rationing), it is, at its core, the story of a woman dissatisfied with the constrictions of traditional domesticity, a wife resentful of the subservient role her husband expected her to adopt. She seeks independence, exhilaration, self-determination, and while her chosen method of achieving these, becoming a gun-toting highwaywoman, may seem a little extreme, the underlying emotional pull clearly had resonances for the women of 1946, re-located in kitchen drudgery after wartime years of comparative autonomy.

Winnington would scoff at such an interpretation, but on closer inspection it becomes apparent that one of his own list of British favourites shares exactly the same fundamental story, for what is *Brief Encounter* but another tale of a woman seeking a world beyond the confines of conventionality? (There is a further subtextual level on which the film works, as a displacement of its author, Noel Coward's homosexuality).[3] A generic gulf separated the look, the style and the appeal of those two films, ensuring that for Winnington and his contemporaries they served as polar opposites of respectable and unacceptable British cinema, but Margaret Lockwood's pulsatingly sinful Barbara and Celia Johnson's tragically hemmed-in Laura were in many ways sisters under the skin. A third, less celebrated, member of their family was the murderous publican played by Googie Withers in *Pink String and Sealing Wax*, turning to murder to escape a loveless marriage in Victorian Brighton. All three films were released in the same month, December 1945, surely more synchronicity than coincidence.

Men also had problems in adjusting to post-war realities, though the films which dealt with their anxieties did not generally have to resort to such elaborate generic disguises. A whole cycle of spiv films showed disillusioned ex-servicemen and borderline gangsters threading their way through a London of bombsites and moral ambiguities, and their bleakness and sourness of tone has led some subsequent critics to compare them to Hollywood's roughly contemporaneous *films noirs*.[4] The startling *They Made Me A Fugitive* (1947) certainly laces its thriller plot with enough urban angst, bastardised Freud and gothic shadows to earn such a comparison, though a year later *Noose* could play the spiv card with a considerably lighter touch. Nigel Patrick's chippily ebullient black-marketeer in that film (one of the most extraordinary performances of the period) being a spiritual forefather of the market traders of *EastEnders* and *Only Fools and Horses*. That female transgressors did not always have to hide behind Gainsborough crinolines was established by *Good Time Girl*, a 1948 cautionary tale of how drinking in the wrong kind of nightclub could lead to a downward spiral of degradation, and the outlandish *No Room at the Inn*, from the same year, where wartime evacuees found themselves accommodated and then terrorised by a heavy-drinking voluptuary with the splendidly over-determined name of Mrs Voray.

Even gloomier than the spiv films in their depiction of a Britain anxiously piecing itself together were a looser cycle of psychological thrillers in which the conflicts are mainly internal, played out in the wracked consciousnesses of their protagonists. Rarely seen now, films like *The Upturned Glass* (1947) and *Daybreak* (1946, a suffocatingly atmospheric transposition of the flavour of 1930s French thrillers such as *Quai des Brumes*) stand with their more straightforwardly criminal peers as telling reminders that post-war audiences were not uniformly seized by dreams of social democratic progress. The wounds of the war were far from healed. This taste for dank morbidity and dark corners can also be detected in that usually most tireless standby of respectable British cinema, the literary adaptation, with the likes of *Uncle Silas* (1947) and, most famously, *Great Expectations* (1946).

A case could plausibly be made for that film's ending, those breathtaking images of John Mills tearing down the curtains in the Havisham house to let the light of day flood in, as a metaphorical attempt to stem the tides of post-war depression and brooding inwardness, and indeed Richard Winnington celebrated *Great Expectations* as the British film triumph he had been waiting for; but the fact remains that it is the earlier sequences of Miss Havisham's lovingly cultivated decay which linger most indelibly in the mind. The film's huge popularity with audiences is also best understood not in terms of a recognition of Winningtonian quality but as part of a broader taste for costume melodrama – Jean Simmons's Estella seems to have learned many of her tricks at the Margaret Lockwood school of entrapment.

So were there no other films that addressed, however tangentially or subtextually, the pressing political concerns of the time? There were a few, though even some of these showed a fondness for period dress, albeit of the recent past. Two film versions of middlebrow bestsellers tentatively considered key issues; *My Brother Jonathan* (1948) told of an idealistic doctor's fight to improve living conditions for industrial workers, and might thus be seen as a metaphorical contribution to the debates engendered by the founding of the NHS, while *Fame Is The Spur* (1947) was a rarity in having politics as the explicit centre of it narrative, tracing the rise to power and eventual disillusionment of a Labour politician modelled without much disguise on Ramsay MacDonald.

Other films from the late 1940s centred on politics tended to be comedies, and while it would be rash to draw definite conclusions from this, it seems noteworthy that 1949 (four weary, still-rationed years into an unexpectedly slow economic recovery, with the optimism of 1945 receding fast) delivered a particularly numerous outbreak of political skits. Some simply placed established comic performers in the novelty of political settings as part of extending their career longevity, so the Lancashire maestro of bodily vulgarily, Frank Randle, stood for the local council in *Somewhere in*

Politics, while Jack Warner did the same as head of his proto-sitcom London family in *Vote for Huggett*. The *Chiltern Hundreds* extracted some lukewarm mirth from the scenario of an aristocratic convert to Labour losing a by-election to the Tory representative, his butler. A fourth political comedy from 1949 was *Cardboard Cavalier*, a costume farce of Cavaliers and Roundheads which clearly sides with the fun-loving former against the pinched and puritanical latter. It's a film which celebrates the joys of gluttony, bawdiness and laughter, activities the Roundheads (several of whom look like none-too-distant relatives of Stafford Cripps) seek to severely ration if they can't ban them altogether.

This hostility towards control and longing for licence finds immeasurably fuller and more important realisation in what could legitimately be seen as the most memorable film of the entire period, yet another political comedy from 1949, *Passport to Pimlico*. A justly celebrated and much-analysed film, its intense topicality at the time of its release means that it remains saturated with prevailing assumptions and preconceptions about British society and indeed 'Britishness' itself.[5]

It is still, of course, far from a documentary (in fact, documentary discourse appears only to be parodied in its delicious fake newsreel sequence). It's a fantasy, a wry meditation on the pros and cons of living in Britain in the late 1940s, a gentle testing of the idea of alternatives, an exploration of ideological tensions for which the techniques of social comedy are particularly useful (and particularly welcome, the preceding post-war years being unusually devoid of substantial comic successes).

Its central comic conceit, that a small district in London discovers via a medieval charter that it is legally a part of Burgundy and not Britain, sets into play a beautifully orchestrated series of challenges to both established notions of national identity and the specific problems of Labour Britain. The running joke that elicited most sympathy from audiences at the time was the impatience with officialdom and bureaucracy (hence the blissful, carnivalesque delirium of the scene where the newly liberated inhabitants shred their ration books and identity cards in the local pub), qualities the film is keen to assign to Labour and Labour alone. Pimlico is an almost Thatcherite paradise of self-motivated small businesses, chafing at State restrictions – 'We're sick and tired of your voice in this country' being one of the more nakedly partisan lines of dialogue, directed from the residents' leader to an interfering posse of civil servants. Yet despite their economic self-sufficiency and hatred of form-filling, the new Burgundians are one-nation Tories, committed to distinctly un-Thatcherite concepts of community and consensus. They believe in teamwork, in the need for national unity in their tiny new nation, and can be seen serving communal meals that recall wartime British restaurants – but they do this only under pressure from outside forces, since to do so voluntarily would be to go further than community and embrace collectivism, and that, crucially, is the step they cannot take.

Pimlico/Burgundy is only prepared to flirt with collective organisation when it faces attack from a large, aggressive, outside power – the narrative twist here reconstructs Burgundy as Britain during the war, small, threatened, plucky and indomitable, all of which, in a devious sleight-of-hand that only becomes apparent after repeated viewings, positions socialist Britain as Nazi Germany. The geniality and warm-heartedness of the film prevents it fully going along that line, but the implication is planted, nonetheless. Britishness (here transposed into Burgundian-ness) thus becomes that which must be protected from the Socialist aggressor, and *Passport to Pimlico* subtly shifts to incorporate a double meaning: it is not only one of the first films to celebrate the Second World War as the good-old-days, but one of the first films of the Cold War too.

As the 1940s became the 1950s, British cinema produced a number of texts that dealt with the Cold War in a more unambiguous way. It largely avoided the McCarthyite excesses of Hollywood, but came close with 1951's bizarre *High Treason*, where a gang of subversives in duffle coats (their socially deviant ranks including cat-loving bachelors and devotees of discordantly modern classical music) storm Battersea Power Station. A less hysterical response to analogous concerns had come a year earlier, in a film also produced by the Boulting Brothers (so much for authorial consistency), *Seven Days to Noon*. Here a nuclear scientist, appalled at the uses to which his research might be put, threatens to detonate a bomb in central London if all further weapons production is not halted. It's a film of considerable tension and real political complexity, but something of a lone, sane, serious voice in the era of not only *High Treason* but a 1951 comedy called *Mr. Drake's Duck*, in which a farmer finds that his fowl is laying uranium eggs, leading to an agricultural nuclear panic, a military intervention and a farce of surpassing fatuousness.

The other vital aspect of Britain's post-war international status was the uncomfortable shift from Empire to Commonwealth. Later in the 1950s, feature films would tackle this directly, but in the Labour era traces of the debates tend to be found only in coded melodramas. Ealing Studios produced three films set in Australia, a trilogy which moved from celebrating the outback as a location for a British Western (*The Overlanders*, 1946), to considering tensions between settlers and colonial government (*Eureka Stockade*, 1949) and, eventually and most contentiously, the struggle between white colonisers and the indigenous black population (*Bitter Springs*, 1950). Backing off from the implications that might arise from any further consideration of the morality of Empire at a moment when large-scale black immigration was an issue of topical concern, Ealing stepped sideways to produce 1951's *Where No Vultures Fly*, the story of a white man's mission to 'civilise' Africa, but in the sense of setting up a wildlife reserve. All the trappings of the colonial adventure, with its increasingly unsustainable fantasy of 'exotic natives' and white-is-right, could thus still be

297

delivered, but cleverly hidden under a layer of animal welfare that no British audience could resist.

Where No Vultures Fly is also a film about Brits in uniform, and its immense popularity parallels that of the rise of the war film. Between 1945 and 1950, almost no films set during the war had been made, the focus being on questions of post-war adjustment, but by the turn of the decade the myth of the war as the good-old-days was strongly asserting itself throughout British popular culture. *Passport to Pimlico* clearly flirts with that myth, but its version of the war did bear some resemblance to the communal struggles fresh in the national memory. When the war re-emerges elsewhere, however, it is no longer the people's war but the prefect's war, the war where gung-ho meets tally-ho, the war won by chaps. A precursor of such antics, though of necessity more downbeat, was 1948's *Scott of the Antarctic*, where the key actors of the war genre-to-be (John Mills, John Gregson, Kenneth More) rehearse their tropes of masculine emotionlessness in a setting that at least has a metereological justification for all those stiff upper lips. The bulk of British war films lie outside the scope of this chapter, but the seeds were sown in 1950 with the success of *They Were Not Divided, The Wooden Horse* and *Odette*.[6]

The last is by far the most interesting and, given the way the genre would later organise its sexual politics, the least typical. It is no less enthralled by the stiff upper lip, but is at least prepared to concede that such lips belonged to women's faces as well as men's. As the eponymous heroine, a British spy captured and tortured in Nazi Germany, Anna Neagle's determination and fortitude go some way towards erasing the reputation for polite froth on which her stardom in the late 1940s had been founded. Neagle's earlier post-war films saw her located in the richer districts of London – *Piccadilly Incident, The Courtneys of Curzon Street, Spring In Park Lane, Maytime in Mayfair*. Such visions of well-heeled metropolitan life offered a form of escapism that was lapped up by those who found Gainsborough's versions a little too vulgar; the critic David Thomson has recalled being 'enchanted' as a child 'by such tales of Samarkand on the other side of the river and thinking how long-suffering of my mother to go on living in South London.'[7]

Though her films belonged to different genres (melodrama, family saga, romantic and musical comedy), Neagle's faintly regal demeanour was unchanged throughout, and it is tempting to see her as an iconic figure for those suburban, *Daily Mail*-reading women who formed the most loyal part of her audience. She stands for a kind of genteel resilience, rising above what her devotees no doubt regarded as the indignities of rationing and the temporary madness of socialist government. *Spring in Park Lane* contains what must be the only anti-nationalisation joke in the history of British comedy – it isn't very funny, just as the Neagle films were not, in any conventional sense of the term, very good, but their success demonstrates how shrewdly they catered to an appetite poorly-served by any other area of British cinema.

With the onset of the 1950s, however, the cucumber-sandwich platitudes of Neagle-land were increasingly under threat, and not just from the changes wrought by the Labour administration. Tensions around class were increasingly giving way to those centred on generation, as youth became a growing focus of social anxiety. The fully-fledged development of youth culture (with its stress on sexuality, consumption and Americanisation) belongs to the 1950s, but another vital Ealing film, a near-contemporary of *Passport to Pimlico*, captures the transitional moment when youth first troubled the established order: *The Blue Lamp*.

Partly a spiv film with the cloudier moral elements ostensibly tidied away, partly a documentary-influenced account of police procedure, partly a hegemonic tract on the centrality of law-enforcement to a sense of national good, partly an early example of the central genre of the 1950s, the social problem film, *The Blue Lamp* is an eloquent distillation of the key ideological issues of its social moment. It has a reputation for banal cosiness (due largely to spawning the

299

ineffably self-satisfied television series *Dixon of Dock Green*), but its drive towards consensus at all costs, its hymn of praise to knowing your place, mark it out as an avatar of the decade to come.

Like *Passport*, it celebrates community, but has a harder edge than the comedy in the way that it treats those who would deviate from the community's norms. When young spiv-turned-murderer Tom Riley (played by Dirk Bogarde with an edge of erotic intensity that at times threatens to upset the rigorously consensual politics of the film) flees into a greyhound stadium to escape the pursuing police, he at first feels secure in the crush of the anonymous crowd. His optimism is short-lived, as the entire stadium, emblematic of not only the immediate community of west London but the nation as a whole, rise against him and hunt him down like a trapped animal. It seems odd, perhaps, that a film so concerned with the machinery of justice fails to include a concluding trial scene with Riley in the dock, but the punishment has already been dealt out, in far more iconographically powerful terms, as the stadium crowd close in on the individual transgressor.

Riley's real crime has not been the killing of P.C. Dixon, but his refusal to accept his station, his youthful disregard for established hierarchies, his infatuation with American culture that reveals itself in his rather risible appropriation of Hollywood gangster slang – he fails to conform and, like Gainsborough's wicked gentlemen and ladies, his punishment must be absolute. As the 1950s begin, there is no place for charismatic, sexy, insolent, on-the-make individualists – they will not reappear in British films until the end of the decade, in forms as varied as Count Dracula, *Room at the Top*'s Joe Lampton, and the whole cackling, misbehaving Carry On crew. But that is another story.

Notes

[1] Richard Winnington, *Penguin Film Review*, Penguin, Harmondsworth 1946, p167.
[2] *Ibid.*
[3] See Andy Medhurst, 'That Special Thrill: Brief Encounter, Homosexuality and Authorship', in *Screen*, Winter 1990; also Richard Dyer, *Brief Encounter*, British Film Institute, London 1993.
[4] See Robert Murphy, *Realism and Tinsel: Cinema and Society in Britain 1939-1948*, Routledge, London 1989.
[5] For the best account see Charles Barr, *Ealing Studios*, Cameron and Tayleur/David and Charles, London 1977.
[6] For a critique of later British war films see Andy Medhurst, '1950s War Films' in Geoff Hurd (ed), *National Fiction*, British Film Institute, London 1984.
[7] David Thomson, *A Biographical Dictionary of the Cinema*, Secker and Warburg, London 1975, p429.

A useful additional reference is Richard Winnington, *Film Criticism and Caricatures 1943-53*, Paul Elek, London 1958.

Recording a Landscape: Growing Up in Dormanstown

Rosalind Delmar

> Perhaps you may never get
> The knack of judging a distance, but at least you know
> How to report on a landscape.
> Henry Reed, Judging Distances, 1946

I was born during a time of death – the last quarter of 1941. In those months as many people died in our locality from war-connected reasons as from other causes. Desperate times call for desperate measures. It was also a period of reform and renewal. Two days after I was born Lord Woolton, Minister of Food, announced the extension of the school meals service to benefit all three million school children (only 300,000 had been covered up till then). He also announced a new policy of making milk freely available to all children at school and during the holidays. With the theme 'no malnutrition for our children' one fundament of the welfare state was being put into place. As I grew up I took these things for granted, expecting them to last forever. But I have lived long enough to see the abolition of free school milk and the dismantling of the school meals service. The concept of universal benefits they heralded looks increasingly fragile.

The 1940s, the time of war and post-war, ended for me as it did for thousands of children the day I could buy as many sweets as I wanted, limited only by the money in my pocket. No longer did I have to compete in school tests for the sweet coupons which would allow me to buy my treats. At about the same time my home town, Dormanstown, was enlarged. Dormanstown (we called it Dormo) had been built after the First World War by Dorman Long Iron and Steel Company to house workers from its Redcar Works, which lay between the mouth of the Tees and Coatham Sands. In the early 1950s Redcar Council built a new estate next to Dormanstown to house the employees of a new giant, ICI at Wilton, which rose up opposite Dorman's latest steel plant at Lackenby. Smoke from its chimneys blackened our homes. A life flanked by fields and farms had ended.

Family

Many newly-wed faces shine hopefully out of the pages of the wartime local newspapers, young men on brief home leave, young women in smart frocks or wedding dresses. My parents had no wedding photos taken; they were not the typical couple. Each had been married before. My father's first wife and my mother's first husband died in the early months of 1940, within three weeks of each other. They were both non-Catholics, although each of my parents was a Catholic. My father was already fifty, with three sons in the Air Force and Navy and a daughter still at home. My mother was approaching forty, with five sons aged sixteen and under.

So I was born into a very crowded household, two families coming together, the first daughter of two from the new marriage, the start of a third family. Whenever I think of our house, I always remember its intimate geography, who slept where and with whom. It was cramped, overcrowded I think now, although I didn't think so at the time. The occupation of the house was broken down by shifts and school hours, so for long periods of the day there might be no-one but my mother there, with perhaps someone on night shift sleeping upstairs or a sick child tucked up on the sofa downstairs.

I remember very little about wartime. A brother in uniform

came home and gave me a toy dog stuffed with wood shavings which I dragged around everywhere on a leash. This was Jimmy, my father's eldest son, who after the war married and went to be a policeman in the Midlands. From the sideboard a cheerful boy wearing a seaman's cap marked 'HMS' smiled out. Leo, his youngest son, had insisted on going to war although only sixteen, and had been killed when his ship was torpedoed. His other son, Mickey, had already been married and divorced, and was a rare visitor.

The only one of my father's older children who lived with us was his daughter Brenda. There was an unhappy relationship between her and my mother. My mother was not at all pleased to have an adolescent girl living amongst her boys, and for her part Brenda resented my mother as the woman who had taken her own mother's place with worrying speed. A pattern developed in which Brenda would borrow money and run away. My father would set off to retrieve her from some police station and there would be hushed discussions about what had happened this time. My mother was very disapproving, as all these adventures made Brenda, in my mother's eyes, an even less suitable companion for 'the boys', as my brothers were called.

As soon as Brenda could leave home properly she did, only returning once, for my father's funeral. She was 'tarted up', as my mother put it, wearing make-up (the most my mother ever put on her skin was Pond's Cold Cream) and I watched fascinated as she painted not only her finger-nails but her toe-nails too. After that I never saw her again.

Although I have a strong memory of prisoners of war singing *Heilige Nacht* at Christmas I have no sense of a division between war and post-war. Life continued wartime rhythms. We children played in tank-traps by the becks when we searched for sticklebacks and newts; we scraped sea coal off the sands at Coatham and packaged it in newspaper cones for the morning fire. In the autumn we went to the fields with our families to pick potatoes and collected hips from the hedges for rose-hip syrup. At the sound of delivery horses' hooves we rushed into the street to shovel up any manure they left behind for the garden. Everyone grew vegetables.

On Saturday mornings one of us had to get up early to queue outside the butcher's for good quality cheap cuts of meat, whether a ration card was needed or not. If one of my brothers went to stay with a friend he took a large piece of bacon with him to help the family cater. Throughout the 1940s my mother did all the baking she could: the bread, the cheese and onion or meat and potato pies for lunch boxes, fruit and jam tarts and scones for tea. For a long time after the war we kept hens which provided eggs. When they were too old for that, my father pulled their necks and we ate them for Sunday dinner. Other Sunday dishes were rabbit, pigeon, roast oxheart and hot tongue.

A Friday barrow brought herrings and other North Sea fish. When one of my brothers left school towards the end of the war he got a job with a local dairy delivering milk on a milk cart pulled by a pony. It was a sign of social status to get your milk from the churn, even though it was the same milk which the rest had delivered in bottles. Although this brother dreamt of being a farmer, he went into the works as an apprentice and worked with locomotives all his life as his father had done before him.

Community

Because everyone in Dormanstown worked in the same works, there was a sense of community even where there was no intimacy. The houses themselves had been built using a new method, Dorlonco, invented by Dorman Long after the First World War.[1] Workers who lived in Dormanstown produced the steel girders which made the skeleton frames of the houses, transported them, and then built the houses in which they were to live. My mother, who went to live there in the early 1920s, told me that a railway line was fed from the works to the town, halting just behind the 'Village Inn', the town's first pub, and that on this line they brought the building materials for the houses.

This in itself must have sponsored feelings of solidarity, of everyone in the same boat. In much the same spirit local men, my father amongst them, built the first hut for Catholic services in Dormanstown. These feelings didn't necessarily overlap into politics, although Dormanstown regularly returned a Labour councillor. My father and one of my brothers were committed supporters of the Labour Party but my mother was not a Labour voter; for her Labour was the party of broken promises. None of the others discussed party politics. What everyone shared was a commitment to the collectivism of trade unionism, an awareness of how everyone depended on everyone else at work, for personal safety, and in the street, for daily acts of kindness, which extended to a sense of 'what about the workers?' rather than to any one political party.

Dormanstown had a special peculiarity, hidden to me and to everyone who lived there. As an industrial village it had been conceived by architects who believed in standardisation: in 'the suppression of rampant individualism for certain general amenities'. One of them, Patrick Abercrombie, gave his name to the outer street which defined our games of hares and hounds. Another, Stanley Adshead, wrote of his creation, 'the standard cottage' that 'it will not be the house of an individual, of an anarchist; but the home of a member of a certain class of the community, of a communist.'[2] Whether it was overall a successful piece of social engineering is not for me to judge, but a sense that we were there to be moulded was certainly present as I grew up and the social architecture may have been one element in this.

We were more like members of a caste than a class. We lived pressed together, with a few educated professionals living near or among us: the doctor, the priest, the teacher – these were the ones who got their milk from the churn. They were authorities, to be respected and deferred to even if they couldn't be obeyed. My mother's greatest dream was to have a son a priest, a daughter a teacher. We never saw a works owner, shareholders were unknown to us and large landowners were only names. We encountered small landowners, farmers or racehorse trainers, and shopkeepers; even then most goods, from tea to towels, were bought at the Co-op. The biggest bug-bears were the management. Behind them were only shadowy figures. My most political brother, who was also a shop-steward in the draughtsmen's union DATA, was particularly annoyed by those who came fresh from university and, with no experience, were given more responsibility than those whose fathers and grandfathers had worked in the works and whom circumstances had robbed of the chance of higher education.

Identities

Each of my parents held allegiances to wider communities than Dormanstown, allegiances which carried with them rigid rules. My father, who had been raised in an orphanage, served as a gunner in the First World War. This military experience formed him. He even named his eldest son after his commanding officer. He believed that might was right and that children should obey paternal discipline without question, but he was too old to enforce his demands on his older children, and my mother refused him any disciplinary rights over her sons, so his potential domain was retricted to my sister and myself. I was frequently berated for 'dumb insolence', but threatened or actual beatings united everyone against him, and he was like a weak old lion. We all believed, rightly, that my mother was the boss in the house. She took his wage packet, gave him an allowance from it, and managed everything. All the same, when he 'performed his ablutions' after coming in from work, with his tattoos on his arms and chest and his heavy belt holding up his trousers the whiff of the army camp seemed to hang about him.

He had a softer side. My mother called him a 'romancer'.

First of all I thought this mysterious term referred to the fairy-stories he used to tell my sister and myself at bedtime. Gradually I came to understand that she meant that you couldn't always believe what he said. For example, had he really, as he claimed, known Trotsky when he drifted around the East End of London at some unspecified time? I had no way of knowing, and was left in a state of uncertainty between his exciting tales of life in Mesopotamia and Manchester and her scepticism. Perhaps it was a love of fantasy which led him to introduce me to the cinema. When I started at the Catholic school a bus-ride away, it seemed that my sister moved swiftly to fill the space I left in the street. One day he found me overcome by upset at my exclusion from play and carried me off to the pictures to find consolation.

My mother was a strong Catholic. No more than my father would she tolerate questioning. Her mental universe was full of absolutes, from the right way to cook a pie or scrub a saucepan – 'Cleanliness is next to godliness' – to iron precepts which told you what to do, say and think. God was good and you didn't question His will; you had to do your best to make your thoughts, words and deeds conform to religious ideals. Holy exclamations and quotes from the Bible were constantly on her lips: 'Jesus, Mary and Joseph!' 'God is Good', 'God is not mocked', 'Vengeance is mine, saith the Lord!' She had also held on to Irishisms. A good story was 'a canny crack', the person who told it had 'the gift of the gab' or had kissed the Blarney Stone.

Both of my parents were children of Irish immigrants. Perhaps in order to celebrate this common Irishness I was to be called Rosaleen, ('Oh my dark Rosaleen, do not sigh, do not weep! The priests are on the ocean green, they march along the Deep') the old romantic name for Ireland, but the registrar seemed not to have heard of it, and wrote me down as Rosalind ('he must have been thinking of Rosalind Russell, she was all the go at the time' said my mother). We went to church on St Patrick's Day, collecting shamrock which we pinned to our lapels. Whilst there we sang 'Hail glorious St Patrick, dear Saint of our Isles, On us Erin's children bestow a sweet smile'. I gained the impression that we, Erin's children, were a huddled group, prone to end up in damp dark cellars or worse. This image drew on visits to my mother's mother who still lived in South Bank, a centre of early Irish immigration and still an immigrant centre to this day. Known to us as 'Slaggy Island' because of the slag heaps which surrounded it, it was a place of grim terraced houses with tiny rooms dark as caves.[3] Here I saw a hunched old woman dressed in black like the witch in Hansel and Gretel; the same woman who, according to my mother, had sent her away at the age of seven to work for and live with a childless aunt.

Perhaps because of this early treatment my mother was as timid as she was strong. The idea of life as a vale of tears, in which suffering was part of the order of things, and in which everyone as well as everything had its place was very much a part of her inner world. Outside this strict regime lay uncertainty and insecurity. In their different ways, each of my parents presented me with a rigid philosophy of life as an experience and confirmation of unescapable rules, governing how you did things. They backed up their view with stories from their bleak childhoods and difficult adulthoods in the Depression. It added up to a view of the world which as a small child I already found deeply unacceptable. I believed that life had more to offer.

The patterns of my life created big dilemmas. Where, for example, did I fit in? Was I English or Irish? Was I even 'real' Yorkshire? I certainly felt urban rather than rural, and joined with other children in making fun of the slow speech of the few girls who came to school from 'over t' hill'. We who lived in the industrial strip of Teesside seemed to have little in common with those from moorland villages. My mother described her first husband, an engine driver whose father had been a blacksmith in the works, as 'a Yorkshireman', so she clearly felt a distinction. But whilst being Irish was her reference point, the real Ireland had no existence for me. Irishness to me was a feeling, suffused with the nostalgia of exile and weakened by the passing of generations. Catholicism was less a focus of identity than a point of difference. Apart from a tug of guilt about Guy Fawkes, I never felt much identity with English Catholics. I was, in the Yorkshire phrase, 'neither nowt nor summat'.

I was a Catholic in a sea of Protestants: they lived around me, I played with them in the street, but they went to different, more convenient schools. The Anglican Church was at the top of our street and I passed it every Sunday on my way to Church but I was forbidden to go inside it except with express permission. My friends belonged to groups, like Brownies, from which I was excluded because of my religion and a vague feeling that Irishness involved Republicanism and therefore an inability to take an oath of allegiance to the Queen. I enjoyed local pleasures as much as any other child, taking a book to read where dog roses encircled a bit of grass on a piece of common near the cinema or taking the dog for a walk along Kirkleatham Lane. Together we played cricket and other street games, and we all went together to pick brambles in the woods above Wilton. But I also experienced interludes of utter isolation.

Her own experiences defined my mother's aspirations for me as for her sons. Thwarted in her desire for a son as priest, she clung to her hope for a schoolteacher daughter who would look after her in her old age. Education, for her was a route to independence and an easier life. Her maiden aunt had refused her the chance to go to a secondary school. She felt she had been made 'to work like a skivvy' from morn to night in her aunt's shop. The skills she developed were a source of pride: she felt a 'good manager', able to make a small income go a long way. But she never felt fulfilled in their use. Because she left her aunt as soon as she could, she inherited nothing, not even the piano she loved to play. She claimed she had been badgered into her first marriage. In her mind marriage and domesticity was a trap, in which you spent your life clearing up after men.

School

She taught me to read by the simple method of drawing an object (like a kettle) on a piece of paper and printing its name next to it. We had newspapers and magazines but few books at home. When I arrived at infant school able to read I was moved up a form, spending the next two years with the older group. But when everyone else 'went across the yard' as we children called the move to junior school, I was left behind because I was too young. I hated the teacher, a harridan with a violent temper who threw whatever came to hand at children who annoyed her. Books sent over from the junior school did little to help. My godmother, a retired teacher, tried to persuade my mother to go to the school and ask for me to be moved up; my mother insisted that the teachers knew what they were doing, and that if this was a good idea, they would already have thought of it. I blamed her for being intimidated instead of protecting me when I was unhappy. I was angry to discover how unsure she was of her place in the world outside of the safety of home and street. Her deference to authority was more powerful than her wish to support my educational needs and in my disillusionment I dimly recognised the limits of that support. Education was, in her view, a means to an end rather than the satisfaction of an intellectual or emotional need. To achieve such satisfaction I would have to rely on myself.

At junior school I was reunited with friends from my first class, now members of gangs and a protective presence in the year above. They told me which teachers to look out for. Being caned was a particular preoccupation. Depending on the teacher, you could be caned for any infringement of school rules – like being inside the school buildings at playtimes. Who used a cane, who used a rubber strap, if you could make it sting less by pulling your hand back at the

311

moment of contact or spitting on your hand before, were all subjects of endless discussion.

Work was geared towards the eleven-plus (which only four of us were to pass) with weekly tests in spelling, maths, grammar. Being a co-operative, hard-working pupil I tended to be put at the front of the class. On a summer's day I could turn my head to see one of the naughty ones climbing silently out of the window at the back of the classroom whilst the teacher was writing on the blackboard in front.

Our school was built on the site of a burnt-out golf club-house, and it was not far over the dunes to the sea-shore. It was to the sands that we were taken for games, and where we ran our end of year races. One magically cold winter when the snow fell and stayed – unusual so near the sea – we built wonderfully huge snowmen, bigger than ourselves, in the school playground. Not long after that a steamship ran aground on the rocks by the shore near the school. I felt compulsively drawn to visit it and watch as the months went by and it gradually broke-up. A few months earlier I had seen on newsreels the heroic Captain Carlsen refusing to leave his ship after it was wrecked off the Atlantic coast. Everyone debated the issue of whether he should leave his ship.

With one, unseen, brother dead on one ship and two away sailing the world, the life and lore of sailors had a special attraction for me. The sea was a mysterious and dangerous place; the North Sea, cold and unswimmable, communicated that as much as any vast ocean. My seamen brothers told me that sailors didn't learn to swim, because it was better to die quickly than fight and die exhausted. Yet all the same, they lived nine months out of every year at sea on their tankers, sending letters with stamps which I collected from Curacao, Meena Al-Ahmadi. Through my brothers I discovered that you could leave home, move on, and in this way free yourself of your parents. I had already decided to follow them, although scholarships rather than apprenticeships and night-schools would have to be my route to a wider world.

Our headteacher was a Scot and carried with him all the

reputation Scots have as educators and educated. Every member of my family has a story to tell about him. Towards the end of my junior school life he conducted an assembly which I have never forgotten. It was on the morning of the execution of Derek Bentley, hanged for a murder he did not commit. We were asked to pray for his soul with the sense that in London a great injustice was being done. For the first time I felt allowed to have my own view about the outside world, and that we and the world were equals. I caught a whiff of a wider view of justice as a yardstick with which those in power could be measured. It wasn't absolutely necessary to put up with everything without complaint. A seed had been sown for the years ahead.

Notes

[1] 'At a time when the building industry continued to suffer from shortages of skilled tradesmen, the system offered the possibility of employing steelworkers and labourers in place of bricklayers and carpenters ... For the steel manufacturers the system represented another outlet for their product when the demand for munitions fell away after the Armistice. The system was marketed as the 'Dorlonco' system and ... became one of the most successful non-traditional building methods of the inter-war years'. Simon Pepper, Mark Swinnerton, *Neo Georgian maison-type*, a study of Dormanstown in *Architectural Review*, 186, August 1980, pp89-92. I am grateful to Andrew Saint for drawing my attention to this article.

[2] *Op.cit.*

[3] Lady Florence Bell's description (in *At the Works*, Edward Arnold, London 1907; reprinted Virago, London 1985, p3) of a typical worker's house in Middlesbrough in 1907 was in most respects still accurate about the houses there in the 1940s and 1950s, 'Most of the houses ... consist of four rooms: two rooms on the ground floor, one of them a kitchen and a living room, which in many of them opens straight from the street, and in some has a tiny lobby with another door inside it – and another room behind, sometimes used as a bedroom, sometimes shut up as a parlour. A little steep dark staircase goes up from the kitchen to the next floor, where there are two more rooms. Sometimes there is a little scullery besides, sometimes a place hardly big enough to be called a room, just big enough to contain a bed, off the kitchen. Such abodes are big enough to house comfortably a couple and two or three children, but not to house families of ten, twelve, and more that are sometimes found in them.'

Name and Place Index

Names and places mentioned in the text have been indexed only when accompanied by further information.

Subject Index

Titles of books and plays are indexed only when they are accompanied by further information.

SUBJECT INDEX